Theoretically grounded and based on extensive original research, this exploration of the experiences of young people in custody in Sweden is a useful addition to the literature on child imprisonment. Its focus on 'open custody' as a potential mechanism for reducing reoffending will be of considerable interest to academics, practitioners and policy makers in a wide range of jurisdictions.

Tim Bateman, *Reader in Youth Justice, University of Bedfordshire, UK*

Tove Pettersson's carefully constructed mixed-method study of youth custody in Sweden presents a rare comparative analysis of the experiences and long-term effects of time spent in open and closed custodial institutions. Her insightful and theoretically-informed inquiry identifies the relevance of young people's contact with their families and the community outside the institution for their successful re-integration following release. Her research adds valuable nuance to our understanding of the impact of youth custody for it illustrates the importance of paying attention to the conditions of confinement. Anyone with an interest in state responses to serious offending by young people will find this book well worth the read.

Caroline Lanskey, *Lecturer in Applied Criminology, University of Cambridge, UK*

Young Offenders and Open Custody

Young offenders given custodial sentences in youth institutions constitute an important group in the context of crime prevention research, given that offenders within this group are at high risk of re-offending or continuing with a criminal career into adulthood. This book explores the significance of custodial openness for children and youths and how this environment affects future desistance from crime.

In *Young Offenders and Open Custody*, Tove Pettersson provides powerful support for the view that the experience of more open custodial forms during the youth custody sentence is of significance both for providing incarcerated youths with a more humane environment and for the likelihood of a positive outcome following their release. Building upon detailed interviews with convicted youths and staff at the special approved homes in Sweden, this book offers unique insights into the effect of punishment on young offenders and their understanding of social control.

Drawing upon quantitative and qualitative data, this book examines levels of re-offending over time among youths sentenced to custody, and considers the impact of more open sentences. This book will be useful reading for students and researchers engaged in youth and juvenile justice, juvenile delinquency, and sentencing and punishment.

Tove Pettersson is Head of Department and Professor at the Department of Criminology, Stockholm University, Sweden.

Routledge Frontiers of Criminal Justice

31 **International Developments and Practices in Investigative Interviewing and Interrogation**
Volume 1: Victims and witnesses
Edited by David Walsh, Gavin Oxburgh, Allison Redlich and Trond Myklebust

32 **International Developments and Practices in Investigative Interviewing and Interrogation**
Volume 2: Suspects
Edited by David Walsh, Gavin Oxburgh, Allison Redlich and Trond Myklebust

33 **Punishing the Other**
The social production of immorality revisited
Anna Eriksson

34 **Improving Criminal Justice Workplaces**
Translating theory and research into evidence-based practice
Paula Brough, Jennifer Brown and Amanda Biggs

35 **Experiencing Imprisonment**
Research on the experience of living and working in carceral institutions
Edited by Carla Reeves

36 **Restorative Justice in Transitional Settings**
Edited by Kerry Clamp

37 **Prisoner Radicalization and Terrorism Detention Policy**
Institutionalized Fear or Evidence-Based Policy-Making?
Tinka M. Veldhuis

38 **Drugs, Evidence, and Policy**
The Shaping of Belgian Drug Policy, 1996–2003
Julie Tieberghien

39 **Restorative Policing**
Concepts, Theory and Practice
Kerry Clamp and Craig Paterson

40 **The Penal Voluntary Sector**
Philippa Tomczak

41 **Transforming Summary Justice**
Modernisation in the Lower Criminal Courts
Jennifer Ward

42 **Stop and Search and Police Legitimacy**
Ben Bradford

43 **Young Offenders and Open Custody**
Tove Pettersson

Young Offenders and Open Custody

Tove Pettersson

Routledge
Taylor & Francis Group
LONDON AND NEW YORK

First published 2017 by Routledge

2 Park Square, Milton Park, Abingdon, Oxfordshire OX14 4RN
52 Vanderbilt Avenue, New York, NY 10017

Routledge is an imprint of the Taylor & Francis Group, an informa business

First issued in paperback 2019

British Library Cataloguing in Publication Data
A catalogue record for this book is available from the British Library

Library of Congress Cataloging in Publication Data
Names: Pettersson, Tove, author.
Title: Young offenders and open custody / Tove Pettersson.
Description: Abingdon, Oxon ; New York, NY : Routledge, 2017. |
Series: Routledge frontiers of criminal justice ; 43 | Includes
bibliographical references and index.
Identifiers: LCCN 2016028736 | ISBN 9781138120921 (hardback) |
ISBN 9781315651446 (ebook)
Subjects: LCSH: Juvenile detention–Sweden. | Juvenile delinquents–
Rehabilitation–Sweden. | Juvenile detention homes–Sweden. | Juvenile
corrections–Sweden. | Alternatives to imprisonment–Sweden.
Classification: LCC HV9182 .P47 2017 | DDC 365/.42–dc23
LC record available at https://lccn.loc.gov/2016028736

ISBN: 978-1-138-12092-1 (hbk)
ISBN: 978-0-367-22626-8 (pbk)

Typeset in Times New Roman
by Wearset Ltd, Boldon, Tyne and Wear

Contents

Figures

Tables

Acknowledgements

In my work with this book, I have been helped by a large number of people, for whose assistance I am, of course, very grateful. First and foremost, however, I would like to thank the youths who have openly and often very candidly shared with me their experiences of being held in a secure institution. Many thanks also to the staff members at special approved homes who have generously allowed me to share their experiences of working with the issues discussed in the book.

I would also like to thank my colleagues at Stockholm University's Department of Criminology, who participated in a seminar to discuss an early draft of this book and provided valuable input. A special thank you to Ingrid Lander and Anders Nilsson, who served as principal discussants and who provided many important comments and suggestions. My colleagues Julia Sandahl and Fredrik Sivertsson have also been particularly helpful, generously making time to discuss a number of methodological issues. I would also like to extend special thanks to Olof Bäckman, of Stockholm University's Swedish Institute for Social Research (SOFI), whose assistance with STATA and the Propensity Score Matching module has been invaluable. The responsibility for any remaining errors and omissions is, of course, mine alone.

Many thanks also due to Elisabeth Nordén, Therese Skrinjar, and Linnea Wätterstam for their excellent work with the data collection process. Finally, thank you to David Shannon, who translated the manuscript from Swedish.

The research has been financed by the National Board of Institutional Care, Sweden.

1 Introduction

> (b) No child shall be deprived of his or her liberty unlawfully or arbitrarily. The arrest, detention or imprisonment of a child shall be in conformity with the law and shall be used only as a measure of last resort and for the shortest appropriate period of time;
> (c) Every child deprived of liberty shall be treated with humanity and respect for the inherent dignity of the human person, and in a manner which takes into account the needs of persons of his or her age. In particular, every child deprived of liberty shall be separated from adults unless it is considered in the child's best interest not to do so and shall have the right to maintain contact with his or her family through correspondence and visits, save in exceptional circumstances;
>
> (UN Convention on the Rights of the Child, Article 37)

The commission of very serious offences by children gives rise to a crime policy dilemma. On the one hand, the justice systems of many countries require such serious offences to be sanctioned by means of imprisonment or some other form of custodial sentence. On the other hand, there are powerful reasons, and a strong desire, to avoid subjecting children to imprisonment and other forms of incarceration. Imprisonment produces a large number of negative consequences and the effects of incarceration are particularly problematic for children. Through the adoption of the United Nations Convention on the Rights of the Child we have accepted a responsibility to protect and promote the rights of children in various ways.[1] This includes a requirement that children should only be subject to incarceration as a last resort. Children are nonetheless sentenced to prison and other forms of incarceration throughout the world. This also raises a large number of questions of relevance to crime policy, some of which are addressed in this book. The book focuses on children who have committed very serious offences, often in the form of serious violent crime, and who have been given custodial sentences as a result. The book examines how incarcerated children and youths experience this situation, how the damaging effects of incarceration might be reduced through efforts to introduce higher levels of custodial openness in various forms, and the significance of custodial openness for the everyday institutional lives of incarcerated young people and for their subsequent re-offending. The book also examines how these children think about their lives subsequent to release, and about their opportunities for living what they themselves view as a better life in the future.

Youth Justice in Sweden, an overview

The way children and youths who commit offences are dealt with varies between different countries (Hazel 2008). Sweden follows what has been labelled the welfare model both in its response to young offenders (Hazel 2008), and in its justice system more generally (Cavadino and Dignan 2006), and there is substantial consensus with regard to avoiding the use of imprisonment for youths (Nordlöf 2005, Proposition 1997/98: 96). When criminal justice sanctions are required, these are as far as possible implemented outside the framework of the prison and probation system (Nordlöf 2005). In Sweden, the age of criminal responsibility is 15, which is relatively high viewed in an international perspective (Hazel 2008). The fact that someone has not reached the age of criminal responsibility does not mean that nothing happens if the individual commits an offence however, but rather that society's response to the offences is implemented within the framework of the social services legislation (Holmberg 2013). For persons aged between 15 and 17, there are special restrictions with regard to the imposition of criminal justice sanctions (such as the use of shorter custodial sentences), which is also the case, although to a more limited extent, for offenders up to the age of 20 (Nordlöf 2005, Holmberg 2013). There are also a number of sanctions whose use is restricted to young offenders: youth care, youth service and youth custody. While there is a deeply rooted tradition in Sweden that children who commit offences should primarily be dealt with within the framework of the social services, a number of reforms have been implemented since the late 1990s with the objective of increasing the prominence of the just deserts principle in relation to young offenders (Holmberg 2013, Tärnfalk 2007, Hazel 2008). These developments reflect a more general trend in the field of Swedish crime policy (Tham 2001, von Hofer and Tham 2013, Cavadino and Dignan 2006), which has also been witnessed in other countries such as the UK and the USA (Garland 2001). In spite of these changes, the various sanctions imposed on young people are still often implemented within a social services framework (Tärnfalk 2007), and Sarnecki and Estrada (2006) have argued that the Swedish response to young offenders has retained its humanitarian focus over recent years, despite a shift towards more punitive attitudes in society at large.

The youth custody sanction[2] was introduced in Sweden in 1999 with the objective of reducing the use of imprisonment for persons below the age of 18. The government bill (1997/1998: 96) outlining the legislation presents a number of reasons for the introduction of the new sanction. One important argument was the goal of meeting the requirements of the *Convention on the Rights of the Child*, which states that there must be an alternative to imprisonment for individuals under the age of 18, that prison sentences should only be used as a last resort, and that children subjected to custodial sentences should not be incarcerated together with adults. The bill also states that imprisonment increases the risk that youths will perceive the sanction as confirming a view of themselves as criminals and that prison sentences are associated with special risks for young people. The bill notes further that it is not reasonable to punish young people as severely as adults. At the same time, it also argues that there is a need for a sanction for young offenders who commit very serious offences that "to a reasonable extent provides a deterrent to crime, clearly marks fundamental boundaries and furthermore meets society's requirements for fairness in the field of sanctioning practice" (p. 153). The restrictive use of custodial sanctions was to continue, which meant that the conditions required for a youth custody sentence were to be the same as they had been for imprisonment. This meant that there must be no possibility of imposing an alternative sanction and that there must be exceptional cause for the imposition of youth custody. While the length of the youth custody sentence was to be specified in proportion to the penal value of the offence, the bill emphasises that the youth's care needs should be ascribed major importance in relation to the *implementation* of the sanction (p. 96). Thus while the sentence length was not to be dependent on the youth's care needs, the contents of the period of youth custody were, which is in line with the traditional Swedish focus on social services care provision in society's response to young offenders.

The state-administered special approved homes were deemed the most appropriate institutions for the implementation of youth custody sentences, and since 1999 youths sentenced to youth custody have served their sentences in one of these institutions. The mission of the special approved homes was, and continues to be, that of assuming responsibility for and providing care to youths, who are (compulsorily) placed in them by the social services as a result of serious offending, substance abuse or other socially destructive behaviour. While these institutions are for the most part secure, the implementation of *criminal justice sanctions* is thus new to them, and the extension of their mission in this way means that they have had to adapt their work to meet requirements that differ somewhat from those placed on them within the framework of their work for the social services.

The *quantitative part* of the study on which this book is based includes the youths sentenced to youth custody between 1999, when the sanction was introduced, and 2006. The qualitative aspects of the research are based on interviews conducted with staff working at special approved homes and with youths sentenced to youth custody who were serving their sentences in these institutions. The responsibilities specified in Section 2 of the Youth Custody Act[3] are of particular relevance to this research:

> The implementation of youth custody sentences is to be formulated so as to promote the convicted individual's adjustment to society and to counteract the harmful consequences of incarceration.

Opportunities to spend time outside the institution and placements in open, as against secure, units may constitute measures of this kind, which can both promote the youth's adjustment to society and reduce the harmful consequences of incarceration.

The introduction of youth custody has largely produced the desired effect in the sense that youths aged 15–17 who commit serious offences are very rarely sentenced to a prison term. Only a very small number of youths in this age-group are still sentenced to prison each year. Figure 1.1 describes the number of youths sentenced to youth custody, prison, probation in combination with imprisonment or forensic psychiatric care for the period since the mid-1990s. At the same time, previous research shows that the introduction of youth custody has led to an increase in the length of the custodial sentences served by this group of young people (Sarnecki and Estrada 2006, Kühlhorn 2002, Pettersson 2010a, 2010b). In practice, the increased sentence length means an even longer period spent incarcerated by comparison with the time when youths in this age-group were sent to prison, since prison inmates are released on parole once they have served two-thirds of their sentences, which is not the case for youth custody sentences. When this is also taken into account, the length of custodial sentences has more or less doubled (Pettersson 2010a, 2010b).

Research has also shown that the introduction of youth custody resulted in a net-widening effect, with youths who committed offences that would *not* previously have resulted in a prison term now being sentenced to youth custody (Granath 2007, Pettersson 2010b). Figure 1.2 shows further that the proportion of incarcerated youths aged 15–17 (a group which since 1999 has primarily been comprised of individuals sentenced to youth custody) has increased substantially since the introduction of youth custody in relation to both the number of youths in this age-group in the population as a whole and the number of 15–17-year-olds convicted of offences. The 5–6 years following the introduction of the youth custody sanction saw these proportions increase to significantly higher levels, after which these levels started to decline.

Thus the effect of the new legislation has been that youths are no longer sentenced to prison, but that the number of youths sentenced to incarceration has increased, and the time they spend incarcerated has also increased. As can be seen from Figure 1.1, however, the number of individuals sentenced to youth custody has declined substantially over recent years, and Figure 1.2 shows that this decline can also be seen in relation to both the number of 15–17-year-olds in the population and the total number of youths convicted of offences. It is possible that part of this decline may be due to a reversal of the above described net-widening effect, as the courts have come to realise that youth custody sentences were in part being imposed for offences for which the sanction was not intended.[4] The decline in the number of youths sentenced to incarceration is not limited to Sweden, however (Bateman 2012, Jacobson *et al.* 2010). Nor is the decline in custodial sentences limited to youths. The number of individuals sentenced to imprisonment has also declined in Sweden. Statistics from the Swedish Prison and Probation Service[5] show a decline in prison numbers for the majority of years between 2004 (5,722 prison inmates on October 1st) and 2014 (4,319 prison inmates on October 1st). Von Hofer and Tham (2013) have shown that

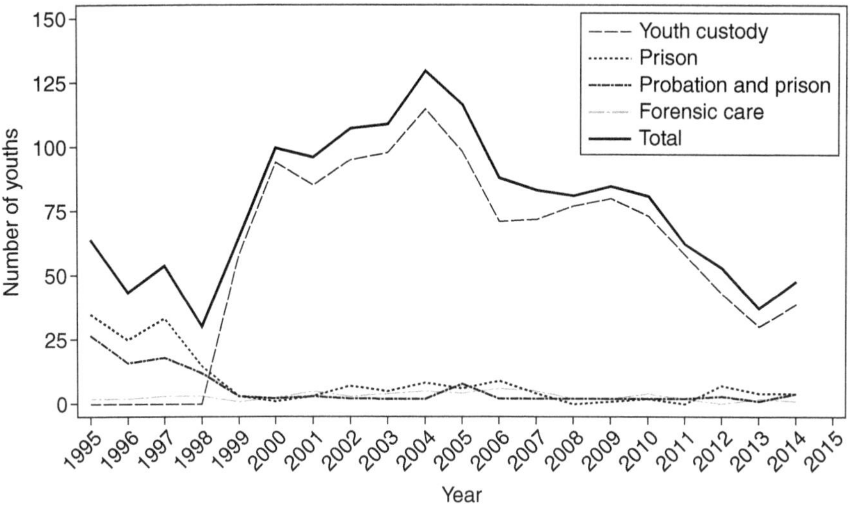

Figure 1.1 Numbers of youths aged 15–17 sentenced to incarceration by the Swedish criminal justice system 1995–2014.

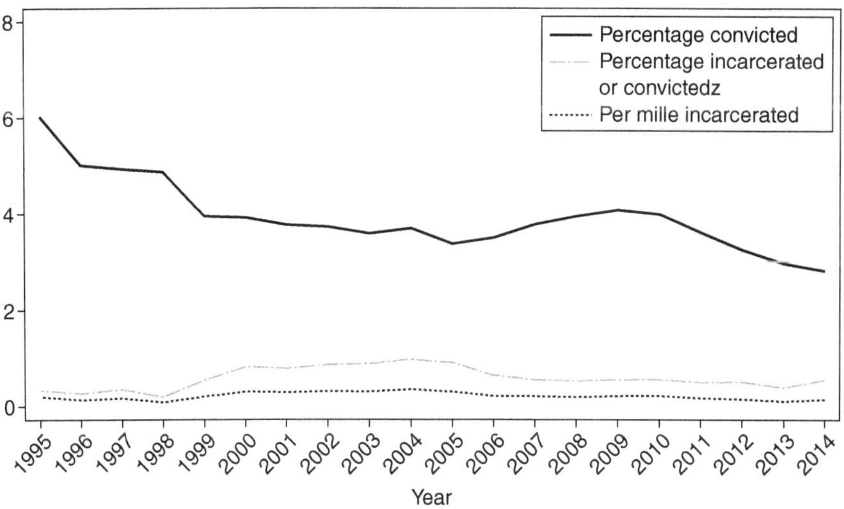

Figure 1.2 Incarceration in the population aged 15–17 (per mille), youths convicted of offences in the population aged 15–17 (per cent), and proportion of convicted 15–17-year-olds sentenced to incarceration (per cent). Sweden 1995–2014.

this decline is also found when the number of individuals sentenced to prison is viewed in relation to the size of the Swedish population.[6]

Given the findings of previous research, which have shown incarceration to produce criminogenic effects (Cullen *et al.* 2011, Durlauf and Nagin 2011, Bales and Piquero 2012, Nagin *et al.* 2009, Nieuwbeerta *et al.* 2009, Gendreau *et al.* 2000, Andersen 2015, Andersen and Andersen 2012) an increase in the number and length of custodial sentences is unfortunate to say the least, and the issue of strategies to reduce the negative effects of incarceration is an important one.[7] Research on the institutional treatment of young people with antisocial behaviour problems show that one important factor for achieving positive treatment results is that this treatment is conducted in forms that are as open as possible, given existing conditions (Andreassen 2003). A previous follow-up study of individuals sentenced to youth custody found a correlation between the frequency of time spent outside the institution and re-offending, with those who did not re-offend within three years of release having more often spent time outside the institution over the course of their sentences. The study was not however able to examine the relationship between time spent outside the institution/custodial openness and re-offending in more detail, i.e. whether periods of time spent outside the institution had an independent effect on the risk for re-offending. At the same time, the study was able to show that the correlation remained following a control for one of the most important factors for the re-offending risk in the form of prior offending (Pettersson 2010a, 2010b). The current study looks at this relationship in more detail and also extends the focus to include the significance of custodial openness for everyday life at the institutions.

Thus this book focuses on a sanction that was formulated in the Swedish context, and that is only found in Sweden. At the same time, youths are subject to different forms of incarceration, in youth institutions or prisons, throughout the world. Questions regarding what happens to young people when they are locked up, and what significance opportunities to spend time outside institutions have for everyday institutional life and for re-offending are thus of interest not only in Sweden but rather irrespective of the form in which youths are incarcerated. Having said this, some scholars have argued that penal policy in Scandinavia is characterised by exceptionally low levels of punitiveness. Before moving on to describe youth care in Sweden, and particularly in the special approved homes, in more detail, I will therefore briefly touch upon this discussion of Scandinavian exceptionalism in the field of penal policy.

Are Scandinavian penal systems exceptional?

Pratt (2008a, 2008b, see also Cavadino and Dignan 2006) has argued that the Scandinavian countries,[8] Sweden, Norway and Finland, are characterised by exceptionalism in relation to punitiveness. By this he means that these countries have exceptionally low levels of imprisonment and that the conditions in prison are exceptionally good. Pratt argues that this situation is due to “the *highly* egalitarian cultural values and social structures of these societies” (Pratt 2008a,

p. 120 emphasis in original). More recently, however, this tendency towards exceptionalism has been under threat as a result of changes in a more punitive direction. According to Pratt, this is due to changes in these countries towards a less egalitarian and homogenous social climate characterised by declining levels of social solidarity. Sweden is particularly vulnerable in this regard, where Pratt argues changes of this kind have been more marked than in Norway and Finland (Pratt 2008b).

Pratt's hypothesis about punitive exceptionalism in Scandinavia has been questioned, however, in a research anthology published by prison researchers from the Nordic countries themselves (Ugelvik and Dullum 2012, Dullum and Ugelvik 2012). Among other things, Pratt's portrayal has been criticised for ignoring a large number of factors that show another side of the picture, such as the use of pre-trial solitary confinement, the prisonisation of Nordic prison inmates, and the way in which the more open conditions produce different forms for the exercise of power. It has also been argued that the positive significance of the egalitarianism of Scandinavian societies noted by Pratt also has its downsides in the form of the exclusion of those who do not happen to fall within the boundaries of this egalitarianism (Mathiesen 2012, Scharff Smith 2012, Neumann 2011, Ugelvik 2012). Pratt (2012) has responded to these criticisms together with Eriksson, and argued that even if certain aspects of the criticisms are correct, Scandinavia may nonetheless be regarded as exceptional in relation to punitiveness. In a later article, Barker (2013) relates to both Pratt's articles and Ugelvik and Dullum's anthology, and argues that in order to understand Scandinavian (in this case Swedish) punitive practice, the welfare state and the punitive elements that the welfare state gives rise to must also be taken into account. Thus, in order to understand the degree of punitiveness in Sweden, one must also direct one's focus outside the criminal justice system and look, among other things, at the ways in which different forms of compulsion are used within the work of the social services.

The anthology editors Dullum and Ugelvik (2012) draw the conclusion that Scandinavia is both exceptional and non-exceptional with regard to punitiveness. They argue that a simple, concise answer is not possible, but rather that certain conditions support the exceptionalist argument while others do not. In a review of the anthology, however, Hörnqvist (2012) notes that while all of the authors criticise Pratt's view, none of the contributions in fact presents a serious challenge to Pratt's arguments, at least with regard to Pratt's central points of departure (that the Scandinavian countries are characterised by low incarceration rates and more open and humane prison conditions). Instead the authors discuss a large number of other factors, on the basis of specific cases from individual countries, and do not present any form of cross-country comparison. Hörnqvist notes that what the Nordic prison researchers have reacted against are not these simple facts, but rather the fact that they have adopted a broader interpretation of what should be included in a punitive system. This view may be linked to Crewe's (2011a) criticism of the current literature on the relationship between political economy and penal severity, which Crewe argues focuses only on a superficial analysis which "stops at the gate of the prison" (p. 525). With this he means that such analyses only compare prison rates, sentence lengths and prison conditions. Crewe does not refer to Pratt's analysis of Scandinavian exceptionalism as an example, although the criticism could also be applied to Pratt's work. Crewe argues that the superficial nature of the analyses means that these do not do justice to the different penal systems' levels of what he refers to as depth, weight and tightness. It is these more nuanced forms of punitiveness that the authors in the Nordic anthology appear to wish to capture, along with Barker in her discussion of the substantial punitive elements that may be found within the framework of Sweden's welfare state and social services.

Shammas (2014) examines the question of Scandinavian punitive exceptionalism from a slightly different angle than the anthology described above. On the basis of the view that Scandinavian prison conditions are in fact exceptional in the way described by Pratt (particularly in open prisons, which constitute the focus of Shammas's work) he discusses how this does not necessarily reduce the harms that prisons produce.[9] At the same time, however, the nature of the consequences of incarceration differ. Proceeding on the basis of Crewe's (2011a, 2011b) analyses of the use of soft power, with a focus on tightness, which Crewe argues is currently exercised in prisons in England and Wales, Shammas develops a conceptualisation of what he refers to as "pains of freedom" (in analogy to Sykes's *pains of imprisonment*). Since Shammas's work is of particular interest to this study, I will be returning to his discussions in the theory chapter.

Youth Justice in Sweden, special approved homes and youth custody

Thus in Sweden, children who commit offences, like children with other types of social problems, are primarily dealt with within the framework of the social services. The majority of measures are implemented in non-institutional care forms and with the (more or less) voluntary participation of the young people concerned. Even in the case of out-of-home care placements, voluntary measures are by far the most common. If the social services assess the child to have particularly substantial social problems and determine that care measures cannot be implemented on a voluntary basis, they can apply for the youth to be placed in a special approved home, i.e. the institutions at which youth custody sentences are also implemented. These applications are made to the administrative court. Special approved homes primarily admit youths who are placed on a compulsory basis in accordance with Section 12 of the Care of Young Persons (Special Provisions) Act (1990: 52), although there are also a number of voluntary placements in exceptional cases.[10] The reasons for such placements are serious crime, serious substance abuse and other socially destructive behaviour. The youths must also have put their health and/or development at serious risk as a result of their behaviour. Youths can also be placed as a result of neglect or deficient care provision, but in these cases they may not be place in a secure unit. A large majority of the youths in special approved homes are admitted in the form of what are referred to as "acute" placements. Such acute placements may then be extended into a treatment placement if the need for such a placement is identified, but these youths are often transferred to a more open form of treatment. Over half of the youths placed in special approved homes are released from the institution after less than three months (annual statistics from the National Board of Institutional Care). Figure 1.3 presents the number of placements in special approved homes, while Figure 1.4 presents the number of youths placed as a proportion of the population aged 15–17 years. As can be seen from a comparison with Figures 1.1 and 1.2, a much larger number of youths are placed in the custody of special approved homes by the social services than as a result of criminal justice sanctions. Approximately one-third of those admitted to special approved homes are girls, which is a much larger proportion by comparison with the gender distribution among youths sentenced to a custodial sanction by the courts. Very few girls are sentenced to youth custody (with girls accounting for 3.7 per cent of youth custody sanctions during the period 1999–2014). The number of girls among those sentenced to a prison term is also small, although they comprise a larger proportion of this group (17.2 per cent). It is not entirely clear why the proportion of girls is greater among those sentenced to prison, but it should be remembered that even though the figures relate to a period of 16 years, the number of individuals sentenced to prison since the introduction of the youth custody sanction is small (amounting to a total of 64 prison sentences for the entire period).

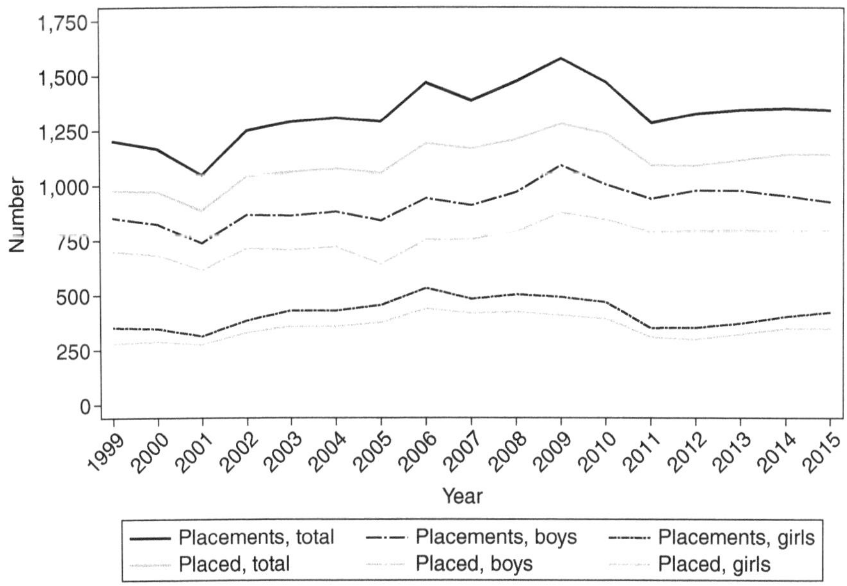

Figure 1.3 Number of placements and number of unique youths placed in special approved homes by year and gender.

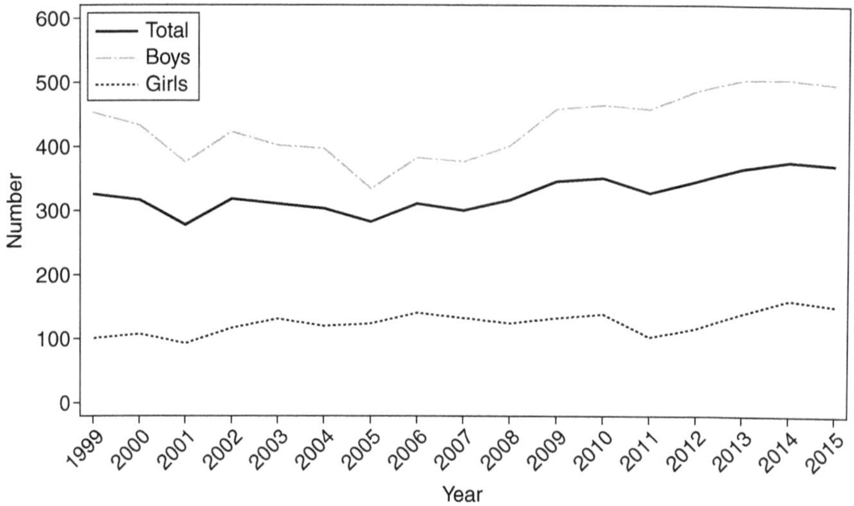

Figure 1.4 Youths aged 15–17 placed in special approved homes per 100,000 in the population aged 15–17, by year and gender.

There are also differences between girls and boys in the reasons for placements in special approved homes. The National Board of Institutional Care's statistics for 2014 show that 44 per cent of girls and 72 per cent of boys had been placed in whole or in part as a result of involvement in crime. A similarly large proportion of girls and boys had been placed in whole or in part as a result of substance abuse – 60 per cent of the girls and 66 per cent of the boys. In the same way as with placements resulting from involvement in crime, there were substantial differences between the sexes in the level of placements related to other socially destructive behaviours, with 84 per cent of girls and 58 per cent of boys having been placed in whole or in part for this reason.[11] The levels may differ somewhat from year to year but the general pattern over time is that boys are more often placed as a result of involvement in crime, girls more often as result of other socially destructive behaviour, while substance abuse problems are found among the reasons for placement for girls and boys to roughly the same extent.

Youths may be placed in special approved homes from the age of 13, or in isolated cases even earlier although this is unusual, and up to the age of 20. The average age among those admitted is 17. The mission of the special approved homes is primarily focused on providing *treatment* to these youths, but also involves holding them in custody both for their own good and the good of others, and conducting assessments on the need for continued treatment. It was first and foremost the special approved homes' focus on and experience of treatment provision that motivated the government to assign the implementation of the youth custody sanction to these institutions rather than to the Prison and Probation Service, for example.

The special approved homes occupy a unique position within the framework of youth care provision in Sweden, not only because they are the only institutions in which youths are placed by compulsory means and that are secure, but also because the staff also have special powers in relation to the institutionalised youths. These include, for example, the power, when necessary, to place the youths in isolation, to conduct searches, take blood and urine samples where there is a suspicion of drug use, to examine their correspondence in certain circumstances and to provide care for an individual youth in a segregated environment. Special approved homes are also the only youth care institutions that are administered by central government.

The work of the special approved homes is conducted in small units with high staffing levels. There are usually around six youths placed in a given unit, although this number is sometimes as low as three. As regards youth custody placements, units with only three places are the most secure and often have the task of taking care of those youths that are assessed to constitute the greatest security risk. On occasion, care may also be provided for a single youth alone in a residential unit for a certain period of time (segregated care provision). The institutions themselves are larger however, having several units.

The mission of the special approved homes varies depending on both the type of crime/reason for placement (with, for example, special units for youths who have committed sexual offences), the length of sentence or of the expected period of treatment, and the assessed risk (for example, absconding). All youths sentenced to youth custody for a period of over two months must also undergo an assessment, which then forms the basis for the formulation of an individual treatment plan. The ideal for the implementation of sentences is furthermore that youths should begin their period of institutionalisation in secure units but that the implementation of the sentence should then gradually move into more open forms. In practice, or course, there is considerable variation in the extent to which these various principles are followed.

Within the implementation process for youth custody sentences there are a number of different degrees of custodial "openness" through which youths may pass during their period of institutionalisation. The most secure forms of custody are found in the *reception units* and the *secure treatment units*. In *locked treatment units*, the custodial experience may be secure or more open, depending on the restrictions applied in relation to the specific individual. The youth may then be moved into an *open treatment unit*, and then to a *pre-release unit*. The release transition process may take place either within the special approved home system or outside this system. When it takes place within the special approved home system, the youth may be located within or outside the grounds of the institution itself during the course of this process. Some institutions have a pre-release unit located in a nearby town or community. Following release, some youths may be offered aftercare measures. Thus there are a number of different steps towards custodial openness that may be taken at special approved homes. An internal review (SiS 2010) found that there are substantial differences between different youths in how far they come along this path over the course of their sentences. In part this is due to differences between different institutions regarding whether or not they have open units, and in part to the fact that there are not always places available in the open units at those institutions that do have them (something that was confirmed in the staff interviews conducted in the current study). In an examination of the pre-release activities associated with the youth custody sanction, it was noted that

> [a]s regards differences between the plans of the different institutions, these seem to have been governed by the motto "use what's available", i.e. those institutions that have access to a pre-release unit of their own have placed more of their youths in these units, while those institutions with no such unit have not chosen to move their youths to another institution for the final period of their sentences. Instead, these youths have often remained in a secure unit throughout their sentences, albeit with the opportunity to spend time outside the unit during the final phase.
>
> (SiS 2010 pp. 14–15)

In other words, this means that there are factors related to neither the youths themselves nor their risk for re-offending that are of significance to the issue of whether youths will be placed in an open or secure unit during the final stage of their sentences. This is of course problematic from the perspective of legal certainty, but paradoxically it is also this factor that provides an opportunity to examine the significance of custodial openness for re-offending, an opportunity that has been exploited in the current study. Thus it is not only risk factors that were present prior to institutionalisation, or what happens during the period of incarceration, that affects youths' chances of moving to a more open unit, even though these factors are naturally also significant.

Hannah-Moffat (2005) has discussed what has now become the relatively dominant perspective of risk and criminogenic needs assessment within the corrections system.[12] This perspective may also be said to have become well-established within the compulsory care system focused on youths in Sweden more generally, and perhaps in particular in relation to the implementation of the youth custody sanction. Hannah-Moffat (2005) has noted that this focus on the assessment of risks and needs directs attention at individuals as active subjects who are responsible for their choices, and as a result directs discussions of the causes of crime away from issues relating to structural factors and the marginalised conditions under which some people live. These are either ignored or regarded as being the result of individual inadequacies, and social problems are thus transformed into individual problems. Special approved homes employ a range of different forms of more or less structured risk assessments, among other things in relation to allowing youths to spend time outside the institution.

Finally, a few words on the concept of open custody in relation to Sweden's special approved homes. In British Columbia, for example, youth custody is divided into secure and open custody. These two forms of custody are described as follows:

Secure custody is for youths found guilty of serious offences or for youth who have a persistent pattern of offending and who cannot be reasonably supervised in a community setting or in open custody.

Open custody is for youths who are deemed by the court to be not yet appropriate for a community setting, but who can manage effectively with less stringent controls and greater privileges within an open custody unit.[13]

Despite the title of this book, the institutions in which the studied youths have been placed are primarily of a kind that would fall within the above definition of secure custody and not open custody. The focus of the book is directed however at the opportunities for being moved to more open custodial forms and at the significance this has for everyday life in the institution and for re-offending. Periods of time spent outside the institution also constitute a means of making periods of secure custody less carceral. As has been noted above, special approved home units are classified into four different levels of custodial security or openness. In the remainder of the book, however, the term "secure" will be used as a generic label for both secure units and locked units, while the term "open" will be used as a label for both open units and pre-release units.

Outline of the book

The remainder of the book is organised as follows. The next chapter locates the questions examined in the book within a theoretical framework, while Chapter 3 presents the study data in more detail. This is followed by three empirical chapters. The first of these looks at the youths' and staff's descriptions of everyday institutional life with a focus on experiences of incarceration and of time spent outside the institution. In the second, the focus shifts to the youths' thoughts about the time following their period of institutionalisation and to the views of staff as to what would be required for the youths not to return to crime. The third begins with a quantitative description of the young persons sentenced to youth custody in terms of the nature of their problems in various areas, including prior criminality, etc., and then presents the results from the re-offending data. The book's final chapter summarises the results by relating the empirical findings to the theoretical framework.

Notes

1 At the time of writing, all the countries of the world with the exception of the USA have ratified the UN Convention on the Rights of the Child, available online at: http://indicators.ohchr.org/ (accessed 19 January, 2016).
2 Chapter 32, Section 5 of the Swedish Penal Code.
3 Swedish: Lag (1998:603) om verkställighet av sluten ungdomsvård.
4 As a result of among other things the higher numbers of youths being sentenced to youth custody than had previously been sentenced to prison, a follow-up study was conducted on the effects of the youth custody legislation. Among other things, this study conducted interviews with judges, and found that many of these felt that they

now had a sanction that they could use in relation to youths whom they felt should be given a custodial sentence, but whom they had previously not wanted to send to prison (Brå *et al.* 2002). Thus the net-widening effect may in part have been due to a perception that it is less problematic to sentence youths to a care-based custodial sanction, which is what youth custody in practice consists in (Pettersson 2010b). This may in part be linked to the Swedish system's strong emphasis on the principle that young offenders should primarily be dealt with within the framework of social services measures.

5 Available online at: www.kriminalvarden.se/forskning-och-statistik/statistik-och-fakta/kriminalvardens-pafoljder/ (accessed 12 January, 2016).

6 The longer term sanctioning trend in Sweden was characterised by a powerful increase in the size of the prison population from the end of World War II until the end of the 1960s, which was followed by a decline until the mid-1970s and then a new increase. The decline in the prison population witnessed over recent years does not however mean that the number of inmates is now low for Swedish conditions. On the contrary, the prison population remains larger today than it was at the end of the 1960s. The highest recorded levels of prison inmates were noted in the years around 2005 (von Hofer and Tham 2013), which was also the case for the numbers sentenced to youth custody.

7 In addition, Palm (2003) conducted a comparison of youths placed in compulsory care in special approved homes by the social services, youths sentenced to youth custody and youths sentenced to prison, and found that the level of repression appeared to be greatest in relation to youth custody sentences. This makes the trend even more problematic.

8 Or rather the Nordic countries.

9 Cullen *et al.* (2011) argue that that opposite is true, however, and that the more gratuitously painful types of prisons produce more harms.

10 Youths admitted in connection with voluntary placements may not, however, be placed in secure units.

11 Youths may be admitted to special approved homes on the basis of more than one of the reasons for placement, which is the case for the majority of placements. Only 26 per cent of the girls and 22 per cent of the boys were placed as a result of only one of the three possible reasons for placement.

12 See Andrews and Bonta (2010) for a thorough description of the risk- and need-perspective in criminology.

13 Available online at: www.mcf.gov.bc.ca/youth_justice/custody.htm (accessed 21 August, 2015).

Bibliography

Andersen, L.H. and Andersen, S.H., 2012. *Losing the stigma of incarceration: Does serving a sentence with electronic monitoring causally improve post-release labor market outcomes?* Odense: University Press of Southern Denmark.

Andersen, S.H., 2015. Serving time or serving the community? Exploiting a policy reform to assess the causal effects of community service on income, social benefit dependency and recidivism. *Journal of Quantitative Criminology*, 31(4), pp. 537–563.

Andreassen, T., 2003. *Institutionsbehandling av ungdomar: Vad säger forskningen?* Stockholm: Gothia.

Andrews, D.A. and Bonta, J., 2010. *The psychology of criminal conduct.* Albany: Lexis Nexis/Anderson Pub.

Bales, W.D. and Piquero, A.R., 2012. Assessing the impact of imprisonment on recidivism. *Journal of Experimental Criminology*, 8(1), pp. 71–101.

Barker, V., 2013. Nordic exceptionalism revisited: Explaining the paradox of a Janus-faced penal regime. *Theoretical Criminology*, 17(1), pp. 5–25.

Bateman, T., 2012. Who pulled the plug? Towards an explanation of the fall in child imprisonment in England and Wales. *Youth Justice*, 12(1), pp. 36–52.

Brå, Statens Institutionsstyrelse and Socialstyrelsen, 2002. *Sluten ungdomsvård – en uppföljning*. Stockholm: Socialstyrelsen.

Cavadino, M. and Dignan, J., 2006. *Penal systems: A comparative approach*. London: Sage.

Crewe, B., 2011a. Depth, weight, tightness: Revisiting the pains of imprisonment. *Punishment & Society*, 13(5), pp. 509–529.

Crewe, B., 2011b. Soft power in prison: Implications for staff–prisoner relationships, liberty and legitimacy. *European Journal of Criminology*, 8(6), pp. 455–468.

Cullen, F.T., Jonson, C.L. and Nagin, D.S., 2011. Prisons do not reduce recidivism: The high cost of ignoring science. *The Prison Journal*, 91(3 suppl.), pp. 48S–65S.

Dullum, J. And Ugelvik, T., 2012. Introduction: Exceptional prisons, exceptional societies? In: T. Ugelvik and J. Dullum, eds, *Penal exceptionalism? Nordic prison policy and practice*. London: Routledge, pp. 1–10.

Durlauf, S.N. and Nagin, D.S., 2011. Imprisonment and crime. *Criminology & Public Policy*, 10(1), pp. 13–54.

Garland, D., 2001. *The culture of control: Crime and social order in contemporary society*. Oxford: Oxford University Press.

Gendreau, P., Goggin, C., Cullen, F.T. and Andrews, D.A., 2000. The effects of community sanctions and incarceration on recidivism, *Forum on Corrections Research* 2000, Correctional Service of Canada, pp. 10–13.

Granath, S., 2007. *Rättsliga reaktioner på ungdomsbrott 1980–2005: Påföljdsval, uppsåtsbedömningar och kriminalpolitik. En kriminologisk analys*. Stockholm: Kriminologiska Institutionen, Stockholms Universitet.

Hannah-Moffat, K., 2005. Criminogenic needs and the transformative risk subject: Hybridizations of risk/need in penality. *Punishment & Society*, 7(1), pp. 29–51.

Hazel, N., 2008. *Cross-national comparison of youth justice*. London: Youth Justice Board for England and Wales.

Holmberg, S., 2013. Påföljdssystemet för unga. In: F. Estrada and J. Flyghed, eds, *Den svenska ungdomsbrottsligheten*. 3rd edn. Stockholm: Studentlitteratur, pp. 313–332.

Hörnqvist, M., 2012. Book review: Thomas Ugelvik and Jane Dullum (eds), Penal Exceptionalism? Nordic Prison Policy and Practice. *Theoretical Criminology*, 16(2), pp. 257–259.

Jacobson, J., Bhardwa, B., Gyateng, T., Hunter, G. and Hough, M., 2010. *Punishing disadvantage: A profile of children in custody*. London: Prison Reform Trust.

Kühlhorn, E., 2002. *Sluten ungdomsvård: Rättsliga reaktioner på de ungas brott före och efter införandet 1999*. Stockholm: Statens Institutionsstyrelse.

Mathiesen, T., 2012. Scandinavian exceptionalism in penal matters. Reality or wishful thinking. In: T. Ugelvik and J. Dullum, eds, *Penal exceptionalism? Nordic prison policy and practice*. London: Routledge, pp. 13–37.

Nagin, D.S., Cullen, F.T. and Jonson, C.L., 2009. Imprisonment and reoffending. *Crime and Justice*, 38(1), pp. 115–200.

Neumann, C.B., 2011. Imprisoning the soul. In: T. Ugelvik and J. Dullum, eds, *Penal exceptionalism? Nordic prison policy and practice*. London & New York: Routledge, pp. 139–155.

Nieuwbeerta, P., Nagin, D.S. and Blokland, A.A., 2009. Assessing the impact of first-time imprisonment on offenders' subsequent criminal career development: A matched samples comparison. *Journal of Quantitative Criminology*, 25(3), pp. 227–257.
Nordlöf, K., 2005. *Unga lagöverträdare i social-, straff-och processrätt.* Lund: Studentlitteratur.
Palm, J., 2003. *Ungdomarnas upplevelse av sluten ungdomsvård: En jämförelse med LVU-placeringar och fängelse.* Stockholm: Statens Institutionsstyrelse.
Pettersson, T., 2010a. *Återfall i brott bland ungdomar dömda till fängelse respektive sluten ungdomsvård.* Stockholm: Statens Institutionsstyrelse.
Pettersson, T., 2010b. Recidivism among young males sentenced to prison and youth custody. *Journal of Scandinavian Studies in Criminology and Crime Prevention*, 11(2), pp. 151–169.
Pratt, J., 2008a. Scandinavian exceptionalism in an era of penal excess, Part I: The nature and roots of Scandinavian exceptionalism. *British Journal of Criminology*, 48(2), pp. 119–137.
Pratt, J., 2008b. Scandinavian exceptionalism in an era of penal excess, Part II: Does Scandinavian exceptionalism have a future? *British Journal of Criminology*, 48(3), pp. 275–292.
Pratt, J. and Eriksson, A., 2012. In defence of Scandinavian exceptionalism. In: T. Ugelvik and J. Dullum, eds, *Penal Exceptionalism? Nordic prison policy and practice.* London: Routledge, pp. 235–260.
Proposition, 1997/98: 96. *Vissa reformer av påföljdssystemet.*
Sarnecki, J. and Estrada, F., 2006. Keeping the balance between humanism and penal punitivism: Recent trends in juvenile delinquency and juvenile justice in Sweden. In: J. Junger-Tass and S.H. Decker, eds, *International handbook of juvenile justice.* Springer, pp. 473–503.
Scharff Smith, P., 2012. A critical look at Scandinavian exceptionalism: Welfare state theories, penal populism and prison conditions in Denmark and Scandinavia. In: T. Ugelvik and J. Dullum, eds, *Penal exceptionalism? Nordic prison policy and practice.* London: Routledge, pp. 38–57.
Shammas, V.L., 2014. The pains of freedom: Assessing the ambiguity of Scandinavian penal exceptionalism on Norway's Prison Island. *Punishment & Society*, 16(1), pp. 104–123.
SiS, 2010. *Kartläggning av LSU-utslussning under 2009.*
Tärnfalk, M., 2007. *Barn och brott: En studie om socialtjänstens yttranden i straffprocessen för unga lagöverträdare.* Stockholm: Institutionen för Socialt Arbete, Stockholms Universitet.
Tham, H., 2001. Law and order as a leftist project? The case of Sweden. *Punishment & Society*, 3(3), pp. 409–426.
Ugelvik, T., 2012. The dark side of a culture of equality: Reimagining communities in a Norwegian remand prison. In: T. Ugelvik and J. Dullum, eds, *Penal exceptionalism? Nordic penal policy and practice.* London: Routledge, pp. 121–138.
Ugelvik, T. and Dullum, J., eds, 2012. *Penal Exceptionalism? Nordic prison policy and practice.* London: Routledge.
von Hofer, H. and Tham, H., 2013. Punishment in Sweden: A changing penal landscape. In: V. Ruggiero and M. Ryan, eds, *Punishment in Europe. A critical anatomy of penal systems.* London: Palgrave Macmillan, pp. 33–56.

2 Total institutions, discipline and power

The questions examined in this book touch upon several different areas of criminology, such as prison research, youth care provision, recidivism studies and life course research. The theoretical framework employed in order to understand and interpret the significance of custodial openness for everyday institutional life and for reoffending, proceeds from a combination of Goffman's (1991) work on total institutions and Foucault's (1991) work on discipline. I will therefore begin by discussing the similarities between the two perspectives, and the ways in which they complement one another, and will then move on to issues of power and resistance at youth institutions and in prison. The discussion concludes by looking at the significance of time and place for the experience of incarceration and at how this also has embodied effects that remain with the inmate even once the period of incarceration is over.

Total institutions and discipline: a synthesis of Goffman and Foucault

The central feature of total institutions is that they break down the boundaries between three spheres – sleep, recreation and work – which in normal life are separated from one another (Goffman 1991 p. 17ff.). The inmates are (temporarily) denied the right to manage their own money, to speak on their own behalf, etc. Another characteristic feature is the management of large groups of people by means of bureaucratic organisation, and to cope with life in a total institution, individuals must adapt. Goffman (1991 p. 61ff.) distinguishes four adaptation strategies, or approaches, among inmates, which may all be used by the same inmate in different situations. The first strategy is labelled *situational withdrawal* and involves cutting oneself off. The second involves adopting an *intransigent line*, which means refusing to engage with the total institution and the conflicts this produces.[1] Goffman refers to a third approach as *colonisation*. This means that "the sampling of the outside world provided by the establishment is taken by the inmate as the whole, and a stable, relatively contented existence is built up out of the maximum satisfactions procurable within the institution" (p. 62). The fourth adaptation strategy is *conversion*. This means that the inmate "appears to be taken over the official or staff view of himself and tries to act out the role of the perfect inmate" (p. 63). Total institutions tend to generate distance between staff and inmates (Goffman 1991 p. 18). The staff often feel superior, while the inmates perceive themselves to be more or less inferior. In combination with other factors, this produces a marked asymmetry in the power relations between staff and inmates, which may, for example, manifest itself in inmates being forced to ask submissively in order to obtain such trivial things as a glass of water, being able to smoke or being given a light for a cigarette, etc.

In *Discipline and Punish* (1991) Foucault describes how society has historically moved from the use of corporal to disciplinary punishments, and how this has affected the whole of society. For Foucault, discipline is

> an art of the human body [...] which was directed not only at the growth of its skills, nor at the intensification of its subjection, but at the formation of a relation that in the mechanism itself makes it more obedient as it becomes more useful, and conversely.
>
> (1991 pp. 137–138)

The use of discipline is about producing obedient and useful bodies. Ugelvik (2011 p. 95 my translation) describes discipline as "an expression of the work of social engineers to change members of society who do not fit in". Foucault's discipline may in part be compared to Goffman's (1991 p. 83) discussion of the significance of the inmates "*self-direct[ing]* themselves" (emphasis in original) in a way that makes their conduct something that they both want and are able to control and change. Goffman's concept of self-directing themselves is however somewhat broader than the conceptualisation of discipline described by Foucault in *Discipline and Punish*, and includes not only the governance of obedient bodies but also influencing the personality. Goffman (1991) argues that total institutions involve new privilege systems that are intended to bring about "personal reorganization", and he describes three central features of these systems:

1 House rules.
2 Rewards. Within the framework of these routines the system offers "a small number of clearly defined rewards or privileges are held out in exchange for obedience to staff in action and spirit" (Goffman 1991 p. 51). These rewards are primarily comprised of things that the inmates would formerly take for granted. An entire world is built up around these small rewards, in a way that can be difficult for an outsider to understand.
3 Punishments. These are described as consequences of breaking the rules. They might mean a temporary or permanent loss of privileges or perhaps of the right to try to earn such privileges. The privileges available in total institutions are not luxury items or special benefits but rather merely the "absence of deprivations one ordinarily expects not to have to sustain" (Goffman 1991 p. 53).

There are similarities here to Foucault's discussions of productive and repressive power (see Hörnqvist 2012), an issue that I will be returning to. Goffman (1991) also notes that release from the total institution often also constitutes part of this privilege system, and describes the movement of inmates from one place to another (e.g. between placements in open or secure units) as "the administrative device for giving them the punishment or reward their cooperativeness warrants" (Goffman 1991 pp. 53–54). One part of cooperating with the system involves showing a willingness to change. Goffman (1991 pp. 138–139) argues that:

> Having every reason to initiate requests for better conditions, he is told that when the staff feel he is "able to manage" or will be "comfortable with" a higher ward level, then appropriate action will be taken. In short, assignment to a given ward is presented not as a reward or punishment, but as an expression of his general level of social functioning, his status as a person.

This is reminiscent of the ways in which other scholars, on the basis of Foucault, have discussed how (showing) willingness to change leads to various benefits (Hörnqvist 2010, Werth 2011, 2013). Foucault (1991) himself refers to what he labels the normalising judgement, which means that all forms of deviation from the rule are punishable. He argues that court sentences are not only punitive legal decisions, but also judgements about whether or not the individual is normal, and about the ways in which the individual can be *made* normal. The micro-economy of the penal system is focused on a perpetual differentiation into good and bad individuals. Discipline imposes exact rewards and penalties, which are gauged to correspond to the exact level or value of each individual.

The resultant penal system integrates the sum of the knowledge that has been collected in relation to the individual. "Small scale legal systems" and "parallel judges" (Foucault 1991 p. 21) are created, in the form of psychiatrists, psychologists, officials concerned with the implementation of sentences, educationalists, etc. Since these may determine whether or not the condemned individual "deserves" to be set at liberty (e.g. in the form of release on parole or periods of prison leave), the task of judging is passed on into their hands. Foucault (1991 p. 126) argues that

> A whole corpus of individualizing knowledge was being organized that took as its field of reference not so much the crime committed (at least in isolation), but the potentially danger that lies hidden in an individual and which is manifested in his observed everyday conduct.

Thus the goal of punishment is to change a "criminal", not to expiate a crime. Goffman (1991) also argues that life in total institutions is related to identifying the types of people who are held in them, and that hierarchies of inmates are established. The measures taken by the management in relation to inmates say something about the way they define what type of people these inmates are. When an inmate participates in the life of the institution, this leads to an identity that corresponds to the institutional management's view of who gets placed in the institution. Goffman (1991 p. 170) argues that "[t]o engage in a particular activity in the prescribed spirit is to accept being a particular kind of person who dwells in a particular kind of world". In a similar way, Ugelvik (2014) shows how resistance from prison inmates constitutes a means of expressing opposition to being (only) a certain type of person, i.e. a prisoner.

One important part of the system is found in what Foucault (1991) labels *the examination*. The examination involves having an overview that enables individuals to be differentiated, rewarded and punished. One manifestation of this examination is being released (being discharged with a "clean bill of health" from Goffman's mental hospital), another may be found in being viewed as having changed sufficiently to be able to spend time outside the institution. Foucault notes that the examination process is immediately guided by the individual being subject to a process of constant documentation. Foucault emphasises the importance of collecting knowledge about the individual as a central element in the disciplining organisation. In this respect, too, Goffman presents similar arguments, among other things when he notes that knowledge about the client is produced for the purposes of control (Goffman 1991, Battershill 1990).

In the power systems sketched by Foucault (and which I feel manifest substantial similarities to those described by Goffman), it is also important that the length of a prison sentence is not determined once and for all. If the length of a sentence were absolute, then the sentence would lose its correctional value, and "(t)he correct duration of the penalty must be calculated, therefore, not only according to the particular crime and its circumstances, but also according to the penalty itself as it takes place in actual fact" (Foucault 1991 pp. 244–245). This is central to understanding the correctional function and potential of spending time outside the institution or in an open unit.

Combining Goffman and Foucault

As can be seen from the above, I feel that there are substantial similarities between the work of Goffman and Foucault in these respects. One difference between the two, however, is that they are interested in different questions, while another is the way in which they choose to examine these questions empirically. Goffman is interested in the interactions that take place within total institutions, and conducted an extensive ethnographic study of these interactions. Foucault, on the other hand, directs his focus at historical processes of change in society at large, and emphasises the role of prisons and correctional techniques as being central to certain aspects of these processes (while also being a consequence of them), and his method directs its primary focus at an analysis of discourses. At the same time, Foucault himself noted that it was essential to study the direct effects of the exercise of power on behaviour (Hörnqvist 2012 p. 56), a view that leans towards a focus on interpersonal interactions. It is possible that the points of departure employed by Goffman and Foucault may be viewed as incompatible, and the two bodies of work have rarely been used in combination, as far as I have been able to ascertain (see, however Petersson 2013, Kivett and Warren 2002). I am not alone in seeing similarities between the two. In a book on Goffman, for example, Burns (1992 p. 158), makes the following observation about Goffman's *Total Institutions* and Foucault's *Discipline and Punish*: "It is at this point that there begins to emerge a quite remarkable coincidence between Goffman's conclusions and what Foucault, later (but almost certainly, quite independently), was to say on the same specific topics".

Hacking (2004) argues that Foucault and Goffman complement one another, and that both are required for an understanding of what he refers to as "making up people". Very briefly, Hacking uses the term "making up people" to refer to the way classifying changes people, but also the way in which the changed people in their turn affect classifications. Hacking's view is that Goffman's bottom-up perspective and Foucault's top-down perspective are both required in order to understand the workings of "making up people". Nor does he view Goffman and Foucault as opposites, even though their respective objects of study, and not least the data they employ, lie at some distance from one another in many ways. Instead, Hacking argues that both aspects are necessary components for this understanding. While Goffman directs his interest entirely at how interactions between people in total institutions form these people (both patients and staff), with no thought for how these institutions have emerged, Foucault is instead explicitly interested in the latter question. In focusing his interest on this topic, however, Foucault also looks at how these institutions (mental hospitals, prisons) form people. Thus, for Hacking, both scholars focus on developing an understanding of issues related to "making up people", but in different ways and on different levels. While the interpersonal level, and how the process of forming people takes place in more concrete terms, does not constitute the central focus for Foucault, I would argue that in *Discipline and Punish* in particular, he presents a large number of concrete, detailed descriptions of how people are disciplined. In this respect, however, Goffman's work is superior as a result of his up-close and comprehensive ethnographic approach. Burns (1992 p. 160, Battershill 1990) describes the links between Goffman and Foucault in the following way:

> It is almost as if Foucault had taken up Goffman's interpretation of the process by which organisations impose an appropriate identity on their members and expanded it into a much wider thesis about how political power is exerted in modern society. The connection is all more striking because neither of them, as far as one can judge, was aware of the other's writing.

Thus combining the two perspectives, in addition to emphasising their similarities, also provides an opportunity to apply different analytical dimensions to understanding the incarceration of (in the current instance) young people.

Power and resistance in youth custody and in prison

For the purposes of this book, the overarching analytical project is not that of understanding how the process of "making up people" (Hacking 2004) functions at the *general* level. At the same time, however, it is clear that what happens within the framework of youth custody sentences is to a large extent focused on making/forming – or perhaps rather *remaking* the youths in question. Central to an understanding of this phenomenon is Foucault's conceptualisation of power (1991 p. 32, see also Hörnqvist 2012) in terms of both productive power and power as a relation. This is largely the view of power that emerges in the *relations* between staff and the youths, and in the *production of actions* that the possibility of spending time outside the institution or of being able to stay in an open unit results in.

In contrast to Foucault, Goffman is not known for his analysis of power, although some have argued that this characterisation is unfair (Burns 1992, Jenkins 2008, Scott 2010). My own view is that Goffman, in *Total Institutions*, is clearly preoccupied with how power relations between staff and inmates are formed and enacted, and Burns (1992, see also Battershill 1990) notes, for example, that there are substantial similarities between the power analyses of Foucault and Goffman in this respect. He writes of Foucault's disciplining, for example, that "the 'disciplining' is [...] a 'privilege and penalty system' of the kind Goffman saw at work in total institutions [which] imposes itself throughout society" (p. 164). Scott (2010) has also argued that the perception of Goffman's inmates as passive and powerless is misleading. In Goffman's discussions of "the underworld" of the patients, for example, their various tactics for getting around the demands made on them by staff and the institutional environment are more reminiscent of the acts of resistance described by Foucault (1991, Hörnqvist 2012, Hörnqvist 2010) rather than they are of passivity. The conception of power that Goffman expresses in *Total Institutions* is thus, in my view, quite compatible with Foucault's power analysis, but since Goffman's analysis is not as explicitly stated, and has further been the subject of less discussion, analysis and exposure in subsequent research, I will be proceeding on the basis of Foucault's writing, and that of those who have themselves published work on Foucault's conceptualisation of power, primarily the work of Hörnqvist (2010, 2012).

Hörnqvist (2010, 2012) outlines a number of central assumptions found in Foucault's conception of power. First, power is understood as both a relation and an activity. Hörnqvist criticises the governmentality research tradition that has followed in the footsteps of Foucault for ignoring the power as a relation aspect and for focusing exclusively on power as an activity. Without an understanding of the workings of power as a relation, however, Hörnqvist argues that it is not possible to differentiate what power is from what it is not. Instead everything is reduced to different activities. Second, Hörnqvist discusses power as both productive and repressive. In order to obtain a view of the potential of power in its entirety, we must examine both its repressive and productive aspects. While repressive power is linked to laws and sets external limits as to what is right and wrong, or whether or not an action constitutes a transgression of a rule, productive power is about *norms*. While repressive power is focused on preventing (unlawful or incorrect) actions, productive power instead involves generating actions.

Finally, Hörnqvist notes that where there is power, there is also resistance, and that what constitutes power and resistance is determined by the internal relations of the involved parties. He argues that "[r]esistance is the activity directed at the opposing party that is engaged in by the subordinate party, whereas the exercise of power is the corresponding activity that proceeds from the dominant party" (Hörnqvist 2012 p. 155, my translation). In my own material, it may be assumed that the actions of staff may primarily be interpreted as the exercise of power, and the youths' actions (to the extent that they act contrary to the intentions of staff) may be interpreted as resistance. This is not necessarily the case in all situations, and this is thus a judgement that must be made in relation to each individual act that is described, and the context in which it occurs. Liebling (2008) notes, for example, that one of the most important results from her study of the introduction of a system of privileges (Incentives and Earned Privileges) in British prisons was that power flowed in both directions between staff and inmates.

Proceeding on the basis of Foucault's work, Ugelvik (2014) has devoted a considerable amount to the question of resistance in prisons. In his ethnographic study of a Norwegian prison, one of the central questions examined is that of what brings resistance among inmates to the fore, and also the significance of this resistance. Ugelvik argues that the inmates "do freedom" by means of their resistance, but also that they "do masculinity". He states that

> the ultimate objective of resistance is not necessarily to successfully evade control. The goal may, instead, be to face that control in a satisfactory way, preferably by making it more liveable and at the same time making yourself more than someone who is being controlled by the process.
>
> (p. 45)

This may be compared with the subtle and well-considered expressions of resistance described by Wästerfors (2009) in a study of boys at a Swedish special approved home (although Wästerfors does not himself use the term resistance). He describes the boys' ability to "use subversive irony or to act 'rudely' in such a discreet manner that it cannot be turned against them" (p. 27). Ugelvik (2014 p. 44) also discusses how the resistance exercised by inmates is of significance to how control becomes formulated, since the staff adapt to the resistance that occurs. In turn, this produces new opportunities for resistance and also moulds the control to this resistance, with resistance and control thus being both interconnected and changeable.

Foucault notes the significance of studying how power is exercised at the micro level (Hörnqvist 2012, Petersson 2013). Hörnqvist (2010 pp. 154–157) argues, in contrast to a number of scholars from the governmentality tradition, that the productive power that is exercised within the framework of (Swedish) prisons, not least in the form of cognitive behavioural programmes, cannot be analysed exclusively as *technologies of the self*, nor even exclusively as *discipline* in accordance with Foucault's original sense of the term (as formulated in *Discipline and Punish*). Instead it contains elements of both. Hörnqvist writes that

> they were found to share characteristics associated with technologies of the self, such as voluntary participation, individualistic responsibility, appeals to existing aspirations and empowerment. At the same time, the programmes contained elements of the opposite: coercion, close monitoring, imposed objectives and limited competence.
>
> (Hörnqvist 2010 p. 154)

He argues further that the description of productive power requires a concept that captures both these forms, since it is "voluntary and involuntary, responsibilizing and de-responsibilizing, authentic and imposed, involving freedom and necessity, empowerment and subordination" (Hörnqvist 2010 p. 97). Hörnqvist notes that it is unclear what is *produced*, and that the research in this field has argued that many different things are produced. For his own part, he argues that the question of what is produced should perhaps be approached a little more modestly than is often the case, and that it is not personality that is produced but, rather, conduct. Hörnqvist (2012, s. 93 my translation) feels that "[i]t is a question of repeatedly influencing which actions will be carried out and not of a once-and-for-all creation of subjects who behave in accordance with their positions".[2] It is on the basis of this perspective that the relations and activities of power are studied in this book. For the purposes of the study presented here, however, there is no analytical reason for separating technologies of the self and discipline. In my analysis, I will therefore make use of Hörnqvist's more composite understanding of the concept of productive power, and will not be distinguishing between the two.

Another of Foucault's (1982) concepts that is of significance to the analysis is that of *pastoral power*. This form of power was originally associated with Christian institutions, but has in today's secular society been reformulated into a form of power exercised through the state. Its importance has not least been emphasised in relation to the institutions of the welfare state, including the various tasks of the social services (Petersson 2013, Järvinen 2002). Ugelvik (2014 p. 48) argues that prisons also constitute part of the welfare state, via their objective of improving people so that they no longer engage in crime, and that pastoral power is also exercised in these institutions (p. 57).[3] Palm (2003), however, feels that this is even more true of youth care institutions than of prisons. Foucault (1982 p. 783) identifies four characteristic components of pastoral power. First, it has the objective of procuring individuals' salvation in the next world. Today this objective has instead become focused on a form of salvation in this life. Second, it involves the pastor (or representatives of the pastor) not only exercising command but also making sacrifices for the benefit of ensuring others' chances of salvation. Third, it is a form of power that focuses not only on the group or congregation, but on every individual within this collective. And, finally, this form of power is exercised within people's minds. It thus requires detailed knowledge about the conscience and also an ability to guide and direct it.

Pastoral power is also exercised within the framework of a benevolent project and is related to the *normalising* task associated with social work (Petersson 2013, Mattsson 2005). Petersson shows, for example, how staff working with substitution treatment consistently describe their control of clients, and their establishment of the conditions and routines that govern access to treatment, in terms of providing support and assistance to clients who lack the ability to cope with their own everyday lives. Järvinen (2002) speaks of the *universe of help* and of how the power exercised by social services officials is concealed and denied through the use of descriptions that present their work in terms of providing help and not of exercising power and control, despite the fact that this work also includes a large number of such elements (see also Johansson and Skrinjar 2001). In *this* universe of help, there is no exercise of power, but rather the provision of (self-sacrificing) help and support to a person who needs to be guided onto the right path to living a good and normal life. Järvinen (2002) argues that his power needs to be exposed and problematised and that it can "only continue as long as those exercising this power perceive that it is not power that they are exercising" (p. 273). For my own part, I am not sure that the exercise of this form of power would cease if all those exercising it were to understand and accept that they are exercising power (which is implied by the above quotation). At the same time, however, I agree that this exercise of power should be exposed and made the subject of reflection, and that it will become more powerful if this does not happen.

Crewe (2009, 2011a, 2011b) discusses how power has changed in prisons in England and Wales. He (2011a p. 524, emphasis in original) argues that "the carceral experience is less directly oppressive, but more gripping – *lighter but tighter*". The former, more repressive power, whose use led to inmates being afraid of staff, and which could also result in inmates being exposed to brutality, while at the same time they were also left more to their own devices,[4] has, Crewe argues, been replaced by what he labels *soft power* (Crewe 2009, Crewe 2011b). The exercise of soft power is more about getting the inmates to govern themselves via the use of the staff's substantial room for discretion. While many inmates appreciate the fact that the former, more brutal, relations between themselves and staff have largely disappeared, and that the staff are no longer disinterested about who the inmates are, this new form of power is at the same time in part perceived as being more ambiguous and less visible. Crewe also describes a number of other consequences of the shift, which has among other things affected staff's attitude to inmates, and I will be returning to these in the book's concluding discussion. It is also worth noting that the use of this form of power was probably already, and it is likely that it remains, more common within the more clearly welfare-focused areas of the societal control apparatus, such as in the area of social services measures (Barker 2013, Järvinen 2002, Petersson 2013).

A further aspect of power in present-day prisons, which is clearly related to youth custody and the opportunities for custodial openness, is what Shammas (2014) has labelled "pains of freedom". This concept links into Sykes's (1958) "pains of imprisonment" and is used to illustrate how more open prisons involve different forms of pains, with the proximity to freedom producing special problems and not least the use of other forms of power. Shammas proceeds from the discussion of Scandinavian penal exceptionalism, which was presented in the introductory chapter, and more specifically the better and freer prison conditions found in Scandinavia, and then builds on Crewe's analyses of the altered power situation in today's British prisons. On the basis of ethnographic data from an open prison in Norway, Shammas describes how the proximity to freedom may be related to five different forms of "pains of freedom": 1) confusion; 2) anxiety and boundlessness; 3) ambiguity; 4) relative deprivation; and 5) individual responsibility (2014 p. 110).

All these forms of pains of freedom, with the exception of relative deprivation, are of relevance to the current study. Confusion is about how the feeling of being in the open prison produces perplexity about being free but at the same time not free, since the inmates move relatively unhindered between the outside and the inside of the prison. In parallel with this substantial freedom, however, the prison's regulations regarding rule violations remain in place. Anxiety and boundlessness relate to how, by contrast with secure conditions, open conditions produce a foretaste of release and, as a result, lead to inmates living in "permanently suspended release anxiety" (Shammas 2014 p. 112). A further aspect is that the contacts with "normal life" associated with various forms of prison leave create stress rather than representing a welcome change. Inmates also spoke of becoming confused when faced with changes that have occurred in society during their period of incarceration, such as technological advances. There was also an ambiguity, a sense of ambivalence towards spending time outside prison, since this on the one hand was good, but on the other created "a taste of freedom" (Shammas 2014 p. 113, cf. McAllister *et al.* 1992), which produced a desire for more and at the same time generated negative feelings because it left inmates unfulfilled. Finally, individual responsibility relates to the way in which inmates in open prisons are faced with having to exercise power over themselves. They are required to *discipline themselves*, so to speak, to follow rules, return after leave periods, etc., a form of disciplining the soul, to use Neumann's (2011) term. Shammas notes that "exceptional penal institutions[5] may perhaps be said 'not to punish less but to punish better'" (with a reference to Foucault's *Discipline and Punish*) and argues that future research should examine other forms of unusual penal institutions.

Finally, another important element in the power relations between staff and youth at special approved homes is found in various systems of privileges, often in the form of a token economy (Franzén and Holmqvist 2014, Kivett and Warren 2002, Liebling 2008). These systems are sometimes related to periods spent outside the institution, as one of the privileges that can be obtained through good behaviour. In this way they become part of the systematised power relations between the staff and youths, with the youths being viewed as being responsible for producing the behaviours that are required in order to receive rewards (Franzén and Holmqvist 2014, see also Werth 2013), while at the same time it is still the staff who assess the extent to which they have performed in accordance with the relevant criteria. Views are divided on whether this constitutes an effective system for achieving desirable behaviours. Franzèn and Holmqvist refer to evaluations that show weak but positive effects of the token economy, whereas Liebling's evaluation of its introduction in British prisons produced findings that instead indicate that the system had the opposite effect. The staff in both studies, however, expressed a belief that the token economy did indeed function as a technique for governing the behaviour of prison inmates (Liebling 2008) and of youths in a special approved home (Franzén and Holmqvist 2014). The same is also true for the staff in Crewe's (2009 p. 108) study, who felt that the use of incentives was an effective means of ensuring inmate compliance. Irrespective of whether or not they are effective, systems of this kind constitute part of the power relations found in prisons and special approved homes.

Criticism of the total institutions concept and the significance of time and place for the experience of incarceration

One criticism that is of relevance to the current study is that which has been directed at researchers who have made use of Goffman's total institutions concept as a description of prisons (Farrington 1992, Moran 2013, 2014, Baer and Ravneberg 2008). Farrington (1992) argues that prisons cannot be described as total institutions in this way, since prisons are linked to the rest of society in a number of different ways. These include services that are provided by the surrounding community (such as food deliveries), the fact that staff live outside the prison and thus take the prison with them into the community, and also the fact that inmates have certain contacts with individuals from outside prison, e.g. in the form of prison visits. In order for prisons to constitute truly total institutions, Farrington argues (as I understand him), they would need to be located somewhere completely isolated, the staff would have to live there and there could be no contacts with the rest of society. Baer and Ravneberg (2008) have also criticised the use of the total institutions concept in relation to prisons primarily on the basis of the idea that such institutions would be completely isolated from external contacts. They instead argue for the use of Foucault's concept of *heterotopia*, which is more fluid and ambiguous, and thus also less associated with dichotomies between inside and outside, staff and inmates, etc. They note, however, that their view is based on their own experiences of visiting prisons in the capacity of researchers, and that it remains to be seen whether the inmates also perceive the boundary between outside and inside as in part somewhat diffuse in the same way as themselves, which would constitute a not entirely unimportant objection in my own view. I would argue, however, that the distinction between outside/inside (although sometimes somewhat blurred), as I interpret it, constitutes one of the factors underlying the pains of freedom described by Shammas (2014), which I view as a very useful concept for the purposes of my own analysis.[6]

In my view, Farrington bases his arguments on a somewhat limited reading of Goffman, using a more restrictive definition of what constitutes a total institution than that employed by Goffman himself.[7] He nonetheless makes a number of important points. One of these is that the perception (or the myth as he refers to it himself) of the prison as a total institution invites an over-simplified use of prisons as a means of dealing with those who are viewed as dangerous criminals and removing them from society. This might in turn contribute to an increased use of prisons as a solution to perceived crime problems. Farrington also refers to the prison as a "not-so-total" institution, and this expression may be said to tie into the subject of the current study, i.e. the significance of opening up special approved homes so that they become "not-so-total".

Another way in which Farrington's criticism of Goffman's total institutions has significance is found in the way Moran (2014) relates to it, when she discusses questions about the effect of prison on the body, and how this means that the prison does not simply "disappear" when an inmate is released. Moran's discussion is based on a study of women in prison in Russia, and she describes how these women perceive the stigma of prison as a "tattoo on the forehead" (p. 41). In this way, prison accompanies the inmate outside the total institution. While the conditions in Russian prisons differ from those found in special approved homes,[8] the sense that having been placed in a special approved home is something that "shows" may also be of relevance in Sweden. Moran (2012b) also argues that this bodily experience of the prison, which remains with the inmate subsequent to release, and which may either take the form of something visible to others (dental status) or something invisible (sleep problems, difficulties being alone or knowing how to act in social situations), is also of significance in relation to the reintegration of inmates into society. Shammas (2014) also describes various forms of bodily reaction among inmates (rashes, cold-sweats) to periods spent outside prison, which he interprets in line with Moran's discussion of the way the experience of prison physically remains with the inmate outside of the prison walls.

In addition to focusing on this bodily link between inside and outside the institution, Moran's (2014, 2012a) work focuses on the field of *carceral space*, an area which combines human geography with criminological/sociological prison research. The research in this field, for example, looks to the perception of time spent inside as an important element in understanding the experience of being in prison (Cope 2003, Moran 2012a, Shammas 2014). Time may be perceived as going so fast that one becomes dizzy, or as moving at a snail's pace and never ending; it may be perceived in different ways depending on whether one is (temporarily) outside the institution or in isolation, and perceptions may vary at different times of day or night. The time spent in prison/institutions is perceived as being lost; while others on the outside move on with their lives, those inside are standing still.[9] Thus carceral space involves a weaving together of one's existence inside and outside the institution.

Another way in which time is linked to the experience of prison, in addition to the link between time and the length of the sentence to be served, is found in the way in which time is subject to continuous controls during a prison sentence. When you have to get up, when you eat, when you go to bed, when you get "free time", when you work or go to school are all things that are often governed in minute detail within the context of a prison sentence or a period of institutional care (Cope 2003, Foucault 1991). Foucault notes that controlling time in this way constitutes one means of exercising disciplinary techniques. The time outside, prior to incarceration or the institutional placement, is instead characterised by having been unstructured, lacking a fixed time-table (Cope 2003). While time in prison is strictly partitioned and controlled in certain respects, there are also long periods that are instead characterised more by inactivity than by such detailed control, such as the period after the day's scheduled activities and during the night (Cope 2003).

Stated briefly, the staff have power over the inmates'/youths' time, the time during which they are locked in,[10] in what ways and on what conditions, and the time when they are permitted to be outside. This careful control of time and space becomes a way in which the micro-power of discipline is exercised (Foucault 1991, Petersson 2013). This power may be used both repressively (punishing and preventing breaches of rules) and productively (rewarding and producing "desirable" behaviour). In this way, power is also exercised over the youths' bodies, that are required to be in certain spaces and places at certain times. Ugelvik (2014 p. 50) argues that at the level of day-to-day interaction, control is primarily focused on the inmates' bodies, ensuring that these are "on the right side of the right door at the right time" (p. 57).

Summary

Goffman's interactionist analyses of what happens between and to people in total institutions and Foucault's analyses of discipline and the exercise of power are both required to understand what happens in special approved homes and to the youths that serve their sentences in these institutions. In many ways the conclusions of Goffman and Foucault are similar, but they contribute to an understanding of inmate life on different levels. Central to any interpretation of the significance of custodial openness for the everyday life of young people sentenced to youth custody and their subsequent reoffending is the issue of how openness is linked to the power relations that exist between the staff and the youths. In this context, both productive power and repressive power are of significance. Where productive power ends in these institutions, however, there is always the possibility of using repressive measures; if productive power does not produce obedient bodies or individuals who engage voluntarily in their own development (in the desired direction), repressive measures will be implemented (Hörnqvist 2010, Ugelvik 2014, Bosworth 2007).

Pastoral power – i.e. the exercise of power within the framework of a generally benevolent project (or to liberate/improve) – is also important to an understanding of the significance of custodial openness. The same is true of the resistance generated by institutional power relations, since this makes it possible for the youths to act with a certain degree of autonomy, but may also serve as an obstacle to processes of change. At the same time as the analysis in this book proceeds on the basis of Goffman's concept of the total institution, an important part of this analysis involves showing how custodial openness may be used to make these institutions less "total", or "not-so-total", to borrow Farrington's (1992) term. To this end, an understanding of how the institution and experiences of incarceration follow the youths outside, and also of the pains of freedom associated with more open conditions, are also of significance.

Notes

1 Goffman notes that, paradoxically, this strategy at the same time requires a deep level of engagement with the organisation.

2 This view can be contrasted with that presented by Crewe (2009 pp. 144–146) in a comparison between an earlier, more authoritarian exercise of power in British prisons, and that of today, which he refers to as neo-paternalistic. He notes that the site of transformation for the authoritarian system was the body and behaviour, whereas in the neo-paternalistic system, it has shifted to cognition, identity and soul.

3 This is at least the case in the Norwegian context, and can reasonably also be generalised to the Swedish and the Scandinavian context.

4 Many activities, such as cannabis use, which are not acceptable today, were tolerated at the time.

5 A concept employed to refer to the more open and humane prison conditions described by Pratt (Pratt 2008a, Pratt 2008b).

6 Moran (2013) argues, for example, that prison visiting rooms should be regarded as *liminal carceral spaces*, a form of space in the borderland between outside and inside for both the visitors and the inmates who receive visits. I see the value of Moran's concept, but for the purpose of the current study, the pains of freedom concept is more useful. The strain that the inmates in Moran's study associated with the visiting room are very reminiscent of those Shammas describes using the pains of freedom concept, such as the pain associated with getting a taste of freedom, as has also been touched upon by McAllister *et al.* (1992). In the current study, it is the reminder that visits provide of the outside world (freedom) that is of primary relevance, rather than the visiting room as a carceral space.

7 The staff of the mental institution at which Goffman conducted his study did not live in the institution, for example, from what I can understand, and nor were the inmates completely isolated from their surroundings. Goffman also describes institutions such as the military and monasteries as total institutions, and these cannot be said to be completely isolated from the rest of society either. Goffman has however been criticised for being unclear in his definition of the term institution, for example (Sundberg 2015).

8 To take one example, Moran's inmates spoke of experiences of very bad dental treatment, which resulted in a perception that their poor dental status would expose them as having been in prison. This is something that is unlikely to be the case among young people sentenced to youth custody in Sweden.

9 Goffman (1991) has also discussed how the inmates in an institution perceived time as having gone to waste.

10 Although not the length of the youth custody sentence that is served.

Bibliography

Baer, L.D. and Ravneberg, B., 2008. The outside and inside in Norwegian and English prisons. *Geografiska Annaler: Series B, Human Geography*, 90(2), pp. 205–216.

Barker, V., 2013. Nordic Exceptionalism revisited: Explaining the paradox of a Janus-faced penal regime. *Theoretical Criminology*, 17(1), pp. 5–25.

Battershill, C.D., 1990. Erving Goffman as a precursor to post-modern sociology. In: S.H. Riggins, ed., *Beyond Goffman. Studies on communication, institution, and social interaction.* Berlin: Mouton de Gruyter, pp. 163–186.

Bosworth, M., 2007. Creating the responsible prisoner. Federal admission and orientation packs. *Punishment & Society*, 9(1), pp. 67–85.

Burns, T., 1992. *Erving Goffman.* London: Routledge.

Cope, N., 2003. 'It's no time or high time': Young offenders' experiences of time and drug use in prison. *The Howard Journal of Criminal Justice*, 42(2), pp. 158–175.

Crewe, B., 2009. *The prisoner society: Power, adaptation and social life in an English prison.* Oxford: Oxford University Press.

Crewe, B., 2011a. Depth, weight, tightness: Revisiting the pains of imprisonment. *Punishment & Society*, 13(5), pp. 509–529.

Crewe, B., 2011b. Soft power in prison: Implications for staff–prisoner relationships, liberty and legitimacy. *European Journal of Criminology*, 8(6), pp. 455–468.

Farrington, K., 1992. The modern prison as total institution? Public perception versus objective reality. *Crime & Delinquency*, 38(1), pp. 6–26.

Foucault, M., 1982. The subject and power. *Critical inquiry*, 8(4), pp. 777–795.

Foucault, M., 1991. *Discipline and punish: The birth of the prison.* London: Penguin books.

Franzén, A.G. and Holmqvist, R., 2014. From punishment to rewards? Treatment dilemmas at a youth detention home. *Punishment & Society*, 16(5), pp. 542–559.

Goffman, E., 1991. *Asylums: Essays on the social situation of mental patients and other inmates.* London: Penguin Books.

Hacking, I., 2004. Between Michel Foucault and Erving Goffman: Between discourse in the abstract and face-to-face interaction. *Economy and Society*, 33(3), pp. 277–302.

Hörnqvist, M., 2010. *Risk, power and the state: After Foucault.* London: Routledge.

Hörnqvist, M., 2012. *En annan Foucault: Maktens problematik.* Stockholm: Carlsson Bokförlag.

Järvinen, M., 2002. Hjälpens universum – ett maktperspektiv på mötet mellan klient och system. In: A. Meeuwisse and H. Swärd, eds, *Perspektiv på sociala problem.* Stockholm: Natur och Kultur, pp. 253–273.

Jenkins, R., 2008. Erving Goffman: A major theorist of power? *Journal of Power*, 1(2), pp. 157–168.

Johansson, P. and Skrinjar, M., 2001. Kontrollanten som hjälpare och hjälparen som kontrollant: Polisers och socialarbetares yrkesroller i arbetet med narkotikamissbrukare. *Nad Publication*, 40, pp. 203–218.

Kivett, D.D. and Warren, C.A., 2002. Social control in a group home for delinquent boys. *Journal of Contemporary Ethnography*, 31(1), pp. 3–32.

Liebling, A., 2008. Incentives and earned privileges revisited: Fairness, discretion, and the quality of prison life. *Journal of Scandinavian Studies in Criminology and Crime Prevention*, 9(S1), pp. 25–41.

Mattsson, T., 2005. *I viljan att göra det normala: En kritisk studie av genusperspektivet i missbrukarvården.* Lund: Lunds Universitet, Institutionen för Socialt Arbete.

McAllister, D., Bottomley, A.K. and Liebling, A., 1992. *From custody to community: Through care for young offenders.* Avebury: Aldershot.

Moran, D., 2012a. "Doing time" in carceral space: Timespace and carceral geography. *Geografiska Annaler: Series B, Human Geography*, 94(4), pp. 305–316.

Moran, D., 2012b. Prisoner reintegration and the stigma of prison time inscribed on the body. *Punishment & Society*, 14(5), pp. 564–583.

Moran, D., 2013. Between outside and inside? Prison visiting rooms as liminal carceral spaces. *GeoJournal*, 78(2), pp. 339–351.

Moran, D., 2014. Leaving behind the "total institution"? Teeth, transcarceral spaces and (re)inscription of the formerly incarcerated body. *Gender, Place & Culture*, 21(1), pp. 35–51.

Neumann, C.B., 2011. Imprisoning the soul. In: T. Ugelvik and J. Dullum, eds, *Penal exceptionalism? Nordic prison policy and practice.* London & New York: Routledge, pp. 139–155.

Palm, J., 2003. *Ungdomarnas upplevelse av sluten ungdomsvård: En jämförelse med LVU-placeringar och fängelse.* Stockholm: Statens Institutionsstyrelse.

Petersson, F., 2013. *Kontroll av beroende. Substitutionsbehandlingens logik, praktik och semantik.* Malmö: Égalité.

Pratt, J., 2008a. Scandinavian exceptionalism in an era of penal excess, Part I: The nature and roots of Scandinavian exceptionalism. *British Journal of Criminology*, 48(2), pp. 119–137.

Pratt, J., 2008b. Scandinavian exceptionalism in an era of penal excess, Part II: Does Scandinavian exceptionalism have a future? *British Journal of Criminology*, 48(3), pp. 275–292.

Scott, S., 2010. Revisiting the total institution: Performative regulation in the reinventive institution. *Sociology*, 44(2), pp. 213–231.

Shammas, V.L., 2014. The pains of freedom: Assessing the ambiguity of Scandinavian penal exceptionalism on Norway's Prison Island. *Punishment & Society*, 16(1), pp. 104–123.

Sundberg, M., 2015. *A Sociology of the total organization: Atomistic unity in the French Foreign Legion.* Farnham: Ashgate Publishing Ltd.

Sykes, G.M., 1958. *The society of captives: A study of a maximum security prison.* Princeton: Princeton University Press.

Ugelvik, T., 2011. Hva er et fengsel?: En analyse av manualen til en sosial teknologi. *Retfærd.Nordisk Juridisk Tidsskrift*, 34(1), pp. 85–100.

Ugelvik, T., 2014. *Power and resistance in prison: Doing time, doing freedom.* London: Palgrave Macmillan.

Wästerfors, D., 2009. *Konflikthantering i ungdomsvård ur ett sociologiskt perspektiv.* Stockholm: Statens Institutionsstyrelse.

Werth, R., 2011. I do what I'm told, sort of: Reformed subjects, unruly citizens, and parole. *Theoretical Criminology*, 16(3), pp. 329–346.

Werth, R., 2013. The construction and stewardship of responsible yet precarious subjects: Punitive ideology, rehabilitation, and "tough love" among parole personnel. *Punishment & Society*, 15(3), pp. 219–246.

3 Studying open custody, re-offending and institutional everyday life

A methodological synthesis

In order to study the issue of custodial openness in relation to re-offending and also its significance for institutional everyday life, this study has collected both quantitative and qualitative data. The qualitative material is comprised of interviews with staff and convicted youths. There are six institutions that have special places for boys serving youth custody sentences and one with special places for girls. Interviews with staff (29 in total) have been conducted at all these institutions. The staff have been interviewed about how youth custody sentences are implemented and about issues related to preparing the youths for the time following the completion of their sentences.

Interviews have been conducted with boys serving youth custody sentences (32 in total) at all of the six institutions that have special places for boys serving this kind of sentence. The boys have been asked about how they experience their time at the institution and about their relations with and opinions about the staff. The interviews focused on the youths' experiences of being incarcerated and their ideas about the time following the completion of their sentence. In these interviews, a special focus was directed at how the youths experience institutional leave and more open forms of custody.

The quantitative data consist of a five-year follow-up of boys sentenced to youth custody between 1999 and 2006.[1] The data include control variables from the time prior to the sentence, variables containing information about the time spent in youth custody (such as instances of institutional leave, but also, for example, information about different types of behaviour during the time spent at the institution) and detailed follow-up data on registered offending.

A non-experimental study always faces the risk that the results in the form of differences in re-offending may in fact be due to other factors related to the risk for re-offending or to the likelihood of being given leave or of being placed on an open unit. At the same time, however, the data employed in this study provide multiple opportunities to include controls for various factors relating to the time both prior to and during the youth custody sentence.

One advantage of using a mix of methods and data is that the different elements contribute *different* understandings and thus allow for the development of deeper insights into the phenomenon under study. The combination of data sources employed in this study should thus not be viewed as a form of triangulation that has the objective of producing more *reliable* conclusions. Instead, following Giordano and colleagues (Giordano *et al.* 2002 p. 991) I have found value in the different forms of knowledge provided by the different data sources. This means that my primary intention is not to identify ways in which the different data sources provide confirmation for one another, even though I do on occasion link the data sources together in this way. At the same time, however, the data from the qualitative interviews are central to interpreting and understanding the quantitative findings and to contextualising these results. The remainder of this chapter provides a more detailed presentation of the data and conduct of the study.

Openness and everyday life at total institutions: qualitative interviews with staff and youths

This study has the ambition of attempting to reflect both the youths' and the staff members' narratives about youth custody, and to allow them to present their stories without the one perspective being viewed as being more "true" than the other. Liebling (2001, see also Presser 2009 p. 185) has argued, against the background of the way in which prison research (by reference to power factors) has placed a greater value on the narratives of inmates than on those of prison staff, that scholars should endeavour to balance competing perspectives in their research. Unlike Becker (1967), in his widely cited article, *Whose side are we on* – in which, according to Liebling, he makes a case for studying one side at a time – Liebling herself argues that a more challenging sociological project would be to attempt to reflect more than one perspective. In order to develop a better understanding of the whole, we need to be able to combine a number of different perspectives. Having said this, however, I would also like to make the point that a theoretical analysis of interview data at times means that the interpretation of what an interview participant has said may differ from the statement itself. This does not necessarily mean that the researcher is "taking sides", but it may generate interpretations that lie closer to the perspective of certain groups than of others.

Given the complex nature of the reality of everyday life in a total institution, it should also be noted that the narratives of neither the youths nor the staff present an unambiguous picture. There are variations both in what a given individual expressed in different parts of the same interview, and within the different groups that I interviewed, which is what would be expected (Holstein and Gubrium 1995, Presser and Sandberg 2015).

In 2011–2012, interviews were conducted with staff at all six institutions with special places for boys sentenced to youth custody.[2] In the spring of 2013 interviews were conducted at one of the two institutions at which the majority of girls sentenced to youth custody are placed.[3] In 2012–2014, interviews were conducted with convicted boys at all of the above institutions for male youth custody placements. The interviews were structured in the form of open thematic interviews. The 32 interviews conducted with youths resulted in a total of just over 20 hours of interview material, while the 29 staff interviews resulted in approximately 27 hours of material. Thus the staff interviews were on average somewhat longer than the interviews conducted with the youths. This was primarily due to the fact that the staff more often spoke in the form of long, coherent narratives. The answers and narratives provided by the youths were generally shorter (although there were exceptions from this pattern), but they did not give the impression of being less willing to be interviewed (see below for a description of certain reservations).

Both the staff and the youths were recruited via so-called *gatekeepers* at the institutions. In all cases I began by asking the institutions' directors for permission to come and interview staff/youths at their respective institutions, and in all cases I was given permission to do so without hesitation. I also specified a number of desired criteria in relation to my interview participants. For the staff, these were that they had worked with the implementation of youth custody sentences and had knowledge about institutional leave, and I also specified that I wanted to interview different categories of staff. At all but one of the institutions, I also interviewed the institution's director (who has a central role in decisions regarding institutional leave and transfers between different units). The other staff interviews were conducted with, among others, treatment assistants, unit managers and psychologists. I have no knowledge of which staff members were actually asked to participate or why these participants were chosen. Nor do I know whether any staff members declined to participate (I have naturally stated that participation was voluntary both in my contacts with the institutions and at the interviews themselves). This may well have varied between the different institutions. None of the staff members interviewed showed any signs of resistance to participating in the study, and all expressed feeling that the questions examined by the study are important. This might indicate that the staff members who were asked about participating (or who agreed to participate) were individuals with an interest in these questions. Many of the interviewed staff members had long experience of working with youth custody sentences and of working at special approved homes, and several of them had been working at these institutions when the youth custody sanction was introduced in 1999. In a small number of cases, the staff members had only been working for a short period of time. Instead of their narratives being informed by extensive experience of special approved homes and youth custody sentences, the relatively inexperienced staff were able to provide more specific knowledge about their impressions of what happens to youths when they experience these forms of incarceration. This is not because this was not visible to other, more experienced, staff members, but the interviews suggest that it was more evident to those with a shorter period of experience of working with incarcerated youths.

As regards the youths, I stated that I wished to interview youths who had started being given institutional leave, but that I was interested both in youths who had only recently been given leave for the first time and youths who had come much further in this process. In the same way as was the case with the interviewed staff, I have no knowledge of how the selection process was conducted, but given the small number of youths who were sentenced to youth custody during this period (the first phase of youth interviews, for example, were conducted when youth custody sentences reached their lowest level since the sanction's introduction in 1999) my impression is that the majority of those who had started being given leave had been asked. I know that a small number of those who were asked about participating declined to do so. At some of the units, however, I know that I interviewed all of the youths who were placed there at the time.

The length of the sentences being served by the interviewed youths varied, and the interview participants included youths serving both short and long sentences. Viewed as a group, however, their sentence lengths were longer than the average for youth custody sentences. This also means that there is an overrepresentation of youths convicted of more serious offences among those I interviewed. Although I did not ask what types of offences the youths had been convicted of, I know from both the nature of the placements, sentence lengths and what the youths themselves said at interview that these offences include everything from the most serious violent crimes – such as murder/manslaughter, rape and robbery – to less serious offences – such as different forms of aggravated property crime. Some of those interviewed had only recently started being given institutional leave, while others had extensive experience in this regard. How far they had come in their sentences also varied. Some were at the beginning or in the middle of their sentences, while some were very close to being released. The interviewed youths were placed on both locked and open units, and some had placements on pre-release units. Thus the youths represent a broad spectrum of those sentenced to youth custody, and of the different experiences and phases that comprise youth custody sentences. This does not, however, mean that the youths comprise a representative sample of the youth custody population generated from random selection.

The staff interviews were structured on the basis of questions regarding the implementation of youth custody sentences at their respective units, questions about institutional leave, about what the pre-release process should look like, and about whether there had been any changes during their time working with youth custody sentences. All of them were also asked what they felt the implementation of the ideal youth custody sentence would look like if they were completely free to make all the relevant decisions, and what prevents youth custody sentences from being implemented in this way today. With regard to institutional leave, we discussed the process by which the youths are given institutional leave, when the youths are able to get leave, what types of institutional leave the youths are given, and what can lead to a youth not being given leave. We also talked about what the staff felt the objectives of institutional leave consist in.

The youths were interviewed about how they experienced their time at the institution, what an ordinary day looked like for them and about their relations with staff. My questions about institutional leave touched upon areas such as whether they had been given leave, for what purpose and how they experienced this leave, when they received institutional leave for the first time and what this experience was like, and also what they thought institutional leave *should* be like. The youths were also asked about how they thought their sentences should be implemented, if they were able to decide this themselves. I also asked them about attitudes towards committing offences subsequent to release and what had been of significance for the formation of these attitudes. If they said that they did not intend to commit further offences, we discussed why and whether the time spent in the institution had contributed to this in any way. We also talked about what might help them to succeed in realising their intention, or alternatively, if they had answered that they felt they would continue to offend, what might lead to them wanting to avoid continued involvement in crime.

The general impression was that the youths were both interested in participating in the study and open to talking, often in a fairly (emotionally) candid way, about their experiences of youth custody, about being incarcerated, and about their thoughts regarding the period following their release. There are several factors that point to this being the case in addition to the contents of the interviews themselves. For example, the staff at different institutions, and on several different occasions, told me that the youths were very interested in participating and that they thought it was important to contribute to the study for the benefit of youths who will be sentenced to youth custody in the future. Some of the youths themselves also told me that they felt participating was important for this reason. On one occasion, staff also told me that one of the youths, who had as yet not been given much institutional leave, was worried that he would not be able to be interviewed. And there were a number of occasions when youths I met on a given unit, who were not included in the study (e.g. because they had been placed by the social services rather than sentenced to youth custody) expressed disappointment about not being interviewed themselves. Some of the youths also thanked me after the interview for being given the chance to participate in the study, and said they thought it had been fun to be interviewed. Palm (2003) also had the impression that many of the youths that she met in her own study were interested in participating and in telling her what life at the institution was like for them. She interpreted this as being due to the youths not being asked about this very often. I believe Palm's interpretation is also relevant to the current study, but with the addition that the youths also seemed to feel it was important to do something, or to be perceived as doing something, that could make things better for youths sentenced to youth custody in the future.

There were a number of exceptions, however. I know that a small number of youths declined to be interviewed. One also changed his mind when I was on site, having first agreed to participate. Two of the interviewed youths did not want the interviews to be recorded. These were among the shortest interviews that I conducted, and one of these youths was the only person to break off the interview.[4] The fact that these interviews were brief may indicate that these two youths were hesitant about being interviewed, and, at least with regard to one of them, I also perceived this to be the case (for which reason I repeated very clearly that he did not need to be interviewed if he did not want to be). The brevity of these interviews was also, however, due to the fact that I was also focused on taking notes, which meant that I was unable to concentrate as fully on the conversation itself.

How then should narratives of this kind be understood and interpreted? Moran (2012) writes that "[w]hatever we do and think about the past and future, we do that thinking or have those impressions *in the present*, and in the context of what the present is like". Järvinen (2004) has argued that life narratives constitute a description of the past, on the basis of a now that is directed towards the future. In the field of narrative criminology, emphasis has been placed on the significance of viewing narratives from a constitutive perspective, rather than as records or interpretations (Presser and Sandberg 2015, Presser 2009, Sandberg 2010) and Sandberg (2010 p. 452) has argued that "[n]arratives are important not because they are true records of what happened, but because they influence behaviour in the future". Although I am not conducting a narrative analysis of the interviews, I share this view and would argue that the interviews with both the staff and the youths should be understood on the basis of this type of perspective. This is also in line with Marunas's (2001) use of narratives. Presser and Sandberg (2015 p. 10) also note that narratives "are part of larger meaning-making structures and that these are embedded in social institutions". This also holds for the narratives of both the staff and youths in the current study, which will be illustrated in my analysis. At the same time, narratives always constitute part of a particular local setting and can only be understood on the basis of this setting (Presser and Sandberg 2015 p. 9).

Thus the interview narratives from the youths should be understood in terms of the interviews having taken place in a very special context, during a period of incarceration, at the same time as they constitute part of a larger context in which issues such as treatment and crime policy are also of significance. I have not devoted any time to attempting to determine whether the youths and staff interviews contain descriptions of "authentic" experiences of institutional care, or whether for example the youths were being "honest" when they described how they view their future and what they need in order for this future to be how they want it to be. The narratives in themselves provide valuable knowledge about these youths' experiences and perceptions about their future.

The staff narratives must, of course, at least in part be understood as having been given by the staff members in the capacity of representatives of themselves as professionals and also in relation to their possibly feeling a sense of loyalty towards describing their own unit/institution as well-functioning. The staff interviews contain a number of statements that suggest this to be the case. In many cases, however, the interviews also contain some criticism of the work conducted at the institutions, which would speak against this type of interpretation. More than anything else, my own sense of the interviews is that they primarily contain conscientious reflections about the questions discussed. Parts of these interviews may also be understood as examples of what Presser and Sandberg (2015 p. 291) have labelled "justifications of harm", and as such they link into the study's theoretical framework, reflecting the concepts of pastoral power (Foucault 1982), for example, and the needs of "helpers" to motivate their exercise of power and control (Järvinen 2002, Petersson 2013).

It may be argued that an ethnographic, rather than an interview-based, approach would be better suited to revealing more subtle forms of power and resistance. One example of the use of this approach is found in Ugelvik's (2014, see also Crewe 2009) study, in which micro-power and resistance constitute a central focus. In a similar way, Wästerfors (2009) has employed the ethnographic approach to describe the less visible dimensions of interactions associated with conflicts at special approved homes. Sandberg (2010), however, argues that the use of interviews does not necessarily constitute a less fruitful approach.

It has not been possible to conduct an ethnographic study within the framework of the current research project, and for reasons of time and resources an ethnographic study would perhaps not even have been the most appropriate option for the examination of such a narrow and specific research question as that discussed here (cf. Sandberg 2010). Since the interviews, in fact, contain a large number of statements that constitute descriptions of micro-power and resistance, I would argue that these interviews have functioned at least as well as an ethnographic study on the same theme would have. One related methodological aspect is that even though I may not have been able to "see" how the youths express resistance, for example, as a result of the use of interviews rather than an ethnographic approach, the interview situation may at the same time have constituted an arena in which the youths were able, even *more clearly*, to reveal and express their resistance to the subject positions they are ascribed as convicted and incarcerated, to *do freedom*, to borrow Ugelvik's term (2014 pp. 238–239). In the same way, the interviews also constituted an arena that provided the staff with an opportunity for what might be termed *doing helpfulness* instead of *doing control* (cf. Järvinen 2002, Petersson 2013).[5] Thus there is nothing to say that interviews cannot contribute important knowledge about the views of the youths and staff members about the subjects discussed.

Finally, something should also be said about my own position. A couple of years prior to the first interviews, I had concluded a period of just under four years' employment at the National Board of Institutional Carc, as head of research at the Board's head office. Because of this, I was well known to all of thc institutional dircctors, who were those who granted the initial permission to conduct the interviews. My previous position at the Board was no doubt a contributory factor in my being granted this permission, but at the same time, my experience from my years working there was that the agency has had a generous approach to allowing researchers access to the work it conducts (not least those whose research is funded by the agency itself), so it is very likely that I would have been given permission to conduct the interviews anyway. Some of the staff members whom I interviewed, but far from all of them, were also people who already knew me. None of the youths knew anything about my earlier work at the Board, however. My knowledge of the agency and its work may have involved both advantages and disadvantages for my research, but I believe it has for the most part been beneficial, since it has provided me with an insight into, and an understanding of, the agency's work that I would otherwise not have had. It is possible, however, that it may also have led to my having blind spots as a result of "preunderstandings", or that I may have been affected by biases. It is naturally not possible for me to say anything about the first of these possible problems, but I do not see the second problem as an issue, since I no longer work for the agency and do not perceive myself as having, or needing to have, any sense of loyalty towards it. And this is also true in relation to the fact that the research project was funded by the agency.[6] On the basis of the approach employed in the study, which views the narratives as being created in an interaction between myself and the interview subjects, these factors will naturally be of significance, but readers must themselves determine in what ways on the basis of the material and the analysis presented in this book.

Analysis

Qualitative data of this kind are extensive (the transcribed interviews comprise just over 1,000 pages of text) and familiarising oneself with the data and then analysing them is a very time-consuming process. In the present context, however, I will only present a brief description of this process. The analysis is, of course, based on the study's aims and research questions but has at the same time involved staying very close to the data. Following several readings of the material, the interviews were thematised[7] and coded using the NVivo software package. The original coding has also been adjusted in the course of the work. Each of the themes were then analysed one at a time. Some of the analyses have related to the entire group of youths, or the entire group of interviewed staff members, while others have been broken down on the basis of, for example, locked and open units respectively, or by institution, when this was viewed as appropriate. The material will not be presented on the basis of these categorisations, however, among other things in order to ensure the anonymity of the participants, but also because I have felt that doing so would not contribute anything of major significance in relation to the study's objective. One result of conducting the analysis close to the data has been that the study's theoretical framework has developed during the course of the analysis itself. Thus the focus on Foucault and discipline has become more pronounced, for example, since the interview data manifested very clear links to these issues.

Open custody and re-offending, a five-year follow-up

The quantitative analyses primarily focus on questions regarding which forms of custodial openness the boys have experienced during their sentences and how (or whether) these are related to subsequent re-offending. The data examined include all boys (with the exception of those sentenced to post-release deportation) who were sentenced to youth custody during the period 1999–2006 for a period of at least two months and at most three years. The restriction to a minimum sentence of two months is due to the fact that the first two months at special approved homes should be devoted to assessing the youths (which does not always happen, however) and those with sentences that are shorter than two months generally have very limited opportunities to be given any form of institutional leave before their sentence has been completed. The restriction to a maximum sentence length of three years was specified in order to give the youths a somewhat longer period at liberty for the purposes of the follow up, and only a small number of youths are given sentences of more than three years.[8] The study includes 611 individuals who have together served a total of 638 youth custody sentences. Since an individual serving more than one sentence may serve these sentences in different ways with regard to the central research question examined in the study – i.e. the level of institutional leave and being released from an open or locked unit – the unit of analysis is *sentences* rather than individuals.

In order to study the significance of custodial openness for re-offending, data have been collected from a wide range of different sources. The composition of this dataset is described in Figure 3.1.

One way of categorising variables in the context of studies such as this one is on the basis of whether they measure what a person "is" (e.g. age), what a person "has" (e.g. a mental disorder), what a person "has done" (e.g. previous offending) and what "has been done to" a person (e.g. exposure to crime) (Nieuwbeerta *et al.* 2009). The current study includes variables from all of these categories.

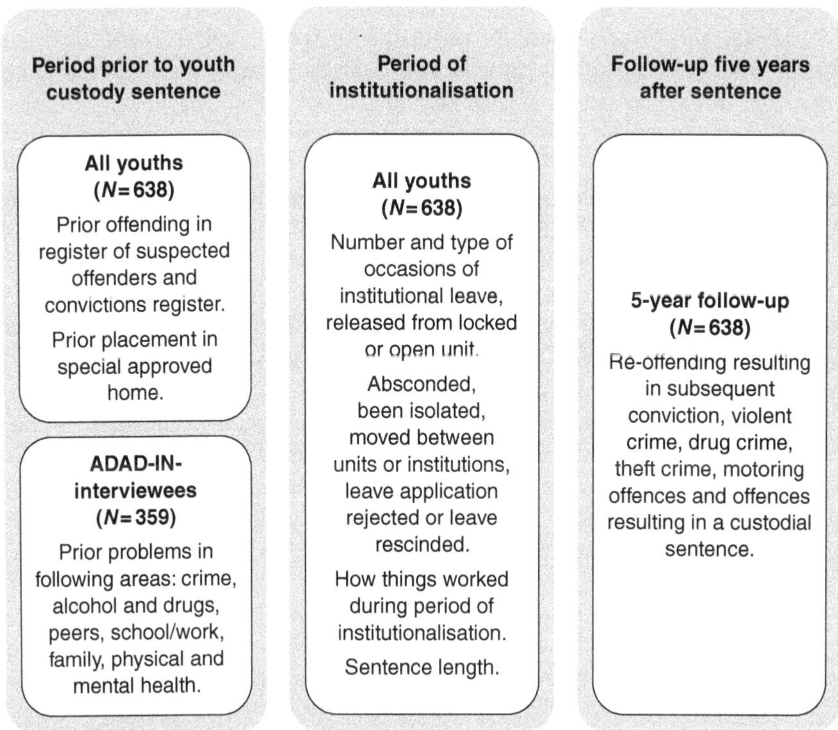

Figure 3.1 Overview of the quantitative data.

In order to control as far as possible for factors that might constitute the real explanation for a possible relationship between custodial openness and re-offending, the analysis needs to include both factors related to re-offending and factors related to the possibility of experiencing more open forms of custody. Thus the analysis needs to include both more traditional background variables and factors related to what happens during youth custody sentences.

The time prior to youth custody

What, then, are the most important risk factors for re-offending that are not related to the youths' experience of the youth custody sentence itself? Risk factors for recidivism are usually divided into the "Big Four" and the "Central Eight", which also include the Big Four (Andrews and Bonta 2010). The Big Four risk factors are prior offending and an early onset of criminal behaviour, an antisocial personality pattern (aggression, impulsiveness, etc.), antisocial attitudes and values, and having antisocial associates. The other four risk factors that are also regarded as central, although not as important as the Big Four, are substance abuse, problems in the family or at school (work), and leisure time activities.

It is well-established that prior offending is one of the strongest predictors of re-offending (Gendreau *et al.* 1996, Andrews and Bonta 2010, Nilsson 2002, Giordano *et al.* 2002). Because the correlation between previous criminality and re-offending is so powerful other factors, such as social measures, contribute very little to the prediction of re-offending (Nilsson 2002, May 1999). Studies have also shown that an early onset of offending, and the type of offence at first conviction are both of significance for the risk for recidivism. Examples of such strategic offences include car theft, theft and robbery (Lenke 2009, Svensson 2002, Brå 2011). Early onset is more significant for the prediction of re-offending however, since a first conviction prior to age 18 produces a very high risk for subsequent offences, irrespective of the offence for which the individual is convicted. All of the individuals included in the current study were convicted prior to age 18, and thus the effect of strategic offences may therefore be expected to be relatively limited for this population.[9]

The study includes detailed information on prior offending. The nature of the boys' prior offending will be presented in general terms. The Propensity Score Matching (PSM) process, and the logistic regression analyses employed in the study, employ measures of prior offending based on *court convictions*.[10] The youths' age at admission to the special approved homes is also included in these analyses.

The material also includes data on previous compulsory care placements in special approved homes[11] made by the social services in accordance with the Section 12 of the Care of Young Persons (Special Provisions) Act (LVU – 1990: 52). These youths may have been placed as a result of failures in care provision or as a result of their own behaviour. The latter reason is more common, and it is only in the case of placements made as a result of the youths' own behaviour, that youths may be held in any form of incarceration. Compulsory placements as a result of the youths' own behaviour may be due to serious offending, serious substance abuse problems or other socially destructive behaviour.[12] Thus, the youths' behaviour must have involved a serious risk to their health and/or development. In exceptional cases, a youth may be placed voluntarily, and in these cases there is also a requirement that the youth may not be subject to any form of incarceration. Only 15 of the 258 youths who had previously been placed in a special approved home had been the subject of non-compulsory placements. Since choosing voluntarily to be placed in an institution of this kind is a sign of a youth having major problems, these youths have been categorised together with the others who had prior experience of special approved home placements. As a group, the youths who are subject to compulsory special approved home placements by the social services may be viewed as being among those with the most serious problems in the areas of crime, substance abuse and other socially destructive behaviour. This variable may thus be regarded as an indicator of the youth having (had) major problems in one or more of the areas covered by the eight risk factors described above.

Some of those who had been placed in accordance with the Care of Young Persons Act (LVU) prior to their youth custody sentence had been placed there while waiting for their cases to come to court, for example, instead of being placed in a remand centre. Unfortunately, it is not possible to reliably distinguish these youths from those whose placements are due to other reasons. In order to compensate for this factor, the variable has been coded in four different ways for those with only *a single* placement based on the Care of Young Persons Act (LVU) prior to their youth custody sentence: 1) all have been coded as belonging to the group with prior LVU placements; 2) only those with a previous LVU-placement that occurred at least three months' prior to the imposition of their youth custody sentence have been coded as belonging to the group with prior LVU-placements; 3) the same coding as for number 2, but with the requirement that the previous placement occurred at least six months prior to the youth custody sentence; 4) the same coding as for number 2, but with the requirement that the previous placement occurred at least 12 months prior to the youth custody sentence. Preliminary analyses were conducted using all four of these variables. There are no major differences in the results when codings 1–3 are used, although the results are affected somewhat when they are based on coding number 4. Since it is likely that many of those whom coding number 4 defines as *not* having had a prior LVU-placement *have* in fact been placed as a result of other reasons than simply waiting for their cases to come to court, this coding was not deemed to be particularly relevant to the analyses, and was not used. Instead, coding number 2 was chosen for the analyses, since this coding was deemed to exclude the majority of those whose earlier placements were specifically related to waiting for their cases to come to court, while at the same time not excluding many whose prior placements had been due to other reasons.[13]

The principal offence[14] in the conviction resulting in youth custody has also been included as a control in the analyses. Here the material has been divided into three large groups: violent crime (murder/manslaughter, aggravated assault, etc.), robbery, and other crimes (including serious sexual offences). The number of sexual offences is small, and it has therefore not been feasible to use them as a category in their own right. The other crimes category comprises different categories of less common offences, such as arson, drug offences and aggravated theft.

Within two weeks of admission to a special approved home, an interview based on the Adolescent Drug Abuse Diagnosis (ADAD) instrument should be conducted with the youth. The interview instrument is based on the original American version developed by Friedman and Utada, and has been translated and adapted to Swedish conditions. The ADAD interview is structured and focused on the youth's situation in nine different areas: physical health, mental health, school, work, leisure time and friends, family, crime and alcohol and drug use (Söderholm Carpelan and Hermodsson 2004). The interviews are conducted by staff members at the special approved homes. For a more detailed description of the conduct of these interviews, see SiS (2011).

The ADAD instrument includes summary items for each section of the questionnaire. These comprise items focused on the youths' perceptions, their level of problems in each area, and how much help they feel they need in that area, and also a so-called interviewer rating. The interviewer-rating is based on a weighting of the youths' answers to specific questions, for which the interviewer is required to estimate the youths' problem levels, and on the youths' estimates of their need for help in each of the life areas covered by the instrument. The method that is used for this weighting process is described in a manual published by the National Board of Institutional Care (SiS 2011).

There are a number of studies that have validated the ADAD interview, either in whole or in part, in a Swedish context. Börjesson (2011) found that the ADAD-interview appears to function well as an instrument for measuring the seriousness of youths' problems and their need for treatment, and that it is characterised by good levels of validity and reliability. The interviewer-rating was judged to be valid, and to give a better indication of the overall level of problems than other summary measures that have been validated.

Innala and Shannon (2007) validated the section focused on crime, and found that the ADAD instrument appears to function as well within its target population as other self-report instruments that have been validated. The only possible problem found by the study was that there was a small group of youths with high levels of registered offending who under-reported their participation in crime.

Data from an ADAD interview are available for 56 per cent of the youths included in the study. For all of the variables on prior offending and recidivism that were collected from the convictions register, those for whom ADAD-data are available have lower levels of involvement in crime prior to the youth custody sentence, and lower levels of re-offending subsequent to release, although the differences are not particularly substantial. Thus those who have been interviewed at admission constitute a less criminally active group and it is reasonable to assume that the level of problems within the study population as a whole is likely to be higher than that shown by the information collected from those who underwent an ADAD interview.

The period of the youth custody sentence

Research has also noted that the risk for re-offending may be related to the degree of openness at an institution during a period of institutionalisation, the issue that constitutes the principal focus for the current study. The literature review on the institutional treatment of young people conducted by Andreassen (2003) points to the importance of establishing pro-social contacts during a period of institutionalisation, and of working with contacts with the wider community, as well as of reducing the level of isolation from the outside world (which instead involves close contacts with other youths who have problems) to the extent that this is possible. Having been subjected to a compulsory placement (as a negative factor) appeared also to be of less significance than the degree of autonomy experienced by the youths.[15] The same review also found that secure institutions produce worse treatment results than open institutions, although this is a problematic comparison since, as a group, the youths placed in open institutions usually have lower levels of problems and thus a lower re-offending risk from the outset. Andreassen argue that the more negative results found for treatment at secure institutions may be linked both to the boundaries imposed by the security measures themselves (locked doors, etc.) and the isolation in relation to the wider community. The study materials include a great deal of information that functions in different ways as a measure of the degree of custodial openness.

Another factor that has been found to be of significance for the risk for re-offending is "prison misconduct" (French and Gendreau 2006) or what has been referred to as "misbehaviour" during the period of institutionalisation (Larsson and Segreus 2005). Others have argued, however, that the link between behaviour in prison and re-offending is not at all clear or self-evident (Crewe 2011). An earlier follow-up of youths sentenced to youth custody found that absconding during the period of institutionalisation was related to subsequent re-offending (Pettersson 2010). It is also likely that "misbehaviour" during the time spent at the institution will restrict a youth's access to more open forms of custody during the sentence. Thus this is a factor that may be assumed to be related to both re-offending and the degree of custodial openness, for which reason it is important to control for this factor when examining the role played by custodial openness. In this regard, too, the study data include a range of information that can provide measures of possible problems – or the absence of problems – during the period of institutionalisation, such as conflicts with staff or other youths.

The data relating to the factors examined in relation to youths' period of institutionalisation are drawn from the youths' journals (although not their medical journals) and files. All of these have been read through and coded on the basis of a number of variables.[16] The variables employed in this area of the analysis have in part been intended to capture whether or not a youth has experienced problems

– or been perceived as problematic – on a given unit, and in part which types of institutional leave the youths have had during different periods of their youth custody sentences. All of the variables have been coded on the basis of two-month periods (0–2 months, 3–4 months, etc.). Some information has also been obtained directly from the National Board of Institutional Care's client administrative system (KIA), such as information on absconding, the units on which the youths have been place, for how long, etc.

If youth custody sentences are implemented in the intended way, the youths should experience a form of "institutional career" in which they move towards increasingly open forms of custody, from an initial placement on a secure or locked unit, to an open treatment unit and above all, ideally also spending time on a so-called pre-release unit at the end of their sentence. It does not always work like this, however, which is not exclusively due to factors related to the youths themselves (SiS 2010). The youths placed in pre-release and open units have been combined in order to produce a larger category (since the numbers released from pre-release units are very small). There are also units that include both open and locked places, and in these cases there is no information available as to which of these types of places a given youth has been placed in. There are 47 youths in the material who have experienced placements on this kind of unit, and based on an examination of the "institutional career" of these youths – i.e. the nature of the units on which they had previously been placed, the nature of their earlier moves between different units, etc. – my assessment was that they had in many cases been assigned to locked rather than open places. In addition, these units have significantly fewer open than locked places (it may, for example, be a question of six locked places and two open places). As a group, the re-offending level of these youths is very similar to that of the youths who had been released from units that only had locked places. Taken together, these factors have led me to classify these youths in the locked category. Preliminary analyses (not presented here) conducted with these youths placed in the "open unit" category led to the same general findings. There are also missing data on this variable in relation to 16 youths, for whom it has not been possible to determine which type of unit they were released from.

Institutional leave is measured on the basis of the number of occasions of institutional leave per 100 days of the placement at a special approved home (hereafter referred to as the sentence length). In addition, the study also includes analyses of the content of this institutional leave.

Good behaviour during the period of institutionalisation may be assumed to be of significance both for the possibility of being given institutional leave and for the risk for re-offending and it is therefore important to control for this as far as is possible. There are a number of factors that may be used to this end in the information contained in the journals (J) and the National Board of Institutional Care's client administrative system (KIA). These factors are:

- Having absconded from the institution (KIA)[17]
- Having been transferred because of staff-perceived problems on the unit (such as different forms of quarrels) (J)

- Having been placed in isolation (KIA)
- Having had a leave application rejected as a result of what the staff have viewed as poor behaviour (J)
- Having approved institutional leave rescinded as a result of what the staff have viewed as poor behaviour (J)

In the PSM, these have been included as individual and (for the most part) continuous variables. In the logistic regression analyses, however, none of the individual variables achieved statistical significance. An additive summary measure of these variables did however show itself to be significant in relation to the outcome, and this measure is therefore employed in the logistic regressions. In order to produce larger groups, and thus make the analysis less sensitive to small frequencies in the categories employed in the analysis, the control variable included in the logistic regression analyses has been dichotomised, with the values "none of these things have happened" and "one or more of these things has happened".

The length of the youth custody sentence may also be assumed to be of significance for the likelihood of re-offending, for example, because those serving longer sentences will have a shorter period in which to re-offend by comparison with those with shorter sentences, or because variations in the length of sentence may produce different levels of harm. The length of sentence was also found to be of significance both for the chances of having had more institutional leave and for the likelihood of being transferred to spend time on an open unit, which further underlines the importance of controlling for this factor. The sentence length has been included as a continuous variable in both the PSM and the logistic regression analyses. Since the factor of interest in the analyses is primarily the time spent at the institution rather than the length of the sentence imposed by the court, the sentence length variable is based on the actual time served at a special approved home. This has been necessary since some of the youths have spent time in remand centres (there is no information available on which these youths are, and how long they have spent on remand), and this time is discounted from the youth custody sentence served at a special approved home. In addition, a number of the youths have absconded for a considerable period of time (and thus have not been at the institutions). Long periods of absconding have thus also been discounted when calculating the length of the period between admission and release.

The period following release: re-offending

The observation period for the follow-up is five years from the date of the court sentence. The follow-up is in part conducted in the form of a presentation of re-offending in general, and re-offending categorised on the basis of different types of crime. The more advanced analyses employ a summary measure. In these analyses, the outcome variable is re-offending that has led to a court conviction resulting in a custodial sanction.[18] The choice of this outcome variable was made in order to restrict the analysis to recidivism in more serious crime, and thus to a relatively limited range of offences.[19] Preliminary analyses (not presented here) have also been conducted using outcome variables based on re-offending resulting in any form of conviction and any form of court conviction respectively. The conclusions that would be drawn on the basis of these analyses are the same as for those based on re-offending resulting in a custodial sentence, although the size of the odd ratios vary somewhat.

Measuring offending on the basis of registered crime, and particularly court convictions, is associated with a number of problems. A large proportion of the crimes that are actually committed are simply not captured by official crime registers, which is particularly true in relation to less serious offending. In the current study, however, the focus has been directed at distinguishing those who relapse into serious offending from those who do not re-offend, or who only relapse into less serious crime, since the study population is comprised of a group with high levels of prior offending, and we know that this group re-offends to a substantial extent. My assessment is therefore that re-offending that has resulted in a new custodial sanction constitutes an appropriate measure in this regard as well.

Some researchers argue that a minimum of five control variables are necessary in order to be able to study the effect of prison sentences on re-offending (Nagin *et al.* 2009, Bales and Piquero 2012). These are gender, race, age, current offence and prior offending. The present study only includes males, and thus gender is controlled for automatically, even though this is not included as a control variable. I have no data on race, but the other variables listed are included in the analyses, together with several additional measures.

Analytical methods: Propensity Score Matching and logistic regression analysis

Since it is relatively clear that the chances of spending time in an open unit towards the end of one's sentence are not independent of factors related to the youths' time both prior to and during their sentences, the analysis must control for such factors in an appropriate way. In studies of this kind it is not possible to employ a randomised control-group design, partly because the study is retrospective but first and foremost because it would not be possible for ethical reasons and reasons of legal certainty. Instead this study employs Propensity Score Matching based on the nearest neighbour method to match the treatment group (those released from an open unit) with the non-treatment group (those released from a locked unit). The propensity score is defined by Rosenbaum and Rubin (1983 p. 41) as "the conditional probability of assignment to a particular treatment given a vector of observed covariates". PSM is now a common and well-established method employed in several disciplines, including criminology, in order to overcome the problems associated with not being able to employ experimental designs based on the random assignment of cases to a treatment and control group (Apel and Sweeten 2010, Nannicini 2007, Becker and Ichino 2002).

The following variables were included in the final PSM model:

- Events prior to the youth custody sentence: prior court convictions (continuous variable), prior LVU placement (dichotomous), and principal offence in the conviction leading to the youth custody sentence (trichotomous).
- Events related to the sentence itself, excluding good behaviour: institutional leave/100 days of sentence (continuous), length of sentence served in days (continuous).
- Events related to good behaviour during the sentence: Rejection of application for institutional leave as a result of poor behaviour (dichotomous), having been subjected to isolation (dichotomous), absconding (continuous), transferred as a result of perceived problems on the unit (dichotomous).

Two further variables that were available to the study had to be removed from the analysis (see below) since their inclusion made it impossible to match on prior offending and prior LVU placement. The models in which the two variables were included over-compensated for prior offending and prior LVU placement, with significant negative differences between treatment and non-treatment groups on these variables shifting to significant positive differences. Since both prior offending and having had a prior LVU placement are central to a study of re-offending among institutionalised youths, the decision was made to exclude the two variables that produced this outcome, since they were regarded as being less important. The variables in question were age at admission to the special approved home and whether the youth had experience of institutional leave that had already been approved being rescinded as a result of poor behaviour. The age differences between the youths at admission are small, with almost all of them having been 16 or 17 when this occurred. Nor was age associated with any significant differences either in re-offending or in whether the youths were released from an open (treatment group) or locked (non-treatment group) unit. The logistical regressions (see below) nonetheless include age. There are no differences at all between those who have had leave rescinded as a result of poor behaviour and those who had not experienced this with regard to either re-offending or having been released from an open or locked unit. My own assessment is that the most important variables have been included in the PSM model. Further, the model already includes a number of different variables that measure good behaviour, which may be viewed as a strength.

Apel and Sweeten (2010) propose that those who employ PSM should endeavour to follow seven recommendations, preferably all, but if this is not possible, then at least the majority of them. In the current study, I follow the majority, but not all of these seven recommendations. I have not, for example, been able to follow the recommendation that all sources of selection in relation to whether or not a youth will be placed on an open unit prior to release should be included in the PSM model. It is likely, however, that all of the central factors related to the likelihood of being placed on an open unit have been included; that is prior offending, prior LVU placement, a range of indicators of good/poor behaviour during the sentence, the offence type that resulted in the youth custody sentence, and the length of this sentence. Nor have I followed the recommendation of testing a range of different matching procedures.

Preliminary analyses (not presented here) showed that the significance of concluding one's sentence on an open or locked unit appears to vary depending on the youths' re-offending risk. This is the case for those with and without a prior court conviction, and for those with or without a prior LVU placement. To analyse this further, logistic regression analyses have been conducted using interaction terms. These logistic regression models have employed so-called combination variables, which have been specified using the categories "no prior court conviction + open unit" and "no prior LVU placement + open unit" as the reference categories, since these were predicted to produce the lowest rates of re-offending.

Following this presentation of the study design, the data and analysis, and of various methodological considerations, the following three chapters present the study's empirical findings. Since the interviews are central to understanding and interpreting the results of the quantitative analyses, I begin by presenting these.

Notes

1 Both boys and girls were included in the study, but the girls are too few to be analysed using more sophisticated methods.
2 Bärby, Fagared, Klarälvsgården, Johannisberg, Sundbo and Råby.
3 Vemyra, which is the institution that has special places for girls sentenced to youth custody.
4 On this occasion I had just asked the youth how he felt about not seeing his family, and he had then told me about how he longed to go home and at the same time became quieter and then answered the following questions more briefly. Shortly after this, he said that he did not have the energy to be interviewed any more, at which point we concluded the interview. Immediately afterwards, however, on the unit, he was once again as bright as he had been prior to the start of the interview. My interpretation was that he found it (too) difficult talking about the things I was asking him.
5 Although it should be noted that they also did the latter in the interviews.
6 The study has been funded by the Swedish National Board for Institutional Care, but this funding was granted on the basis of a research application submitted to the Board's scientific council, which is made up of external scholars who have the task of assessing which research projects will be granted funding.
7 Examples of the themes employed include all of the narratives on institutional leave, on the first experience of institutional leave, on being incarcerated, on custodial openness, on the objectives associated with institutional leave, changes since the introduction of the youth custody sanction, etc. Some of the themes have been coded for both staff and youths, others only for the one group or the other.
8 During the period 1999–2007 (the original data set includes the year 2007, but those admitted in 2007 could only be followed up for three years, and have therefore been removed from the analyses presented in this book) there were 26 individuals who had been given sentences of over three years.
9 A more detailed analysis of re-offending on the basis of different categories of offences (not presented here) has shown that this assumption is correct.

10 The use of court convictions, as against all convictions, means that the least serious offences are excluded, since offences that have resulted in waivers of prosecution and summary sanction orders are not included. The use of all convictions produced a poorer matching and court convictions are also better at distinguishing among those with a somewhat more serious history of offending in a group in which a very large proportion have some level of prior offending.
11 That is, placements at the same type of institution in which youth custody sentences are served.
12 See the introductory chapter for a more detailed description.
13 This assessment is in part based on information from the interviewed youths who described having been placed on the basis of the Care of Young Persons Act while waiting for their sentences and how long these placements had lasted.
14 That is, the most serious offence in a given conviction.
15 Since all of the youths were placed in institutions, these results are not an effect of differences between outpatient care provision and institutional treatment; that is, the results cannot be viewed as the same as those found in research that has studied the criminogenic effects of incarceration.
16 I have myself participated in this work by reading a number of journals and files during the process of writing the project plan for the research, and also during the initial phase of the data collection process, and the coding schedule was formulated on the basis of this work. The remainder of this extensive work has been conducted by Elisabeth Nordén and Linnéa Wätterstam.
17 The absconding measure also includes instances when the youths have returned late to the institution, even if they have returned voluntarily, since such incidents are registered as absconding and cannot be distinguished from instances of intentional absconding.
18 Usually in the form of a prison term, but there are cases where the youths have been sentenced to a new period of youth custody.
19 When a measure based on all convictions is employed, for example, this variable includes everything from shoplifting to homicide.

Bibliography

Andreassen, T., 2003. *Institutionsbehandling av ungdomar: Vad säger forskningen?* Stockholm: Gothia.

Andrews, D.A. and Bonta, J., 2010. *The psychology of criminal conduct.* Albany: Lexis Nexis/Anderson Pub.

Apel, R.J. and Sweeten, G., 2010. Propensity score matching in criminology and criminal justice. In: R.A. Piquero and D. Weisburd, eds, *Handbook of quantitative criminology.* New York & London: Springer, pp. 543–562.

Bales, W.D. and Piquero, A.R., 2012. Assessing the impact of imprisonment on recidivism. *Journal of Experimental Criminology*, 8(1), pp. 71–101.

Becker, H.S., 1967. Whose side are we on. *Social problems*, 14(3), pp. 239–247.

Becker, S.O. and Ichino, A., 2002. Estimation of average treatment effects based on propensity scores. *The Stata Journal*, 2(4), pp. 358–377.

Börjesson, J., 2011. *Psychometric studies of the Swedish version of the Adolescent Drug Abuse Diagnosis (ADAD) instrument.* Umeå: Institutionen för Psykologi, Umeå Universitet.

Brå, 2011. *Strategiska brott bland unga på 00-talet.* Stockholm: Fritzes.

Crewe, B., 2009. *The prisoner society: Power, adaptation and social life in an English prison.* Oxford: Oxford University Press.

Crewe, B., 2011. Soft power in prison: Implications for staff–prisoner relationships, liberty and legitimacy. *European Journal of Criminology*, 8(6), pp. 455–468.

Foucault, M., 1982. The subject and power. *Critical Inquiry*, 8(4), pp. 777–795.

French, S.A. and Gendreau, P., 2006. Reducing prison misconducts: What works! *Criminal Justice and Behavior*, 33(2), pp. 185–218.

Gendreau, P., Little, T. and Goggin, C., 1996. A meta-analysis of the predictors of adult offender recidivism: What works! *Criminology*, 34(4), pp. 575–608.

Giordano, P.C., Cernkovich, S.A. and Rudolph, J.L., 2002. Gender, crime, and desistance: Toward a theory of cognitive transformation. *American Journal of Sociology*, 107(4), pp. 990–1064.

Holstein, J.A. and Gubrium, J.F., 1995. *The active interview*. Thousand Oaks: Sage.

Innala, C. and Shannon, D., 2007. *En kriterievalidering av brottsfrågorna i svenska ADAD-instrumentet*. Stockholm: Statens Institutionsstyrelse.

Järvinen, M., 2002. Hjälpens universum – ett maktperspektiv på mötet mellan klient och system. In: A. Meeuwisse and H. Swärd, eds, *Perspektiv på sociala problem*. Stockholm: Natur och Kultur, pp. 253–273.

Järvinen, M., 2004. Life histories and the perspective of the present. *Narrative Inquiry*, 14(1), pp. 45–68.

Lenke, L., 2009. Ungdomsbrott och återfall, 1969–1975. In: H. von Hofer, ed., *Leif Lenke In Memoriam*. Stockholm: Kriminologiska Institutionen, Stockholms Universitet.

Liebling, A., 2001. Whose side are we on? Theory, practice and allegiances in prisons research. *British Journal of Criminology*, 41(3), pp. 472–484.

Maruna, S., 2001. *Making good: How ex-convicts reform and rebuild their lives*. Washington DC: American Psychological Association.

May, C., 1999. *Explaining reconviction following a community sentence: The role of social factors*. London: Home Office.

Moran, D., 2012. "Doing time" in carceral space: Timespace and carceral geography. *Geografiska Annaler: Series B, Human Geography*, 94(4), pp. 305–316.

Nagin, D.S., Cullen, F.T. and Jonson, C.L., 2009. Imprisonment and reoffending. *Crime and Justice*, 38(1), pp. 115–200.

Nannicini, T., 2007. Simulation-based sensitivity analysis for matching estimators. *Stata Journal*, 7(3), p. 334.

Nieuwbeerta, P., Nagin, D.S. and Blokland, A.A., 2009. Assessing the impact of first-time imprisonment on offenders' subsequent criminal career development: A matched samples comparison. *Journal of Quantitative Criminology*, 25(3), pp. 227–257.

Nilsson, A., 2002. *Fånge i marginalen. Uppväxtvillkor, levnadsförhållanden och återfall i brott bland fångar*. Stockholm: Kriminologiska Institutionen, Stockholms Universitet.

Palm, J., 2003. *Ungdomarnas upplevelse av sluten ungdomsvård: En jämförelse med LVU-placeringar och fängelse*. Stockholm: Statens Institutionsstyrelse.

Petersson, F., 2013. *Kontroll av beroende. Substitutionsbehandlingens logik, praktik och semantik*. Malmö: Égalité.

Pettersson, T., 2010. *Återfall i brott bland ungdomar dömda till fängelse respektive sluten ungdomsvård*. Stockholm: Statens Institutionsstyrelse.

Presser, L., 2009. The narratives of offenders. *Theoretical Criminology*, 13(2), pp. 177–200.

Presser, L. and Sandberg, S., 2015. *Narrative criminology: Understanding stories of crime*. New York and London: New York University Press.

Rosenbaum, P.R. and Rubin, D.B., 1983. The central role of the propensity score in observational studies for causal effects. *Biometrika*, 70(1), pp. 41–55.

Sandberg, S., 2010. What can "lies" tell us about life? Notes towards a framework of narrative criminology. *Journal of Criminal Justice Education*, 21(4), pp. 447–465.

SiS, 2010. *Kartläggning av LSU-utslussning under 2009.*

SiS, 2011. *ADAD – Adolescent Drug Abuse Diagnosis. Manual.* Stockholm: Statens Institutionsstyrelse.

Söderholm Carpelan, K. and Hermodsson, A., 2004. ADAD och utvecklingen av ett dokumentationssystem för ungdomar. *Nordisk sosialt arbeid*, 24(2), pp. 110–123.

Svensson, R., 2002. Strategic offences in the criminal career context. *British Journal of Criminology*, 42(2), pp. 395–411.

Ugelvik, T., 2014. *Power and resistance in prison: Doing time, doing freedom.* London: Palgrave Macmillan.

Wästerfors, D., 2009. *Konflikthantering i ungdomsvård ur ett sociologiskt perspektiv.* Stockholm: Statens Institutionsstyrelse.

4 Youth and staff narratives about youth custody sentences

This chapter describes how the youths and staff talk about everyday life at the institutions and the role played by different aspects of custodial openness. It is important to understand the functions that the staff feel that institutional leave serves, or should serve, and staff and youth narratives on the factors of significance to whether or not a youth is given institutional leave. These narratives show that institutional leave plays a central role as a disciplinary technique via the specification of good behaviour as a condition for being granted leave. The chapter therefore devotes a substantial amount of attention to this issue. The central focus on good behaviour has consequences for the everyday life of the institutions, both for the youths' experiences of their period of institutionalisation and for the power relations between youths and staff, which is discussed in the chapter's final section. However, in order to understand how and why opportunities for more open forms of custody are so important for everyday life in the institutions we first need to understand how the youths experience being incarcerated, and the chapter therefore begins with their narratives on this issue.

The experience of incarceration

> Yeah, yeah, it's crazy, being able to open your door, I'm telling you! There on [name of locked unit] there's maybe seven, or five doors to every exit. So you're constantly asking, "Can you open this door? Can you open that door? Can you open my toilet, can you …". I mean *totally* … you know, the whole time, it's like this, and it's, I mean it's a bit degrading, I mean it's a bit degrading, you know. Here you feel free; you can open whatever you want.
>
> (Lucas, youth)[1]

In the above quote, Lucas describes the difference between being on a pre-release unit and a locked unit. When I had arrived at the institution on the previous day to conduct interviews, it was Lucas who had been standing outside, and who had let me in with his own key (and at the time I had not really understood whether he was a member of staff or was one of the institutionalised youths), and we had just spoken about this. At the same time as having a key and being able to unlock the door for me, he was careful during the interview to note that he is not free. He has rules to follow and times he must keep to, and even if he has a greater degree of freedom and a key, he cannot come and go as he pleases. This captures several aspects of the narratives of youths who live under more open conditions in special approved homes. These youths are well aware that they are still not at liberty. Thus being on an open unit or in pre-release activities does not mean that the youths are left to themselves to do what they want. Instead these units often still have very clear rules, although these now involve the youths themselves having more responsibility and being less micro-managed.

The youths' perceptions of this situation vary, which I will be returning to. To begin with, however, I would like to note that many of the youths interviewed described the opportunity of being transferred to pre-release as something desirable while they were placed in secure units. The reason given for describing pre-release and more open forms of custody in positive terms, in addition to the aspect of openness itself, was that these custodial forms give the youths the chance to start living their lives in a new way. The youths felt that these more open custodial forms gave them the opportunity to test their ability to cope with the responsibilities that come with freedom, and to make a start on things that may be able to improve their opportunities for a life away from involvement in crime, such as going to school, working and dealing with social situations without being constantly monitored. These factors are reminiscent of the reasons emphasised by staff for giving the youths institutional leave. One of the youths expressed a need to spend time outside the institution without always being monitored, since life in general does not consist of monitored situations. Having to take responsibility was also emphasised as being valuable.

Most of the youths that I interviewed (and most of the youths serving youth custody in general, since only 4 per cent are released from a pre-release unit) were placed in some other type of unit at the time of the interview. How did these youths experience being placed in locked and open units respectively? I will begin with two narratives that perhaps reflect what might be expected, i.e. that the youths prefer more open to more secure conditions. In the first narrative, a boy describes the experience of being placed in a secure unit, while, in the second, a different boy describes being placed in an open unit.

> I'm a person too, I'm not like an animal. Being locked in the whole time, you have no choice, you don't know what to do, you have nothing planned, nothing, I mean nothing.
>
> [...]
>
> You wake up and you have nothing. You just sit, like. You can't talk with other kids, with staff.... You know that you are totally locked up. Then ... that's the way it is. It was terrible actually. I can't like say [explain] */No ... was it tough?/* Because all the kids were unhappy. Everyone had their problems and [there were] conflicts every day. Every day kids screaming, it was really no fun at all.
>
> (Kim, youth)

OSCAR (youth): It's much nicer here; I feel much safer than over there [a locked unit].
TOVE: Mm, okay. What is it that makes it feels safer?
OSCAR: I don't know actually
[Describes what it was like being in a locked unit, that it's cramped, that the youths get on each other's nerves, etc.]
OSCAR: Yeah, it got too much. I mean I became very, very, very restless. I can't cope with being in that kind of environment. */No. Okay. And here you can simply/* Yes, I mean I know that I can open the window, the door, and so on, but it's still not free "free", I mean. It's better than over there anyway.

The first narrative describes how confined one can feel on a secure unit, how the lack of choices and variation in one's daily life creates a feeling that could almost be described as that of being a "caged animal". Kim, in describing this experience, does not primarily blame the staff, however, even though he did not feel that he'd had good contacts with the staff on that particular unit. Instead he emphasised that the staff were also restricted by the rules and demands that are associated with the secure conditions. He said that they could not, in fact, behave very differently since they also had to follow the prevailing rules and regulations. The second quote, which describes an open unit, instead shows how the perception of having more freedom, even if Oscar was well aware that he was still not free, produces a sense of safety. By contrast with being in a locked unit, where it was cramped and the youths would get on each other's nerves, Oscar also felt less restless in the open unit.

Not all of the narratives show the youths preferring open units to secure and locked units, however. Several of the boys also talked about difficulties linked to being placed in more open forms, as is exemplified in the following description, from Peter.

TOVE: What was it like living in that flat in the centre of town? You were living there for two months?
PETER (youth): It was bloody awful!
TOVE: Was it?
PETER: Yes.
TOVE: Why?
PETER: Because you're so close to being free, but still so confined. You have the opportunity to go out into town and that … it's just that … you're in town, you're 18 years old and you're allowed to be out until eight; it's difficult for you. It's just difficult. You're free but … you just feel like they're treating you like a child the whole time. If it's going to be open, then it should probably be a bit outside town, not in the *middle* of town; that just isn't good at all. It isn't. I mean you're in the middle of town, you can meet the wrong people. You *can* meet really good people [as well]! You can end up in the wrong company in [name of town]; you can do other stuff there; it doesn't help you at all.

TOVE: Okay.
PETER: It doesn't.
TOVE: No. What did it feel like moving back here then, afterwards?
PETER: It felt bad to begin with, you know, but I feel that it was a lot better for me, that from here it's a lot easier to plan; you've got time; you don't have anything that distracts you. It's better.

In this case, the proximity to freedom did not make Peter feel safer but instead had the effect of making things feel more uncertain. A number of the youths spoke of how more open placement forms served to remind them that they were not free, since freedom becomes closer while at the same time remaining at a considerable distance. Similar narratives have been presented by McAllister *et al.* (1992) on the basis of their interviews with youths serving custodial sentences. Some of the youths described being given "tasters of liberty" (p. 90) as stressful, and in some cases as being so stressful that some of them had no desire to be given leave more often (which they were generally given less often than the youths in the current study). Similar narratives have also been described among youths interviewed by Cope (2003) in American prisons, and among the female prison inmates in Russia interviewed by Moran (2013), and there are clear parallels here to Shammas's (2014) concept of *pains of freedom*. Neumann (2011) has discussed this issue in relation to an open prison in Norway, and argues that the inmates are "forced to impose on themselves the image of prison discipline and to conduct a self-control that can be extremely challenging" (p. 151). According to Neumann, these inmates experienced "imprisonment of the soul" to a greater extent than inmates in high-security prisons (where it is rather a question of an unequivocal incarceration of the physical body). Being close to things that are happening – in a town, for example – further underlines the experience. Peter's narrative also describes an anxiety about being tempted to do things that are not good, and that he did not seem to want to do, which several of the other youths also spoke of. Nor is the final part of the above quotation, where Peter describes being in a more secure placement form as being easier for him, unique to Peter's narrative. In the following quotation, Samir explains how he felt about being placed on a secure as against an open unit.

SAMIR (youth): You feel relief when you're here.
TOVE: Here?
SAMIR: Yes. I know that that's how it feels for me anyway. [I] sleep better, I don't know, [it] feels better to be inside this.
TOVE: Does it? Why's that?
SAMIR: I don't know.... Others might have said this too [...] that you feel relief when you're sitting here.
[...]
SAMIR: How you think, you don't need to get a headache, sitting here, [with] the fences all around. You know that you can't go out, so you cut off these ideas about wanting to go out.

TOVE: Yes, okay. And then it's easier?
SAMIR: Yes.

Once again, it is the proximity to freedom and the choices, but also the temptations, that this proximity involves, that make being placed on a secure unit seem easier. The above quotation may be compared with Goffman's (1991) concept of institutionalisation, with life becoming easier as inmates adapt to conditions inside the walls of the institution. Although proximity to freedom is sometimes perceived as being difficult to handle, however, it must be remembered that it is still the experience of incarceration that forms the basis for these feelings. In the absence of incarceration, the youths would not experience reminders of freedom as troublesome.

Although the youths often described experiencing incarceration as being difficult in various ways, many of them nonetheless spoke about gradually becoming used to being locked up, like Samir below, an issue that is also touched upon by Goffman (1991).

SAMIR: I mean … when you're in for such a long time, I don't know if it's because you're young or not, but you, you cut of all these kinds of feelings. Do you know what I mean? You don't feel like you're missing anyone. You just don't care.
TOVE: Because you can't cope with thinking about what you're feeling?
SAMIR: Yeah. To begin with it's difficult, to begin with it's shitty, the first three months, until you realise that you've ended up, until you've woken up to – Wow, am I here, you know? You think – what, is this real? You know, you look around … and then understand that you've ended up here.… I don't know. It gets easier day by day.
TOVE: Okay. You get used to it.
[…]
SAMIR: The only hope you have left is getting out some day, feeling that freedom and (inaudible)
TOVE: Yes. What was it that meant that you, after a few months, that you got used to it? Was it that you started shutting off, thinking about it, and that before you'd been feeling?
SAMIR: You don't choose anything yourself. You just don't have the energy to care. You just move away from your thoughts.
TOVE: Okay, it's just about letting the time pass in some way?
SAMIR: For example, if I've been playing FIFA today, then when I go to bed I think about FIFA. And "when I play tomorrow I'm going to do that", you know what I mean, you become like a child almost. Then, wake up the next day and think, er, tomorrow I have school, then I'll play, do some training, okay. So you get yourself focused on the schedule. Because you know you can't do any more than that.

Thus adapting to the conditions of incarceration in part involves shutting oneself off. Samir's narrative also shows that he experiences institutionalisation as resulting in a form of infantilisation. One way of shutting off is thus to concentrate on things that might otherwise seem unimportant, and focusing all one's attention on these, such as thinking about what to do in order to do better next time you play a computer game.

Some of the youths also spoke about two special forms of incarceration: being placed on remand, as several of the youths had been prior to being sentenced, and being placed in isolation. The material includes only a small number of narratives about being placed in isolation, but these are very consistent with one another. Isolation is perceived as being very stressful and is something that most often happens at units where there are no opportunities for the youths to be given any form of institutional leave (see the discussion below on the use of isolation as a disciplinary technique in the absence of opportunities for institutional leave). The few references to isolation that the material contains[2] describe a solitary room with a plastic mattress and staff who then leave the youth there alone.[3] The youths interviewed by Hermodsson and Hansson (2005), who had been placed in special approved homes by the social services, spoke about the experience of isolation in a similar way. The described experience is one of have being alone in dealing with one's anger, and thereafter one's loneliness, sometimes for a relatively short period of time, but sometimes for several hours. The material also contains narratives from individuals who had been placed on remand with maximum restrictions (but these are also uncommon). One narrative that deviates from the pattern of descriptions of being left alone, and that also includes a description of feelings experienced as a result of what can lead to isolation, may serve to illustrate the experience of isolation among the youths interviewed. The quotation is long, but is presented in order to describe a range of factors related to isolation.

MELVIN (youth): When I, I mean … er. .. questioned, then on occasion I've got into a conflict, or maybe shouted and started yelling. And then I've been pinned to the floor, regarded [as] being too aggressive and then they take you down using what they call "No Power, No Lose".[4]… Yes, then you're lying down and … they sound the alarm and half the unit turns up. And that just triggers it, that half the staff from [name of institution] are standing there looking at you. And the worst thing is that it's only two or three of them who, or … *at the most*, at the most eight or nine of them have jumped on me. And it's only eight, nine who *intervene* but there's still 30 people standing there, and the other 20 are standing and *looking*. It's really tough / *Unpleasant/* Yes, and then they just throw you into isolation … and just dive out. And just leave and let you freak out in there, you know, they don't care if you injure yourself. I've stood there and butted my head against the wall but they don't give a damn about [it].

TOVE: Aha, so the staff just leave /*Kind of, yes*/ they don't stay there?

MELVIN: No, they don't stay there.

TOVE: They don't stay there, you're left by yourself in there?

MELVIN: Yes.

TOVE: Okay, how …

MELVIN: It doesn't always happen. It happened once on [name of locked unit], then, then … a really nice staff member, I mean I'll never forget what he does for me. He stayed, even though I'd been swearing at him, kind of told him to "go away, I don't even want you here, go away". But he came and opened the door and.… And … and sat himself down and talked to me. I'll never forget that, you know, that he showed that trust in me. Not like all the others [who] just went away.

TOVE: Okay. So he made an attempt /*To communicate*/ to understand what you wanted?

MELVIN: Yes, which led to a very good relationship, even today, always when I see him, say hi and hug … yes. He's really nice that guy.

TOVE: Yes.… This thing with isolation then, do you stay there long, or?

MELVIN: It depends on how it's prioritised. I've also been in isolation here on [name of locked unit 2], and then I was there between ten at night and one in the morning. I've been in isolation on [name of locked unit 1] from four … or 16.00 until 19.00. And then I've been in isolation on, I mean over there I was chaos and it was like isolation every day kind of thing. Or not exactly every day, but …

TOVE: Often?

MELVIN: Yes, quite often. So over there I was, I mean there's been *one* hour's isolation, a half hour's isolation, but over there time goes so slowly. You just sit there, nothing happens. It's worse than your room, there you've at least got a book to read, there [in isolation] you've got nothing.

TOVE: The room's completely stripped bare?

MELVIN: We have the isolation room over there, you can see what it's like. I mean in my eyes, you wouldn't even put a dog in there. It's so bad.

TOVE: Yes, and so you have to sit there for several hours then, on your own?

MELVIN: Yes, and then there's a metal door and the frames are hard and there's just a *mattress* in the room, *nothing* else /*No*/ You're freezing once the adrenaline has gone. Everything, everything becomes … against you.

Thus isolation produces a good deal of emotion in those who experience it. And a large proportion of those sentenced to youth custody have experience of isolation. Of those given a youth custody sentence between 1999 and 2006, 45 per cent have been subjected to isolation at some point during their sentence. Just over 20 per cent have experienced isolation on more than one occasion. Experiences like those described by Melvin can also be viewed in relation to discussions of how time may be perceived differently depending on the situation, and how this is an important part of understanding experiences of incarceration (Moran 2012a, Cope 2003). Ugelvik (2014 p. 58) argues that the power of staff in relation to inmates may "be exercised in less invasive and more humane ways than normal. A smile, a look, a chat, a cup of coffee make the walls, locks, keys and uniforms more bearable." Melvin's narrative illustrates how being treated with what is perceived as consideration can be of major significance, and how the experience of this kind of treatment can make a staff member very important to a specific youth. Several of the interviewed youths spoke of how important the experience of friendly treatment can be, not least the feeling that a member of staff really cares about them (cf. Hill 2005).

The youths' narratives about the experience of spending time on remand vary, and since such experiences are not actually part of the institutional care provision that constitute the focus of this study, I will only discuss them briefly. These experiences are nonetheless of interest, however, in part because they constitute part of the youths' experience of being in a secure environment, and in part because the time spent on remand precedes the period of the institutional placement itself, and thus constitutes a form of frame of reference for the experience of serving a youth custody sentence in a special approved home.

Often, when the youths spoke about time spent on remand, they discussed it in relation to their experiences of their current institution (in part because I sometimes asked them to compare remand with the institutional placement). The youths had often experienced harsh restrictions at the remand centre, and had largely spent their time there alone. Some spoke of this experience as having given them time to reflect, while others instead described it as very stressful. Benjamin described sitting in isolation at a remand centre by saying that "it does strange things with your mind, you could say". Those who had spoken of it as an opportunity for reflection, or as giving them something to think about, did so on the basis of finding themselves in an extreme situation. The time spent on remand had also preceded their convictions, which made the situation somewhat special, although they had all been convicted by the time I spoke to them. The reason some of them had experienced their time in the remand centre as calm and as an opportunity for reflection was ascribed to their often having been left alone, by contrast with the situation in their current institution. Here demands were made on their attention by both staff and other youths, but perhaps primarily by the staff. At the institutions they were expected to follow their treatment and engage in other activities, and these were perceived as "disturbing" them. At the same time, the youths' experiences of being on remand must be viewed in relation to the fact that for most of them these experiences had been relatively short-lived (few spoke of having been on remand for more than a month). Some said that there were not many differences by comparison with being placed in a secure unit at a special approved home, but said that the locked and open units at the institution were more open than the environments they had experienced while on remand. Others however said that there were substantial differences between the special approved home and the remand centre. The similarities between the secure conditions in special approved homes and at remand centres are perhaps not surprising. In both cases, the experience involves an intensive form of incarceration.

Just as the remand centre may constitute a frame of reference for the youths' perceptions of the subsequent institutional placement, some of the youths' preconceptions about being placed in an institution of this kind appear to function in the same way. Some youths (who had not previously been placed in a special approved home) described their expectations about what it would be like to come to the institution. In several of these cases, the youths described having felt very anxious; they had felt that it would be like in the movies, that they would have to "fight every day". When this anxiety showed itself to be unfounded, they had felt relieved and they said that it was nothing like as bad as they had thought it would be. Several of the youths interviewed by Hermodsson and Hansson (2005) had the opposite experience. Some of these youths had expected, or felt, that they would be going to a place where they would be given help and the opportunity to rest, and unlike the youths sentenced to youth custody that I interviewed, the experience of the locked institution had been a shock and had been much worse than they had been expecting. These youths had often been the subjects of emergency placements and had either not been given information about, or had not had time to develop an understanding of, what was actually going to happen prior to their placement. Although the experiences of the youths interviewed in the two studies differ, in both cases they are based on the youths' expectations about what it means to be placed in a youth institution.

The youths often described the experience of incarceration as having been very stressful, particularly to begin with. The interview material includes a large number of narratives in which the youths speak of "getting used to" being incarcerated. What it is that they describe having got used to varies somewhat, however. Some spoke of how they had got used to the rules of the institution, or to withdrawing and keeping out of the way, in relation to both the staff and other youths, because doing so made life easier, exactly the kind of strategies described by Goffman (1991). As has been discussed above, part of this process of adaptation appears to involve "shutting off". Others described how they had got used to the slow tempo, which was in turn associated with a sense of despondency that many experienced in connection with their incarceration (cf. Cope 2003). Every day is the same, and there is no real difference between weekdays and the weekend. Some of the youths even described themselves as becoming ill as a result of the tedium. Tore described what it was like waiting for something in the locked unit in which he was placed, which might actually involve waiting for a few months, but "particularly when you're placed here [locked unit] and the days pass like … like years" (cf. Moran 2012a).

Other youths also spoke of a tormenting inability to sleep, of the many hours during which they were locked in their rooms, when they were expected to sleep but unable to do so. One of these youths, Leon described this experience in the following way:

LEON (youth): I've had problems sleeping … which I'd never had previously … before I came here. I find it really difficult to sleep in the evenings.

TOVE: Why's that? Is it *only* the bed [he had previously spoken about the beds being hard] or is it something else too?

LEON: No it's the ideas that come up. I don't know, maybe you get depressed or something.… You like sit and think, the family … the distance, freedom, this place … I mean, it gets too much. Every day that passes, I mean, you do

> *exactly* the same thing; the week is over, it begins with the same thing again; the week is over, it begins with the same … I have … when you lived at home, then when it was like Monday, you'd say "Oh, it's Monday again," and when it was Friday, then just, the weekend at last. It feels, it feels, I mean, you lose that feeling like, for example when you, on Fridays, you know, that then, on Saturdays you've probably got the day off, ah, then you think "it feels so good", you can have a lie in, and like that kind of thing. Here you don't think about those things any more. I used to love the weekends. And now they don't matter … you don't think about it, because it's just the same thing.

Thus the time in the institutions is described as being monotonous, with one day being just like another. Both adults and youths serving prison sentences have described their experiences in the same way (Moran 2012a, Cope 2003). In an interview study of youths serving long prison sentences, Cope (2003) describes how they developed different strategies to cope with their perceptions about the passage of time. One of these involved attempting to view the period in prison as a parenthesis in relation to life outside, and one example of a way of achieving this was to try and sleep away as much time as possible. When it was difficult to sleep, not least during the evening, if the youths had been asleep for a large part of the day, several of them used drugs as a means of getting to sleep. None of the youths I interviewed spoke of taking drugs at the special approved homes, but they did experience sleep as constituting a problem, and they did also express a desire to get through their time at the institutions as smoothly as possible. When they were unsuccessful in this, life became difficult to deal with. That is why different ways of trying to "shut off" feelings became so important.

The first experience of going out on leave

One way of examining the youths' perceptions about both incarceration and what it is like to be given institutional leave is to look at how they spoke about their first leave experience. All of the interviewed youths were asked about this, although sometimes their answers were not about the first time they were given leave to spend time outside the institution but rather the first time they had been able to travel home to their families. In a majority of the interviews, however, the youths spoke about the feeling of being able to spend time outside the institution for the first time. The length of their period of incarceration prior to this varied between the youths, in part depending on the length of their sentences, but sometimes also as a result of other factors.

Several of the youths' narratives describe how good it felt to get out of the institution for the first time. A more uncommon narrative was that the youths could not really remember what it had been like. A reasonable interpretation of this latter type of narrative is that the first experience of leave was not a particularly big thing for these youths (provided that it not was because they did not want to talk to me about what it had felt like, and my sense has rather been that the youths had a fairly unproblematic attitude towards their first leave experience). Patrik described the first time he was given leave for a home visit in the following way:

> It was totally … I couldn't believe that I had been able to go home, if you can put it like that; I couldn't. It felt really strange; I mean, yeah, I've got a girlfriend and that; I've been together with my girlfriend for three years in August, and that's something that's really, really tough, it really is tough. So it was totally wonderful being able to get home and see my family. But er … yes, it was a strange feeling. Fucking wonderful feeling. It feels like you've missed a lot, and you have.
>
> (Patrik, youth)

Patrik's description focuses primarily on how good it felt to be able to go home for the first time, even though the experience also felt strange to some extent. The narrative shows that it is not only family members that youths may miss and whom they (risk) losing contact with during their youth custody sentences. In this case there was also a girlfriend whom Patrik wanted to see. The quotation concludes with a description of a feeling of having missed a great deal during the period of incarceration. This was something that several of the youths took up, and which also constitutes one of the problems associated with incarceration in general, not least when this occurs in youth, when there is a lot going on in life (see Moran 2012a). This may include friends graduating from upper secondary education, or the youths' family and friends experiencing things that they themselves cannot participate in. The youths' narratives also describe the possibility of being able to experience at least some of these things by being present for them while on leave, and several of the youths stated that it was important to be able to spend time outside the institution in order to maintain these contacts.

Goffman (1991) argues that many of the inmates of total institutions experience the time spent in these institutions as being wasted and having been taken from their lives (see also Moran 2012a). One type of experience is that of being completely exiled from one's life. According to Goffman, it is against this backdrop, among other things, that the demoralising effect of long or indeterminate sentences may be understood. Several of the youths in the current study also expressed major indignation at the way in which the social services are able to place youths in special approved homes without knowing when these placements will end, and the youths were grateful that they themselves at least knew when their sentences would end.[5] Goffman (1991, p. 67) argues that:

> However harsh the conditions of life in total institutions, harshness alone cannot account for this sense of life wasted; we must rather look to the social disconnexions caused by entrance and to the failure (usually) to acquire within the institution gains that can be transferred to outside life – gains such as money earned, or marital relations formed, or certified training received.

While the special approved home youths may do some of the things described by Goffman, such as acquiring some degree of education, this type of experience is very real to them. Life moves on outside the institution, while they are no longer a part of it but are instead in a bubble in which time is perceived as standing still. Institutional leave can contribute to reducing the level of dissolution in their social relations outside the institution, and may also provide benefits that remain with them subsequent to release, if the youths are given the opportunity to participate in activities which give them experience that may be of use to them in their subsequent lives. Both youths and staff members also emphasised such factors as being one of the benefits of institutional leave.

Thus the youths' narratives include a number of positive descriptions of their first experience of institutional leave (or their first period of home leave). Some described that it felt good, but at the same time strange and different, to be outside the institution. This was how Leon described how it felt: "Different. It … yeah, I don't know, you got like … the feeling of freedom, but confined freedom. It's like … letting you stand in a glass frame; you can see freedom but not touch." For Leon it felt like this every time (at the time he was interviewed, Leon had to date only been on monitored leave, and he said that the feeling was in part linked to this factor). In the context of a narrative about his first home visit, another youth spoke of how, at the beginning, being in the institution had felt more like being "at home" than when he was actually at home, but that this feeling had passed with time. A number of youths also spoke of how it felt like people were looking at them (cf. Moran 2014, Moran 2012b), while others described not being used to being out among other people, and that things move so fast, and there is so much happening, that they become confused; Rickard described that, "your brain can't keep up", because he was used to being in isolation. The youths themselves (as well as some of the staff) linked these experiences to the youths having been damaged by their period of institutional incarceration. This view is also in line with the research on carceral space, which has described how the experience of time varies with context, and where among other things time has been described as passing much more quickly on the outside (Moran 2012a).

Some of the youths spoke of unpleasant experiences of their first time outside the institution, however. Adam described his first time outside the institution in the following way:

ADAM (youth): Yes, I've been out several times.
TOVE: Yes, how did you feel about it the first time?
ADAM: It was tough (sighs). I … I got into a cold sweat, I … I … my heart … I mean, my heart beat increased, you could say. I, er … I almost fell apart the first time. I wasn't used … to so many people as I could see, and it felt the whole time as though someone was behind me giving me strange looks … for example, when I went to the kiosk for the first time, there were two … er … two … an older couple, in their seventies maybe, who were behind me, and I felt the whole time that they were going to attack me.

TOVE: Oh. I see.

ADAM: So I never took my eyes off them. So it was tough … it was. And even today, it's still tough when I go out but … I'm learning, but it's a lot better when you go out. You get to practise and it's so much better when you get outside, so that you don't, like I have done, shut down … out … because that can be really tough when you get to be free.

TOVE: So it's good to get out nonetheless so that you /*get used to*/ so that you get used to it.

ADAM: Yes.

TOVE: Yes. But it's easier now than it was the first time, even if it's still tough?

ADAM: Yes, it's much easier now.

As can be seen from Adam's narrative, he experienced feelings that might almost be described as dread and also felt suspicious about people around him. A little later in the interview, he spoke of how the staff understood this, and that they could help him in trying to make the experience easier, and also that he did not want to avoid going out, because that makes the situation worse. Things had improved but he still felt it was tough. Similar feelings about coming home after a period in custody have been described by youths in interviews in England and Wales (Bateman *et al.* 2013, Hazel and Bateman 2013). These youths' narratives also at times include descriptions of traumatic feelings due to both feelings of stress and paranoia, and also the fact that the youths do not know how to behave in relation either to people around them or their own families (Hazel and Bateman 2013). The study's authors also note that there is a lack of research in this area, which is also true in relation to reactions to, and experiences of, institutional leave.

The interviews contained further narratives, like the one above, about how difficult it can be to leave the special approved homes for the first time. Samir, who had not been outside the grounds of his institution for over a year and a half, described his first experience of leave in the following way:

TOVE: How did it feel the first time, if it was after a year and eight months?

SAMIR (youth): I mean, it was a sick feeling. I don't want to remember days like that.

TOVE: You don't want to remember it?

SAMIR: No, that's the truth, I swear.… Imagine being inside for a year and eight months … you're there the whole time; you have this space, a hundred metres to be in the whole time. Then suddenly you see people around you. /*Yes*/ Because me in particular, I, I've been in one of these secure units.

TOVE: Yes. Was it unpleasant?

SAMIR: Yeah, bloody hell. Kept looking around the whole time, to see if someone was following you, you check whether, yes it … you can't describe it.

This narrative describes something similar to Goffman's (1991) description of *institutionalisation*, and during the interview, Samir described himself specifically as being institutionalised as a result of his long stay in a secure unit. This type of reaction involves life inside the (total) institution becoming easier to cope with, while what is outside appears unpleasant and difficult to handle. Thus one of the reactions that the youths described was that incarceration led to their adapting to life in the institution, which resulted in life inside feeling familiar and safe while what was outside, "normal" life, came to appear frightening and unfamiliar.

One important aspect of the youths' narratives, however, was also that they described this initial insecurity and discomfort as passing once they were able to get out a little more often. There was thus a point to being outside the institution; it served to "de-institutionalise" them. Institutional leave, both in the form of home visits and participating in activities in the local community outside the institution were thus described in the boys' narratives as being a means of reducing the effects of processes of institutionalisation.

Having institutional leave

In addition to asking the youths about their first time outside the institution, I also asked more general questions about institutional leave and their experiences of it. Many spoke of it feeling good to get out, away from the institution. Leave could serve both as a breathing space and as an opportunity for the youths to be themselves, viewed in relation to having to maintain a façade during their time in the institution. A number spoke of how they had learned to appreciate small things that they had previously taken for granted – nature, flowers, being able to buy oneself a drink, etc. The youths described how they had realised that they had previously had unfettered access to these things without ever having thought about it. These experiences are very reminiscent of Goffman's (1991) descriptions of how inmates lose things that had previously been taken for granted. Alexander spoke about having met a girl while on leave, who had said that she understood what it was like to be incarcerated, because going to school felt like being locked up. He went on:

> Believe me, it's not the same; when you're locked up in here you're *screaming* like an idiot to be able to go back to school. Even if you hated it before, you realise now that you love it because you can see how free it actually is, to get to go to school and to be there. Not like here, having to be in school here [at the institution] and sit locked-in in a classroom.
>
> (Alexander, youth)

What had previously been experienced as tough or irritating, or had even been something the youths hated, may be transformed in the light of the current experience of incarceration into something desirable and longed for. Several of the other youths, like Alexander, said that you couldn't understand what it meant to be incarcerated if you had not experienced it yourself. This was the case both for the staff and for other people that the youths met. This view was also linked to some of the youths speaking of how they may themselves work in similar institutions in the future, in part because they know what it's like and will be able to understand the youths who are incarcerated, in part because they felt that they would be able to make such institutions better places than they are today.

Thus the youths spoke of themselves as having been *damaged* by their institutionalisation, and also described needing to practice being outside in order to cope with it, and that the experience of being on leave felt strange. Adam exemplified this by saying that if you put a person in a cave for several months, then when they came out, the person would have become stupid. Adam argued that being incarcerated in an institution was exactly the same. Others described, in the same way as in relation to their first experience of leave, how things happened (too) quickly on the outside, if there were large numbers of people and the youths were no longer used to meeting lots of people. Some said that irrespective of how difficult it felt, being outside the institution was something you had to expose yourself to and practice coping with. Adam said that "irrespective of how tough it is, I have to deal with it, because I've got eight months left … and that's not so much. So I have to start … practicing, no matter how tough it is." Thus he felt that it was necessary to force himself to practice, since he "only" had eight months left of his sentence. This shows how much he perceived himself to have been affected by the experience of incarceration, and how difficult it felt to be outside.

The material also includes narratives about how institutional leave makes the possibility of obtaining one's freedom by absconding more tangible, and how this can lead to difficult feelings about returning to the institution. Peter described this in the following way:

PETER (youth): Your first leave, that's quite good because you travel by car; you know there's no stress. You're at home with the family; it's quite good. It's the first unmonitored [leave] that's quite difficult.

TOVE: Okay. Why is it difficult?

PETER: You leave here, you're at home, I was at home by twelve. Then the train leaves at seven, so you've got like six hours at home, then you have to go to the train, and it's like you feel it churning in your stomach when you know that you are travelling back here *voluntarily*. Am I really going to go back? So it … I can understand that a lot of people choose to run off on their first unmonitored [leave] because it's bloody difficult, it's not easy sitting yourself down on that train. Really.

This quotation shows how difficult the decision to return to the institution and the incarceration this involves can be for the youths, and there are clear parallels with Neumann's (2011) concept of disciplining the soul and Shammas's (2014) pains of freedom. The youths in McAllister *et al.*'s (1992) study also spoke of similar fears that the freedom associated with leave might tempt them to abscond.

This worry about absconding also illustrates the level of responsibility that is placed on the youths when they are given the chance of going on unmonitored leave. This is a responsibility that the majority of the youths cope with well. The study's quantitative data do not show exactly how common it is for youths to abscond from unmonitored leave. However, an estimate based on the data that are available on absconding[6] indicate that this happens in connection with *at most* 6 per cent of the occasions on which youths are given unmonitored leave, and this represents an overestimate of the real number of incidents of absconding of this kind. Further, in some of these cases of absconding, the youths return to the institution voluntarily, and it is rather a question of returning later than the time that had been agreed in advance.

Thus the picture that emerges of institutional leave, both in terms of the youths' first experience of leave and their descriptions of subsequent leave experiences, just like the experience of being incarcerated, is both varied and complex. The experience of being outside the institution can take several different forms, not all of which involve good or positive feelings, even though the desire to be outside is there nonetheless. Having illustrated the youths' experiences of being incarcerated by means of narratives focused on their experiences of custodial openness, secure environments and different forms of institutional leave, I now move on to look at the views of staff as to why the youths should be given institutional leave. I will then examine what the youths and staff describe as being necessary for a youth to be given leave or to be moved to a more open unit.

Why should youths be given leave?

All of the staff interviewed in the study were asked to describe the objectives associated with giving the youths leave. The answers of different staff members varied, but they were also concordant in a number of respects. One central theme in the staff's answers was that of the youths being able to maintain contact with people outside the institution, first and foremost their families, which involved not only parents and siblings but also other relatives who have an important role in the youths' lives. Other (pro-social) contacts were also emphasised, such as (non delinquent) friends. The family is viewed as central for a number of reasons, in part because the youths are young, and because their sentences have "taken them away" from their parents at an age when their peers are usually still living at home. The family is also viewed as central because the youths will often return to the family home following the completion of their sentences (65 per cent of the youths in the study were released to the parental home). This means that it is in the home environment that desistance from crime has to be made to work if recidivism is to be avoided. Some staff noted that there may be problems in the youths' relationships with their families that need to be worked on during the youths' time at the institution, and that in these cases it was important to be able to test the effects of this work in the family environment. According to some of the interviewed staff, home visits during which the youths were accompanied by staff could also present an opportunity to find out about these types of problems. Such visits may thus be used as an opportunity to obtain knowledge about the youths, which may then be used for exercising control (Goffman 1991, Foucault 1991) dressed up as providing help (Foucault 1982, Järvinen 2002, Petersson 2013).

Another common reason described for the youths to be given institutional leave is that they need to practice coping with things outside the institution. Several of the interviewed staff members argued that the youths being able to do well and cope with things (such as getting up in the morning, arriving on time and not getting into conflicts) at the institution becomes meaningless if they are unable to do the same things outside the institution. It is on the outside that they need to be able to avoid getting into conflicts and doing "stupid things" or failing to deal with the routines required to cope with school or a job. Staff members also maintained that it is easier for youths to involve themselves in activities subsequent to their release from the institution, such as various forms of leisure time activities, if they have started participating in these activities during their time at the institution. Some also added that it can quite simply be fun for the youths to get away from the institution, and that this can be of value in itself. At the same time, these staff also said that they think that institutional leave should also serve other purposes than simply being fun. Another reason that was given was that it may be important for the youths to test things that they would not otherwise get the opportunity to experience.

Among the things that the staff described the youths as needing to practice were things that they had "learned" or been practicing in the context of various treatment programmes. The staff said that the youths also need to test out what they had learned in situations outside the institution, since that was the context in which they would need to consistently put this knowledge and the skills they had learned into practice. The staff also spoke of the need for social skills training, which involved learning to travel between different places on public transport, going for a coffee, ordering in a restaurant or café, practising social interactions with people the youths meet and so on. Other activities that the staff felt it was useful for the youths to practice included going to a school outside the institution and participating in different types of leisure activities. This focus on practising various activities may be compared with Foucault's (1991) description of how the recurrent practice of sometimes simple and routine tasks constitutes a central element of discipline. Although the staff argued that what the youths needed to practice were not things that the *youths themselves* found to be simple and routine, but were rather things that the youths found difficult, the examples described nonetheless reflect relatively simple and routine activities, of a kind that a "normal" person would be expected to cope with (quite easily).

Closely linked to this theme, there were also a number of descriptions of the youths needing institutional leave in order to feel that they were *not failing*, because it may be important for them to experience being successful at doing things that they are supposed to do. In this context, staff argued, the strict forms and rules associated with leave may make it easier for the youths to get things to work, and may give them a sense of not failing. Some of the staff emphasised that the youths are used to failing, and that they need a counterbalance to this experience, i.e. a way of practising being successful.

One very common theme in the staff's narratives about the objectives associated with institutional leave was that it should reduce the harmful effects of incarceration. Many of the staff said that the youths quickly become institutionalised (Goffman 1991), which among other things leads to the youths feeling uncomfortable spending time outside the institution and sometimes wanting to stay there instead. The staff argued that this made it very important for the youths to spend time outside the institution, since incarceration produced problems and almost paranoid reactions (a view that corresponds well with the narratives of the youths themselves). The following narrative, from Hanna, may serve as an illustration.

> I [...] became really worried in the beginning when the boys had been out to buy clothes, [with] staff; you travel to [name of shopping centre] and buy clothes and they're almost shy of people, experiencing almost panic from being out among people, almost feeling like they've got "I'm a criminal" written on their foreheads, and wanting to get back to the unit. This worried me a great deal, but incarceration has these effects on youths.
>
> (Hanna, staff)

The similarity with Moran's (2014, 2012b) description of how female prison inmates described feeling like their experience of prison was tattooed on their foreheads is striking. Similar descriptions can also be seen in the interviews with youths, as when they spoke of how people could "see from looking at them" that they were from a youth institution when they were out on leave.

A further benefit of institutional leave described by the staff was that it was good for the staff to see how the youths functioned outside the institution. In this sense, as with the use of home visits to observe family relations, leave functions as part of the individual-focused knowledge collection process described by Foucault (1991). The staff also felt it was important for the families to see that things were happening, that the youths were making progress with their behaviour. Some of the interviewed staff members said that institutional leave can also provide an opportunity for more personal conversations between the youths and their contact persons or other staff members. Some of the youths also spoke of feeling that it was easier to talk to staff members when they were with one of them outside the institution. The fact that it is difficult to have an intimate or confidential conversation within the framework of the institutional environment may, in some ways, be interpreted as constituting one of the harms that institutionalisation results in.

There are also examples of the staff members describing occasions when they have to try to motivate youths who do not *want* to go outside the institution, sometimes by more or less forcing them out. There were also isolated descriptions of this kind among the interviews with the youths. Some youths, for example, felt that it may be easier simply to sit out one's sentence rather than devoting time to applying for leave, a view which they sometimes justified by saying that leave was monitored anyway, which they felt they could just as well do without. Besides the fact that it may be simpler just to sit out one's sentence, the youths' interviews also included another narrative about their reluctance in relation to institutional leave, which differed somewhat from those described by staff members. Alexander said that the reason he had not applied for leave was not because it felt *comfortable* not to do so (as the staff argued), but rather because he felt *insecure*. He also said that he intended to apply for leave at a later date. In line with the staff's descriptions of how they would step in and put "pressure" on youths with such tendencies in order to get them out anyway, Alexander described that in his case the staff had taken over and ensured that he spent time outside the institution.

Thus, according to the staff, there are a number of reasons why it is important for the youths to have the opportunity to spend time outside the institution. But what is it that determines which youths are given leave and why?

Doing good behaviour

Rules governing whether youths are given institutional leave

The rules that govern whether or not youths should be given leave describe several factors that are to be taken into consideration, and within the framework of these rules good behaviour is central in a number of ways. For example, the staff fill in a form in connection with applications for leave, which requires them to state whether the youth has been (is) behaving well, the youth's attitudes towards drugs and substance abuse and whether the youth is following the specified treatment plan.[7] Another factor that affects the chances for being given leave is the length of the youth's sentence and how much of this sentence has already been served. Previously, youths were required to have served half their sentence before they could be given monitored home leave, and two-thirds before they could be given unmonitored home leave.[8] These strict regulations based on the sentence length have since been toned down, however, in favour of a more individually based assessment. When the first staff interviews were conducted, this process had only just begun, whereas the shift had become clearer by the time of the final interviews, among other things as a result of the publication of new directives on improved pre-release activities for those sentenced to youth custody (Justitiedepartementet 2011). These directives opened the way for increased opportunities to give the youths institutional leave, and also to give them leave at an earlier point in their sentences. They have also involved increased opportunities for control, however, in the sense that youths may now be fitted with electronic ankle tags when they spend time outside the institution. The intention is to make it possible to give youths leave *earlier* in their sentences, but it also involves a risk for increased levels of supervision (so-called net-widening) if tagging is employed in cases where the youths would previously have been given leave even without an ankle tag.

Being given institutional leave

The youths mentioned a number of different factors in their descriptions of what was required in order to be given leave or to be able to move to a more open unit. Some of these were not using threats or violence and not getting into arguments with other youths or with staff. These factors were mentioned, or rather briefly listed, by many of the youths, and with the exception of isolated objections, the youths viewed it as unproblematic and quite natural that this was (and should be) the way things were. One of the objections that was raised related to the issue of the interpretation of whether a certain situation had really involved a threat, or whether it was rather a question of inexperienced staff, for example, over-interpreting a situation that more experienced staff members would have been able to deal with in a better way. Another objection that was raised in relation to the use of conflicts as a natural and unproblematic criterion was that it is not always so easy to avoid becoming angry and upset given the situation that the youths find themselves in. Leon elaborated on this in the following way:

> If someone is sitting irritating you, for example, if we say some other kid is irritating you. Then they [the staff] say "focus on yourself". It's impossible to focus on yourself when someone is sitting there poking you. You tell them to pack it in. If he doesn't listen, you tell him again. If he doesn't listen, you raise your voice or you get … and you start to like have a go at them and it.… I mean that's what happens, even if you don't hit them, but you start like having a go … because you can't take it anymore. But they say "focus on yourself" and if we [the youths] say that "he's doing it, it's obvious that I'm going to want to do it too", but they say "no, you mustn't do it. Just because he did it, doesn't mean that you have to do it." I know that *too*, but whatever you do they say "focus on yourself" and that's not that easy when seven other kids live here, plus the staff, come and have a poke at you; plus that you've got so many thoughts going around your head, without any answers. You *can't* always focus on yourself. You can't, like … and you don't know what to do with that [all the thoughts] either.
>
> (Leon, youth)

This narrative shows how the staff responsibilise the youths. They are themselves to assume responsibility for behaving correctly, irrespective of what other youths do and irrespective of the stresses produced by life in the institution. This is reminiscent of the responsibilisation practices engaged in by staff both in prisons (Bosworth 2007), and in the probation service (Werth 2013).

Something else that the youths spoke of in the interviews was that you cannot bring drugs into, or use drugs, in the institution. This was not mentioned as often as threats and violence, but was viewed as being even more self-explanatory. None of the youths expressed any objections to this. Some youths also spoke of not being allowed to have other things – such as telephones, knives or lighters, in the unit – and in these cases the youths did not appear to have any objections either. Some also mentioned that not having absconded was one of the criteria for good behaviour in relation to institutional leave, once again without raising any objections to this. A small number also said that the length of one's sentence also matters in relation to being able to spend time outside the institution.

The thematic category that dominated the youths' discussions, however, which may in part be due to the fact that I asked follow-up questions in order to clarify what it might mean in practice, involved the importance of "doing what you're supposed to" in various contexts. The reason I asked follow-up questions was that the youths in the majority of cases initially only referred to this by saying that what was required was that they exhibited "good behaviour" (which sometimes also included the criteria described above, such as not being violent). It is also here that the picture of the youths' views about what is required of them becomes more complex. By contrast with the categories of behaviour mentioned above – such as not being allowed to bring in drugs, which the youths appeared to regard as being quite reasonable – if they want to be able to be given institutional leave, the youths' opinions on the issue of "good behaviour" or "doing what they're supposed to" were divided. Some youths described the requirement to always do what they were supposed to as being relatively uncomplicated and reasonable, while others described their experience of this requirement as almost producing a form of paralysis. I will begin by describing what the youths mentioned as examples of what constitutes good behaviour. Since this statement gives a fairly overwhelming impression in the interviews, I will initially simply present a number of the descriptions related by the youths by listing them one after the other, in order to attempt to communicate the feeling these produced in the interviews (these descriptions are taken from interviews with a large number of different youths). As will become apparent, the list presented below contains descriptions of what is regarded as both good behaviour and bad behaviour.

> You don't participate in the daily activities, don't have your therapy, don't participate in the treatment, you're perceived as being argumentative, you have to participate in everything that happens, do the cleaning twice a week, quite simply go along with everything, don't follow the routines and so on, get up in the morning, aren't there for the school day, don't get up in the morning, refuse to go and shower after sports class, refuse to go down to sports class, do what you're supposed to, follow the routines, wake up in the morning, do the cleaning, go to sports class, go to school, don't wake up in the morning, unpleasant attitude, unpleasant, choose not to follow the rules, do what you're supposed to do in the unit and be nice and so on, don't go to school, don't wake up, don't do what … they're supposed to do every day, be nice and pleasant, participate in your activities, clean up when they say "cleaning", participate, positive, helpful and stuff like that, do what you're supposed to, be nice, respectful, listen to the staff, argue with the staff, not be the kind of person who causes problems, how you react to staff if they tell you to go and clean your room, show that you've chosen to actively

> participate, treat people with respect, be helpful, do your bit, if you happen to say a bad word, not being on time, play truant, keeping to your schedule, no arguing, wake up a minute late, participating in everything that's been scheduled, get up in the morning, following all the routines.

As can be seen from the above excerpt, the experience is one of micro-management of the youths' daily lives. It involves both concrete activities and more general statements about "following all the routines" and about how the youths react to staff demands or rebukes. The impression given is that it is quite simply a question of doing everything that the staff have decided must be done in the context of the daily activities of the institution; that is to say, it is a question of disciplined behaviour (Foucault 1991). This feeling of micro-management is illustrated by expressions such as, "I mean, everything you do here has consequences. Everything you do, everything you don't do, everything has consequences" (Leon, youth) and "But almost everything is wrong, so we could say, there aren't that many things we can do" (Casper, youth). Both these comments were made after the youths had listed the various things that they must, or must not, do. Crewe (2011) describes similar tendencies towards increasing levels of behavioural micro-management in prisons in England and Wales. This is what Crewe is referring to when he describes how the exercise of penal power has become "tighter"[9] by comparison with an earlier period when the inmates were left to themselves to a greater extent, provided that they kept to the more general rules that were to be followed. For Crewe, one consequence of this has been that "with appropriate behaviour defined so narrowly, prisoners feel encircled by 'eggshells', and deemed responsible for any breakages" (p. 520).

Writing about correctional institutions, Foucault (1991 pp. 128–129) argues that what these are primarily trying to produce is

> the obedient subject, the individual subjected to habits, rules, orders, an authority that is exercised continually around him and upon him, and which he must allow to function automatically in him.

The youths' narratives about what good behaviour involves manifest clear parallels to the contents of the above quote from Foucault. The central focus on good behaviour being about doing everyday things in the right way involves submitting to habits and rules in a way that is made a continuous, ongoing part of daily life. This can also be compared with what staff members in others studies have described as youths acting "like clockwork", which is not exclusively viewed as something positive, since it may involve superficial adaptation instead of real change (Hill 2005, Franzén and Holmqvist 2014, see also Goffman 1991, Petersson 2013). I will be returning to this point later in the chapter, in connection with a discussion of the consequences of discipline.

Another similarity with Foucault's (1991 p. 149) description of correctional institutions is that the work of these institutions manifests itself, among other things, in a substantial focus on schedules, which become increasingly detailed.

The youths' descriptions of how they have to get up at exactly the right time, and of how they must keep to the schedule determined for them, constitute examples of this parallel. At the same time, there are a number of elements described by Foucault, such as the precise training of the body (e.g. in the form of shouldering a rifle), that have no equivalent in today's Swedish youth institutions. Nor can Foucault's description of discipline as in part being intended to combat idleness be fully applied to the context of Swedish youth institutions. It is true that the youths are to engage in activities that constitute a "full day", which may include school, participation in treatment and leisure time activities, but the youths' institutional day also includes a good deal of time when they are relatively unoccupied (cf. Moran 2012b, Cope 2003).

The fact that good behaviour constitutes the fundamental criterion for being given institutional leave can be seen both from the emphasis that the youths placed on this factor, and how often they spoke of it in the interviews, but also from the fact that they stated quite explicitly that good behaviour was of primary importance. However, while there was consensus among the interviewed youths about the importance and the content of good behaviour, there was less agreement with regard to their *opinions* about the role of good behaviour. Some of the youths did not actually express very much of an opinion at all, but for the most part simply listed various examples so that I would understand what they meant by "good behaviour". Some of them, however, concluded their descriptions about the expectations placed on them by saying that meeting these expectations was not particularly difficult, but actually relatively easy:

TOVE: What does ... what does it mean, then, good behaviour?

RICKARD (youth): Yes, well, it's just this, how you behave, don't take drugs in the unit or just generally like ... Yeah.... You're calm ... do what you're supposed to do, you go down to school every day, you take part in sports ... yes. It's fairly simple.

The youths who stated that this was something simple and straightforward were the exceptions, however. There were many more who expressed having been negatively affected to a greater or lesser extent by this institutional micro-management of their daily lives. I will be returning to this point later when I discuss how the good behaviour criterion serves a disciplinary function through the way it is linked to the possibility of being given various forms of institutional leave.

Finally, a number of the youths also stated that there was an expectation placed on them to show that they wanted to change, to look to the future. Mohamed expressed this by saying that the youths were expected to "show that you want to get out of here in every possible way". This involves a requirement to show willingness and a desire for "improvement", to be one of those who can be "normalised", to use Foucault's terminology (1991 p. 21, see also Bosworth 2007, Werth 2013). The requirement to show in every conceivable way that one wants to get out of the institution also functions as a powerful disciplinary tool.

Only those who do everything that the staff say that they need to do in order to be "made normal" can meet this criterion. This requirement is likely to greatly restrict the opportunities for protesting against various elements of treatment provision or about activities that the staff say are necessary.

What, then, did the staff say about the criteria for being given institutional leave? In their interviews, the staff described a somewhat larger range of criteria than the youths, but the descriptions of the two groups were largely similar. Like the youths, the staff said that it was important not to have absconded, but the staff also added that if a youth was deemed to be at *risk* of absconding, then this too could be a reason for not being given leave. Thus it was not merely a question of not actually having absconded. In their descriptions of the propensity to abscond, the staff also related absconding to the notion of protecting the community. Another criterion taken up by the staff in relation to institutional leave was an assessment of the risk for re-offending (or sometimes the risk of relapse into substance abuse). As has previously been noted, both of these factors (the risk of relapse into crime and substance abuse respectively) are among the formal criteria that the staff are required to assess when youths submit an application for leave. The use of risk assessments in relation to both absconding and recidivism may be viewed as part of a trend towards an increasing use of risk analyses within both the corrections (Hörnqvist 2010) and substance abuse treatment systems (Petersson 2013). The length of the sentence being served was a further, more formal criterion of this kind that was mentioned by the staff. As has been noted above, the application of this criterion had initially also been very strictly regulated, but over the course of the period during which the interviews were conducted, the implementation of these regulations came to be increasingly less stringent. In some cases, the staff also said that being given institutional leave (too early in the sentence) can undermine the fact that youth custody is a penal sanction, and that as such it should be "disagreeable".

The staff also mentioned a number of factors related to various aspects of the youths' situation that could also constitute an obstacle to being given leave, primarily in the form of home leave. One of these factors was if it was felt that the family had too many problems. According to the staff, this was sometimes relevant since it resulted in them being unable to identify a functioning "leave address" (if it is not possible to find a functioning address within the immediate family, the staff attempt to identify other addresses, such as those of other relatives, for example). The staff said that this sometimes resulted in the youths not wanting to go on home leave. Some staff also spoke of cases where the parents did not want the youths to come home. Other family-related factors that may serve as an obstacle to home leave are if the victim of the offence for which the youth has been convicted is a family member, and it is not possible to arrange for this person, or persons, (who might, for example, be siblings), to be somewhere else when the youth is to be given home leave. Other obstacles might involve the presence of a threat to the youth, for example from former friends or individuals from criminal gangs. According to staff there may also be a threat from the local community as a result of the offences for which the youth has been convicted. In such situations, the personal safety of both the youth and accompanying staff becomes an issue that may serve as an obstacle to home leave.

Other reasons given by staff – not in relation to institutional leave, but that may rather serve as an obstacle to moving to more open forms of custody – were a lack of places on open units or that the institution simply did not have an open unit. Some staff also stated that the institutions had been forced to transform units that had formerly been open into locked units due to a lack of demand for places in open units. These same factors have also identified in an internal study conducted by the National Board for Institutional Care (SiS 2010). Some staff members also stated that the youths had to show a willingness to change in order to be able to move to a more open form of placement or to be given leave.

As was the case in the interviews with youths, however, the dominant factor described by staff in relation to the possibility of being given institutional leave was good behaviour. In the same way as in the youth interviews, follow-up questions were required in order to get a picture of what good behaviour involves. To begin with, the staff had only mentioned it as one, and often the most important, factor for being granted leave. What, then, does the term good behaviour mean to the staff? Like the youths, the staff mentioned violence, threats, taking drugs, bringing drugs and other prohibited items into the institution and absconding as examples of bad behaviour.[10] In the same way as the youths, however, the staff often returned to more general criteria for good behaviour in the form of "doing what you're supposed to". As I did with the youths, I will simply list a number of the factors described in the staff interviews in order to provide a sense of what the stream of descriptions of good/bad behaviour looks like.

> Doing your chores, keeping your room tidy, getting up in time for activities in the morning, completing their activities, that you participate in activities, that you participate in programme activities, that you participate in structured conversations with your contact person, get up in the morning, attend lessons, that you do those kind of things [assigned cleaning chores], are active [in school] [...] it's not enough just to turn up and sit and sway back and forth on a chair, how you behave towards other students, how you behave towards staff, how you interact with people, not participating in everyday life, being motivated in treatment, being on time, getting involved in activities, getting up in the morning, how you interact with other people, participate in treatment programmes, go to school, participate, don't follow your activity plan, don't participate in treatment, refuse to go to school, good conduct in relation to us, do what [you're] supposed to, eating breakfast, making your bed, coming to morning assembly, follow rules and routines, being like a good friend.

As can be seen from the factors listed above, the staff's view of what good behaviour consists in is much the same as that described by the youths. Both staff members and youths sometimes said that the important factor was the issue of cumulative bad behaviour, not that one of these criteria would by itself prevent the possibility of being given leave. But there were also others who said that the opposite was true, and that you had to do absolutely everything right in order to be able to spend time outside the institution. While good behaviour constitutes the dominant criterion for the possibility of institutional leave, and was viewed as a relatively natural requirement by both youths and staff, there were isolated individuals who had objections to this. The following quotation, for example, illustrates the concerns expressed by Elisabeth about the central role that good behaviour at the unit plays in relation to being given leave. Just prior to this quote, Elisabeth had described that it was primarily good behaviour that was important in this regard, and she continued:

> I guess it's more that people see it as a punishment, and that they don't think so much about what is best from the point of view of treatment, but instead just relate to good behaviour goals and not so much treatment goals. Which is easier, of course, because it's easier to measure good behaviour. But the major risk is that those youths who are at very high risk for recidivism, but who are able to do what they're supposed to on a locked unit, can very easily go out too soon, and maybe those who have more of a problem with like impulse control and find it difficult to do what they're supposed to and who say the wrong things in the wrong situations and so on, they don't get to go out and maybe then don't get the treatment that they need. And I'm not sure that it's the right youths who don't get to go out, so to speak; I think that's what I can say is the biggest risk.
>
> (Elisabeth, staff)

The issue of what should determine which are the "right" youths to be given the opportunity to spend time outside the institution becomes complicated as soon as the strict application of a principle based *exclusively* on the length of sentence and time served is abandoned (and such a principle has never been in place in relation to the youths in the current study, although the sentence length has been of major significance in the past and continues to play a role). According to Elizabeth, however, having such a clear focus on good behaviour as the central criterion constitutes an easier option for the staff than if they instead used criteria based on a more treatment-focused perspective. The focus on good behaviour also produces other benefits for the staff, as will be seen below.

Institutional leave as a disciplinary tool

Both Goffman (1991) and Foucault (1991) describe the position of power occupied by staff in relation to inmates as being an important factor for getting the inmates to act in accordance with rules and routines in the everyday work of the institution. Although this power is not exercised forcibly through the imposition of punishments, but rather via the possibility of obtaining rewards, these rewards are nonetheless associated with both the threat and the possibility that they can be taken away from the inmates. In the everyday life of special approved homes, as described by both youths and staff, institutional leave constitutes a form of reward that can generate good behaviour. In work focused on prisons, Hörnqvist (2010) has noted that the possibility of being moved to a more open unit functions in a similar way, and Werth (2011, 2013) has described the ability of probation staff to send clients back to prison as a powerful disciplinary tool for ensuring good behaviour.

The fact that it was my follow-up questions that produced the stream of descriptions of what good behaviour consists of, and that virtually all of those interviewed had initially simply referred to "good behaviour" (or "bad behaviour") as a criterion for (or an obstacle to) being given institutional leave, without providing any details as to what this meant, may be interpreted as indicating that good behaviour constitutes a category that is taken for granted by those I interviewed, both youths and staff. The fact that the descriptions of what "good behaviour" comprises are also characterised by a high degree of consistency among those interviewed may also support such an interpretation. Both staff and youths also mentioned the concepts of a "week inside" and a "month inside" as consequences of "bad behaviour". Evidence for the central significance of good behaviour in relation to the possibility of obtaining institutional leave is also found in a number of narratives from both youths and staff which describe losing the opportunity to spend time outside the institution as the only consequence of bad behaviour. The following example is taken from my interview with Adam.

TOVE: Are there other consequences of getting into arguments than not being able to go on leave?

ADAM (youth): How do you mean?

TOVE: I, I mean, you said that, actually, you could be moved to another institution, but is there anything else if you get into an argument or something, does anything else happen, was there something else that you weren't allowed to do as well, other than … you got a week inside?

ADAM: Yes. No, everything just goes on as usual. I watch TV as usual, I play the PlayStation as usual … I do my thing here, but I do my stuff in *here*.

TOVE: Yes.

ADAM: I just can't leave the grounds.

TOVE: Yes okay, so actually the only consequence […] is that you don't get to go out?

ADAM: Yes.

TOVE: Yes. And this happens to all the kids sort of every now and then, or?

ADAM: Yes.

Bad behaviour can in some cases also lead to a youth being moved to another unit or institution, which can also be seen from the youths' journals, but the main consequences are related to the possibility of spending time outside the institution. Some youths spoke, however, of other sanctions, such as having to go to bed an hour earlier ("If you're a second late, then you've got oversleeping, and then you have to go to bed an hour earlier" (Leon Y)) or having gaming time rescinded, and thus forfeiting the opportunity for institutional leave is probably not the only consequence of bad behaviour. It nonetheless appears to constitute a very central theme, and to function as a reward that it is important for the youths not to forfeit.[11]

The youths' interviews also included descriptions of the staff using the forfeiture of institutional leave as a threat (cf. Wästerfors 2009 p. 46). Sebastian, for example, described how there are times when a youth does not have the energy or does not want to go to physical exercise classes. The staff then start to threaten that "you're going to wreck your leave". He said that he first became angry when things like this happened, but that he then thought "who cares" and did what they wanted. But the most common type of description of how the opportunity to spend time outside the institution affects the youths' behaviour, and of how they do exactly what the staff want them to, does not involve references to explicit threats, even though the possibility of being able to rescind leave nonetheless constitutes a central pre-requisite. Instead, the most common type of description instead lies very close to the use of what Foucault (1991) and Hörnqvist (2010, 2012) have described as productive power. It is first and foremost the implicit, rather than explicit, threat of institutional leave being rescinded that functions as an effective correctional technique for ensuring that the youths follow the routines and treatment measures involved in the everyday work of the institution, and that they do not protest or get into conflicts with the staff or other youths. Thus it is first and foremost the possibility of receiving this *reward* that makes the youths compliant and well-behaved.[12] Although Goffman and Foucault have different perspectives and points of departure, this can also be compared to Goffman's (1991 p. 83 emphasis in original) discussion of how inmates "*self-direct themselves*" in the sense that it is something that the inmates both want and can themselves influence and change. Institutional leave, and the associated requirements for good behaviour, quite simply function as a simple and effective technique for getting the youths to self-govern. On the basis of the interviews with a number of youths, the reason this functions so effectively is because the desire to spend time outside the institution is very strong. Soltan described this in the following way:

SOLTAN (youth): Do you know what I think?

TOVE: No.

SOLTAN: If they get a student[13] to aim for something, if we say to a student now that he will get leave in a month, then I think he does, if he wants to get leave then he does, he behaves exactly as he should just in order to get there, because if he ... if you're just here and don't have anything to aim for, then I don't think things will go well. That's what I think.

TOVE: Institutional leave is needed because ...

SOLTAN: Yes, you know, I promise you, institutional leave, *everyone* behaves themselves, *everyone*. *Everyone* who wants to be given leave, they'll find it easy to behave well. Without any effort. I know this myself; to begin with it was catastrophic when I came up to [name of secure unit], you see. I had nothing to aim for; I was just there; I didn't think about, I thought I'm going to be here for a good long time, and I've got nothing to aim for. Then after a while I started to think, I have to get outside, because I've been here such a long time. So I behaved myself for a period of a few months, then I got to go out. Then (inaudible) [name of pre-release unit], behaved for two months maximum, got to move there, and then it's, if you want to get to move to [name of pre-release unit], pure good behaviour, you do it easily. In order to have the best situation possible, that's what I think.

As can be seen from Soltan's description, the powerful desire to get outside the institution, and to have the best situation possible (represented in Soltan's description by being placed in the institution's pre-release unit), produces a powerful incentive for the youths to behave in exactly the way the staff want them to. Soltan described how he himself, following an initial period of incarceration during which he did not feel there was anything to look forward to, decided to start behaving well in order to make progress through the system that regulates the opportunities for custodial openness in institutional care. But Soltan also argued that this incentive is the same for the incarcerated youths more generally. It can also be noted that Soltan said that it did not take very long to move along to more open forms of custody, once he had started to behave well. If institutional leave is to function as an effective disciplinary technique, then this is probably precisely what is required, i.e. that it becomes clear relatively quickly that it is important to have behaved well over a period of time.

The staff members' narratives also contain descriptions of how effective institutional leave is as a means of getting the youths to do what the staff want them to. It was not uncommon for the staff to emphasise that the fact that good behaviour is a criterion for institutional leave makes it easier for them to get the youths to do what they are "supposed to". One clear example of this can be seen in the following description of how the staff are assisted by the youths' desire to spend time outside the institution.

TOVE: If we're thinking about, institutional leave, there's a youth custody "ladder" and that's based on good behaviour and that kind of thing. Are there big *differences* between the youths, or do they cope with this more or less *as well as* each other, or?

RASMUS (youth): Mm, they cope with it [... pause six seconds] of course we have students that, that don't ... because all the boys we have, they're completely aware about ... about how they *stand* and when they can get to go *home* and when they'll be getting institutional leave, and they're very focused on that. You could say that it helps us in the sense that ... it's a very

> good motivator, I can say. For, *for* activities, *for* counselling and so on, and it means that in some way we're, instead we used to devote three months to motivating a boy to sit down in a drug counselling session. Here the boy sits down for the drug counselling immediately. So he's motivated by the fact that he knows that he *has to* participate in that counselling. But naturally we only have drug counselling with those who have a drug … but *everyone* who is placed here naturally has crime-programmes, since they've been convicted of something by a court, but you still have those who, you're sitting in that situation, then [you see] that he's not particularly interested *but* you like talk about the programme, you talk about it. And it's much, much easier to implement a treatment programme when you have this motivator to begin with. I mean we don't really have any students who say "I really don't give a damn about it", because then they know that, "Okay, we can take a walk out here, inside the fence, but anything else just isn't going to happen."

Although this quote from Rasmus shows the substantial importance of institutional leave in relation to the smooth running of the unit and for getting the youths to participate in treatment measures, this does not mean that the staff did not problematise this situation. Although it makes things easier, this does not necessarily mean that it is always viewed as a good thing. A little earlier in the same interview, Rasmus had spoken of the goals associated with institutional leave, and among other things he said the following:

> It's a bit like you can imagine, like I often say on the unit, I mean, we can actually get our boys to do *anything* at all, as long as they're in here, but that is of absolutely no interest. Of no interest *whatsoever*. Because if it isn't like something that they can implement and use themselves when to get out to Angered, to Sergels Torg, or wherever the hell it is, then what we do here is completely meaningless. So like the idea in some way is that from the first day that they arrive here, that everything we do, we do it so that they'll be able to cope by themselves on the outside.

In this part of the interview Rasmus instead expressed misgivings that the youths may just do as they are told, without this leading to anything very beneficial, although he did not link this specifically to institutional leave. The risk of the period spent at the institution resulting in superficial adaptation would nonetheless appear to be very real in Rasmus's description of the motivating effects of institutional leave.

At the same time, it is not only institutional leave that may function as a correctional technique. The threat of having one's sentence extended by means of the Care of Young Persons Act – i.e. of having to remain in the institution following the completion of the youth custody sentence via a compulsory placement determined by the social services – may produce the same effect. This was mentioned less often in the interviews, however (which may in part be due to the subject matter that the interviews were focused on). The descriptions provided during the interviews may be interpreted as indicating that different forms of possible punishment are available depending on the type of unit and the legal grounds for a given youth's placement (Youth Custody Act or Care of Young Persons Act). Thus there are different forms of "threats", or of possible rewards, associated with these conditions that the youths must relate to. The interviewed youths, who had been sentenced on the basis of the Youth Custody Act, stated that it was easier for youths placed on the basis of the Care of Young Persons Act to get leave (a factor which was also mentioned in some of the staff interviews), but that, on the other hand, the youths placed on the basis of the Care of Young Persons Act have to live with the pressure of not knowing when they will be released from the institution. If these youths do not behave themselves, they risk having their placements extended by six months (at a time).[14] On secure units, where youths often begin their placements, and where there are few opportunities to be given leave, some of the youths identified isolation as the "tool" that the staff have available to them as a means of getting the youths to behave well. But the interview narratives suggest that the possibility of being given institutional leave functions as a considerably more effective means of generating good behaviour than the possibility of either isolation or an extended placement on the basis of the Care of Young Persons Act. Adam described the situation in terms of a form of trading system, in which the youths provide the staff with a calm environment, while the staff give them institutional leave in return.

ADAM (youth): Or yes … I mean the kids give the staff a hard time and … and vice versa. Because there on [name of secure unit] the only … you give and give as one of the kids, *you give*, it's like … you behave yourself, you act in way that gives them a calm work environment, you follow the rules, you follow the routines. But what do they get back? Nothing. They can't go out; they get nothing; but in principle they get to eat the little food that they're given, which is hardly enough. And then watch TV. But here you give and take. I give, nice and calm, so that it's nice and calm here … and so they give me my leave. And in that way you get along well.

TOVE: Mm. Yes … what is it that you do as a youth [when you] give the staff a hard time, how … like you said that you did sometimes, what do you do?

ADAM: Yes, for example, you might not bother getting up in the morning … naa, I'm not going to get up, or when it's time to go to bed, er, they stay up in the corridor and refuse to go into their rooms … er, or … yes, that's kind of what it is in principle, or like … avoiding going down to sports class … and then … so it's like those three things.

TOVE: Yes okay, you avoid doing what you should do. What it is that you're supposed to be doing basically?

ADAM: Yes.

TOVE: Yes. And how do the staff react to that?

ADAM: Yes, well, obviously it's isolation every which way. That's what they're like [on the secure unit].

As can be seen from the above excerpt, Adam felt that there was little room for manoeuvre in relation to the staff. It is possible to imagine much more serious incidents that could be resorted to in order to "cause problems", but instead the behaviour is restricted to not keeping to scheduled times and not following routines. The fact that acts of this kind cause problems shows how tightly governed activities at the institution often are. The acts constitute a form of resistance to the power of the staff, and similar strategies of resistance – involving the use of delaying tactics and taking longer over things than necessary – have also been identified by Petersson (2013). In this way, assuming control over one's time becomes a part of strategies of resistance (cf. Moran 2012a). The fact that the risk of isolation and of having one's period of institutionalisation extended constitute less effective tools can be understood on the basis of Foucault's (1991) argument that the more effective correctional techniques are those that are based on rewards rather than punishments, and also Goffman's (1991) argument that rewards constitute more effective means of achieving desired behaviour.

Foucault (1991) also argues that one important aspect of disciplinary power is that the exercise of this power is relatively invisible. Previously, the exercise of power involved the public display of the ruler's power, whereas with disciplinary power it is the subject against whom the power is exercised that is most visible, whereas those exercising this power instead become invisible. Power that is not exercised via the use of force, but rather by generating actions without the use of visible coercion, is more effective and less likely to be questioned, and in this way the exercise of power is also made invisible. Linus described the use of the token economy in place on his unit in the following way:[15]

LINUS (staff): I don't force anyone to clean the toilet; I don't force anyone to participate in ART;[16] don't force anyone. It's a choice they make if they want to fill in the pyramid and earn an extra 150 crowns. This [the different parts of the token economy system] is formed, so that in seven to eight days they can fill it in.

TOVE: Okay. Yes.

LINUS: And it's a choice they make.

TOVE: Yes. Do most of them usually choose to do it?

LINUS: Yes.

TOVE: Yes, so most of them fill these things in?

LINUS: They might resist to begin with when they come here, "no bastard's going to get me to do the cleaning". No, no, it's voluntary. So we only have cleaning the unit on Wednesdays, so then he has to wait another week for cleaning the unit. We have ART on Tuesdays, social skills training. If he won't do it, then he has to wait another week; if he won't do it then, he has to wait another week again, so he might only have that square left, and he'll have to wait a whole week.

TOVE: Okay, and then you don't … you get to do the shop,[17] but you don't get to go to the cinema or those kind of [activities] …

LINUS: No. If you refuse to do certain things, you don't get to go out. But you still get to go out to do the shop.
TOVE: Okay. But do they usually do it?
LINUS: Yes.

In this way, the staff do not need to rely on more visible forms of power, such as various forms of punishment, but can rather sit back and relax and wait for the youth to settle himself into line and do what he is supposed to. The acts of resistance that the youths may engage in are effectively neutralised by the staff without any major effort on their part. They can wait the youths out, because they know that they have the power to make decisions about something that the youths really want. The power that is actually exercised, via the ability to give the youths institutional leave, is on the one hand very clear, since Linus is very aware of the effect this has on the youths, but on the other hand also invisible, since it does not need to be made explicit (once the youth has realised how the system works) in the staff members' interactions with the youths. This is reminiscent of both Bosworth's (2007) and Werth's (2013) arguments about the strong emphasis placed on prison inmates and released inmates themselves choosing to follow the right path and to behave correctly, and the way the role of the prison service and probation staff, and the responsibility involved in this role, is downplayed. There are also striking similarities with Crewe's (2011) description of the ways in which prison inmates describe the consequences of not participating in treatment programmes. They are given the choice to participate, or not participate, in programme activities, but if they choose the latter, they do not get out of prison.[18]

Not all of the interview narratives can be interpreted quite so easily as descriptions of the use of productive power, in which the youths are presented as *wanting* to behave well in order to be given institutional leave, and as transforming themselves in the context of this process (Foucault 1991, Hacking 2004). As has been noted by a number of scholars in the context of earlier studies of prison and probation systems (Bosworth 2007, Hannah-Moffat 2005, Hörnqvist 2010, Werth 2013, 2011), the power that is exercised by the staff in relation to the youths includes both productive and repressive elements, although in the current study the interviews were dominated by narratives that described productive power.

If we now accept that opportunities for institutional leave and the possibility of being moved to more open forms of custody serve a central function in disciplining the youths into good behaviour in the daily life of the institution, what consequences does this have (in addition to the youths becoming compliant) for the time spent in a given unit, and for the power relations that emerge between the youths and the staff?

The consequences of discipline

The disciplinary function served by the criteria for good behaviour associated with institutional leave results in a number of consequences according to both the youths and staff members interviewed in the study. In this section, I will describe some of these consequences, such as perceptions of powerlessness, superficial adaptation and also consequences that affect the relations between youths and staff.

Some of the youths described how their relations with staff, as a result of the staff's superiority in being able to interpret what should be regarded as good behaviour, led to them giving up, and just keeping quiet, since they felt they could never win, whatever the situation. Many of the youths expressed a sense of hopelessness at the impossibility of even trying to object to the staff's ideas about how things should be. Similar descriptions can also be found in the interviews that Hermodsson and Hansson conducted with youths at special approved homes (2005). This sense of hopelessness need not be directly linked to institutional leave, but may instead rather be associated with the absence of any possibility for negotiation as to what good behaviour involves. There are nonetheless implicit links to the possibility of being granted institutional leave, however, since leave is something that the youths desire, and since being regarded as well-behaved is central to being granted leave. Lucas spoke of this in the following way:

LUCAS (youth): I mean, being locked up is itself a punishment … I mean, if you're locked up, then you can't take it if someone comes along and kind of … say there's a cup here, it's supposed to stand five centimetres to the right … and yeah, we'll say that I'm staff and I can just move it. But instead of doing that, they knock on your door and call you and ask you to move it. I mean, small things like that, it just gets to be **too** much. It's actually, it's nothing, they could just have moved it without … but there's this itch somewhere, but you know, but it's difficult; I don't know why you'd do that kind of thing. That's one example, so.

TOVE: Okay, so some of the staff do petty things …

LUCAS: Yes, yes petty, irritating stuff, they talk the whole time about … they're flexible when *they* want to be and then when they kind of can't be bothered to do a thing, then you have to go by the rules, I mean like completely.

TOVE: Okay. Why do you think some of them are like that? Or have they said something themselves?

LUCAS: I mean, I don't know; you never even get to know, because when you ask them, they say "that's the rules". I mean, you can … I can't explain for you until you've lived it, you have to */No I understand/* have experienced it.

TOVE: Yes. Okay, but it's a bit like when they *want* to?

LUCAS: Yes.

This is reminiscent of Goffman's (Goffman 1991 p. 61) discussion of different adaptation strategies, in which one strategy involves withdrawal and cutting oneself off. Parts of Lucas's narrative also bring to mind Goffman's discussion of the "looping" effect, by means of which the smallest expression of disaffection may result in additional punishment from the staff. Kivett and Warren (2002

p. 16) have argued that this looping can also result in an escalation of the conflict(s), whereas if the staff instead chose to ignore some of the rules, the conflicts might de-escalate.

While the majority of the staff gave the impression that they thought this form of adaptation was a good thing, there were also staff members who questioned this. Indications of such a view can be seen in the earlier quotation from Rasmus, where he speaks of the youths perhaps not actually being particularly interested in participating in drug counselling, but rather doing it because they knew they would not otherwise get the chance to spend time outside the institution. The staff spoke of *superficial adaptation* (cf. Goffman 1991), or of the youths only adapting in order to "sit out their sentence". Wästerfors's (2009) research also describes similar processes, such as how the boys "sit out" conversations in which they have to participate and how they gradually learn that this is what they have to do in order to get through them more quickly. According to the staff, one way in which this manifests itself can be seen in the way the youths know what is required of them on the surface and ensure that this is what the staff are given. Prior to the description presented in the following quotation, which constitutes an example of this, Hanna had just spoken about how many youths describe being in an ambivalent situation, in which they on the one hand (dare to) hope and dream of a different kind of existence than continued involvement in crime and (sometimes) drugs, while on the other hand they experience continuous setbacks and difficulties related to their earlier offending and experiences, such as already having such high levels of debt that they will never be able to pay it all off.

TOVE: But there are also those who like have no motivation *at all* to *stop* but who are just going to sit out their sentence and then get out and go *back*. What would you say, have you encountered those too?

HANNA (staff): They may well exist, but they wouldn't put it like *that* of course. /*No okay*/ They know exactly, because then it would be difficult to get institutional leave and other things. /*Yes*/ So there you find, because there you've also got this superficial adaptation in some way. That "okay, I'll play by the rules", there is that of course; we work against that too, and it's also a consequence of incarceration, naturally, that you *learn* what you're supposed to say, *how* you should express yourself in order to get benefits during your time here. /*Yes*/ How far down did that treatment reach? I mean, you understand, we don't get any further than superficial adaptation. *That* can also be the case of course.

Hanna thus described how the youths were well aware of what they needed to show and say to the staff in order to be regarded as being worthy of rewards. Goffman (1991) argues that the majority of inmates simply "lie low" in order to avoid problems and to make their stay in the institution as easy as possible. The youths learn how they need to act in order to avoid problems and negative consequences, but it is actually only a question of adapting to the conditions of the institution, and not of any real change in attitude (cf. Hill 2005, Werth 2013). There is thus an awareness among some of the staff that adaptation and the mechanisms of governance which link institutional leave to good behaviour may well produce superficial adaptation rather than an actual change in attitude among the youths, with these staff arguing that the youths merely adapt in order to make the time pass as painlessly as possible.

The material also includes examples of how the staff get the youths to steer one another in the direction of good behaviour in order to produce a peaceful environment on the unit (Goffman 1991, Foucault 1991). One such narrative started with a focus on how the staff at one unit had started working to follow the rules more clearly. The staff had previously made exceptions to the rules now and then, and according to Robin (a staff member) this had led to the youths pushing the limits and to things getting rowdy on the unit. When they subsequently worked at observing the rules more strictly for a few months, things calmed down, as Robin explained:

ROBIN (staff): And then it fell into *place* somehow. And then what happened was that, instead, when we got a new student in, then these old students were so highly drilled into, or *attentive* of the fact that "we actually *want* it like this"; it was nice and calm and everybody did what they were supposed to. And they, the students, were happy and satisfied, so the staff were happy and satisfied, and it was easier to work and you could concentrate on what was *important* instead of moaning on, "No, you can't go into the kitchen now because it has to be *closed* for half an hour. You can get some water somewhere else." Erm … so then it was, you got to hear from the new students that the old students told them that "We want to have it this way on this unit; we want it to be nice and calm. We don't want a load of crap, and you make sure that you behave yourself too, and it works like this." So then we got to harvest the goodies, or the fruit, of it all, of the tough job we'd had for two months. And then that culture has lived *on* a bit at the unit.… Every now and then you know it's like happened that someone, maybe someone with a very *powerful* personality, has you know tried to disrupt this.

TOVE: Okay. In relation to *you* or also to get the other youths to go along with it?

ROBIN: Yes, to get the other youths to go along as well. /*Yes*/ But then we've closed ranks again and … the other students are aware of course, that "naa, this was like how we *didn't* want it to be", and then it's actually happened that *the group* has turned *against* this person who's been trying to cause problems for everyone. And so far there hasn't been *one* of those personalities who has like driven it further, but rather "Okay, I give up; I'll get into line and this is the way we'll have things."

Thus the staff's work becomes easier if they can get the youths themselves to want peace and quiet and to want everyone to follow the rules. Here it is possible to distinguish a process that begins in the exercise of repressive power, in the form of a patrolling of boundaries (Hörnqvist 2012) whereby the rules and their observance are re-established, but which is then transformed into something which might rather be interpreted as a form of productive power, in the form of the youths themselves maintaining order because they want life on the unit to be peaceful. This narrative is not in itself directly related to institutional leave, but since good behaviour is required in order to be given leave it is nonetheless interesting to examine how good behaviour may be of significance for everyday life at the institutions and for the power relations between staff and youths. The narrative also represents an example of the way in which those who exercise power become invisible, as described by Foucault (1991). In the above narrative, the youths may be said to have taken over the disciplinary work of the staff, and largely made it their own. In this way, they keep one another in line and the staff no longer need to repeatedly rationalise and justify the rules. On the topic of productive power, Hörnqvist (2012 p. 62) writes that "the individuals are involved, in short, as active subjects in the maintenance of order, and by this means, collective subordination is linked to individual ambitions", which is clearly exemplified in Robin's description of the youths' behaviour. It should also be noted that the examples described by Robin relate specifically to everyday rules and routines, and the micro-management of daily life, such as how the youths are not permitted to go into the kitchen for a certain period of time. The quotation also exemplifies another phenomenon, namely the way in which rules and routines themselves constitute arenas of conflict. If there had not been a rule stating that the kitchen had to be closed for half an hour, the discussion would never have arisen to begin with.

Another aspect of the power relations between youths and staff described in the interviews is the way in which the youths may be forced to ask nicely in order to obtain small things, which they would be able to do for themselves in the context of life outside the institution without even stopping to think about it. There were also descriptions of the staff using their position to regulate petty things and minor details in a way that seemed unnecessary to the youths concerned. Such descriptions are reminiscent of Goffman's (1991 p. 45) discussions of how inmates are required to ask submissively for trivial things that they had previously taken for granted, and they are related to the micro-management that youths perceive their daily lives to be subject to.

Several of the youths also described a perception that it was impossible to reason with the staff (see also Hermodsson and Hansson 2005). Lucas spoke of how it had taken considerably longer for him to start being given institutional leave than had been the case for some of the other youths. When I asked why this was, he said that he hadn't asked because he had not felt there would have been any point in doing so.

TOVE: Why was that?

LUCAS (youth): I mean, to be completely honest, I don't know; I don't care about stuff like that, so I don't even ask.

TOVE: No okay. That's simply the way it is?

LUCAS: Yes. I don't like to ask that kind of... that kind of questions.
TOVE: You don't?
LUCAS: Because I'll get, I'll get a no and then nothing else, you see? There's a bit of... oh, I don't know, it's a bit unfair in here.
TOVE: Yes. In what way is it unfair?
LUCAS: Kind of, kind of... you just have to take it and swallow it, I mean, you know. There's nothing, you can't do anything; there's no arguments, you can't... have a discussion with those who work here, you know.
TOVE: Mm, so you can't win them [the discussions] or?
LUCAS: No, you can't, they've always got to be right.
TOVE: Okay. Are all the staff like that?
LUCAS: No, not all of them. Some are really good, some are ... [they] don't know what they're talking about.

Unlike earlier examples, which could be related to what Goffman (1991 p. 41) refers to as "looping", Lucas did not refer to the threat of consequences when describing why it was meaningless to try to discuss things with the staff. This need not mean, of course, that the threat of consequences in relation to protests or objections does not constitute part of why these things are perceived as meaningless, but above all this narrative illustrates the nature of a power constellation between youths and staff, as perceived by Lucas, which is based on the staff (always) being in a position to determine what is right and what is wrong. This position is so powerful that the staff do not need to motivate their determinations, and a simple "no" is sufficient in response to any questions. For Goffman (1991 p. 54) the privilege systems related to following staff rules that are developed by total institutions lead to "the over-all consequence [...] that cooperativeness is obtained from persons who often have cause to be uncooperative". In the above narrative, Lucas describes feeling neglected by the privilege system, but the power dynamic that he identifies at the unit nonetheless means that he will not tell the staff about this.

Although they are uncommon, the staff interviews also contain descriptions of staff members not always thinking that it is a good thing for the youths to adapt so much that they no longer express dissenting opinions. In response to a question I had asked about whether the youths often appealed against decisions, such as having an application for leave rejected, Rune said that in fact the youths' appealed in this way far too seldom. He said that generally speaking it was not good simply to say that something was wrong, but if youths were able to convey *why* they thought a decision was wrong, and had objective reasons for doing so, then he felt that they should appeal. He pointed out that the youths have their rights, and that they should actually invoke these rights sometimes. He continued with this line of argument by relating it to what it usually means to be young.

> If you're young, then you're supposed to be opportunistic too, you're supposed to question things, you're supposed to make things a bit bloody difficult for the adult world, and now I even swore.

> [...]
>
> No but I think you should actually be able to *do* that, if you do it in a, in a satisfactory way. [Not] when there's a veiled threat or something like that, not in *that* way, but by, yes, by not submitting to everything that ... comes along.
>
> (Rune, staff)

Thus the staff can also see the value of the youths not completely submitting to rules and routines at the institution, but rather also being able to question and discuss things that they feel are unfair or unreasonable. However, there were several among the interviewed youths who described feeling that it was pointless to discuss this kind of thing with the staff, and the above quotation from Rune's interview also suggests that there is too little protest at times. How much adaptation is healthy, and what are the consequences when the youths adapt too much?

Summary

The contents of this chapter show that the youths' experiences of being incarcerated are complex. What is perhaps the natural, intuitive understanding, that more open forms of custody are better and easier to live with, is sometimes reflected in the contents of the youths' narratives, but not always. The youths' narratives also contain ideas about it being easier to "shut off" difficult emotions in a more secure environment, in which they are not confronted with their lost freedom in the same way. More open forms of custody also place more demands on the youths to participate in disciplining themselves, which they sometimes experience as difficult. At the same time, the reason for this is naturally the way it restricts the youths' freedom, and they generally view more open forms of custody as being desirable. The youths' narratives about institutional leave, both their first experience of leave, and subsequent, more regular experiences, are also characterised by ambiguities. Youths who perceive spending time outside the institution as a positive experience and as a relief are found alongside youths who instead have experienced, or who continue to experience, near-paranoid feelings in connection with time spent away from the institution. These latter experiences show that the youths undergo a process of institutionalisation over the course of their sentences, which then manifests itself in an adaptation to the institution and in difficulties being outside. At the same time, it is also important to note that these youths describe these experiences as being worst at the beginning, and as successively improving as they are able to spend more time outside the institution. Thus institutional leave contributes to diminishing the effects of these processes, or to turning them around, which is something that can be seen in the narratives of both youths and staff.

In order to be given institutional leave, good behaviour is central, with this meaning that the youths must do exactly what the staff feel they should do, and must behave in the way the staff feel they should behave. Some degree of good behaviour is in many ways a pre-condition for everyday life to function in institutions of this kind. At the same time, the link between good behaviour and institutional leave, as a result of the powerful desire of the youths to be able to spend time outside the institution and of the way the staff make use of this fact (both consciously and unconsciously), also generates discipline, superficial adaptation, feelings of powerlessness and sometimes destructive relations between the youths and the staff. I will return to the issue of the possible consequences of this in the concluding chapter.

Notes

1 All names are fictitious. Whether the interviewee was a youth or a member of staff is indicated.

2 Although only a few of the youths described having been placed in isolation, some of them spoke of this having happened repeatedly. It should also be noted that I did not ask any questions specifically focused on experiences of isolation.

3 According to the rules that regulate the special powers of the special approved homes, staff should be in close proximity during the implementation of isolation. It is not possible to say whether these narratives mean that the youths have in fact been left entirely alone, or whether the staff have remained nearby without the youths being aware of this. What is of significance in this context, however, is that irrespective of whether or not the staff have been present (at a distance), the youths appear to have *perceived* themselves to have been left completely alone.

4 "No Power, No Lose" is a method for dealing with conflict situations that is primarily intended to avoid such situations ending in isolation and the use of the floor restraint technique but where the last resort nonetheless involves physically restraining the youth.

5 The social services have the opportunity to decide that a youth custody placement will continue, subsequent to the end of the sentence, on the basis of a placement based on the Care of Young Persons (Special Provisions) Act, with the youth thus staying on in the special approved home. Some of the youths spoke of the risk of this happening, but the vast majority did not expect this to be the case for them. Nor is it a particularly common occurrence. Seven per cent of those included in the current study were released from youth custody sentences into continued care at a special approved home.

6 This estimate has been calculated on the basis of a combination of information showing that a given individual has absconded while on unmonitored leave and information relating to the minimum number of times that the youths in the study have been given unmonitored leave. The latter figure is based on data on whether the youth had *any* unmonitored leave during each of the two-month periods that the youth custody sentence has been divided into, which thus constitutes an *underestimate* of the actual number of times they had been given leave of this kind.

7 Compare Foucault's (1991) discussion on how the emergence of the possibility for "examination" in the system of discipline was accompanied by the emergence of continuous documentation.

8 Recommendations and guidelines from the National Board of Institutional Care.

9 For Crewe (2011 p. 522) this means that

> the power is experienced as both firm and soft, oppressive yet also somehow light. It does not so much weigh down on prisoners and suppress them as wrap them up, smother them and incite them to conduct themselves in particular ways.

10 These factors were sometimes mentioned separately as being factors that in and of themselves affected the possibility of being given institutional leave. It is likely however that the staff who mentioned them separately in this way would also regard them as forms of bad behaviour.

11 It should, of course, be remembered that this study is specifically focused on institutional leave. More general themes were however discussed during the interviews, and there were substantial opportunities for both youths and staff to discuss other factors if they had wanted to do so. The focus of the study is nonetheless likely to have resulted in a certain bias towards the significance of institutional leave. This does not mean that leave is not a central factor, however, but rather that other central factors may perhaps have become less prominent in the interviews.
12 It could be argued that the threat of rescinded leave and the possibility of being given leave are so similar that it is not meaningful to distinguish between the two. There is a clear difference however between engaging in good behaviour in order to be given the opportunity for leave and refraining from bad behaviour in order to avoid losing something one has already earned the right to.
13 "Student" is an expression sometimes used by youths and staff to describe the youths placed in special approved homes, and in this context it means 'inmate' rather than 'student' in the educational sense.
14 According to the Care of Young Persons (Special Provisions) Act (1990:52), decisions on placements at special approved homes should be reviewed within six months and then continuously reviewed at intervals of at most six months (§13).
15 The token economy is based on a system whereby youths complete, or "fill in" various "blocks" by doing the things required in relation to each specific block. In this way, the youth earns various benefits, the nature of which depends on the type of block completed.
16 Aggression Replacement Training, one of the CBT-based treatment methods that is often used at special approved homes.
17 This involves travelling to the nearby community and buying things, such as sweets and cigarettes, for yourself and the other youths, when it is your turn to do so.
18 My understanding of Crewe is that the consequences of non-participation were not related to the issue of being granted institutional leave, but rather that of having an indeterminate sentence transformed into a fixed-term sentence.

Bibliography

Bateman, T., Hazel, N. and Wright, S., 2013. *Resettlement of young people leaving custody: Lessons from the literature.* London: Beyond Youth Custody.

Bosworth, M., 2007. Creating the responsible prisoner: Federal admission and orientation packs. *Punishment & Society*, 9(1), pp. 67–85.

Cope, N., 2003. 'It's no time or high time': Young offenders' experiences of time and drug use in prison. *The Howard Journal of Criminal Justice*, 42(2), pp. 158–175.

Crewe, B., 2011. Depth, weight, tightness: Revisiting the pains of imprisonment. *Punishment & Society*, 13(5), pp. 509–529.

Foucault, M., 1982. The subject and power. *Critical Inquiry,* 8(4), pp. 777–795.

Foucault, M., 1991. *Discipline and punish: The birth of the prison.* London: Penguin books.

Franzén, A.G. and Holmqvist, R., 2014. From punishment to rewards? Treatment dilemmas at a youth detention home. *Punishment & Society*, 16(5), pp. 542–559.

Goffman, E., 1991. *Asylums: Essays on the social situation of mental patients and other inmates.* London: Penguin Books.

Hacking, I., 2004. Between Michel Foucault and Erving Goffman: Between discourse in the abstract and face-to-face interaction. *Economy and Society*, 33(3), pp. 277–302.

Hannah-Moffat, K., 2005. Criminogenic needs and the transformative risk subject: Hybridizations of risk/need in penality. *Punishment & Society*, 7(1), pp. 29–51.

Hazel, N. and Bateman, T., 2013. Young offenders' trauma on release from custody. European Society of Criminology Conference, 5 September, 2013, Budapest, Hungary.

Hermodsson, A. and Hansson, C., 2005. *Demokrati i det lilla? Ungdomars delaktighet i sin behandling.* Stockholm: Statens institutionsstyrelse.

Hill, T., 2005. *Allians under tvång: behandlingssamarbete mellan elever och personal på särskilda ungdomshem.* Linköping: Institutionen för beteendevetenskap, Linköpings Universitet.

Hörnqvist, M., 2010. *Risk, power and the state: After Foucault.* London: Routledge.

Hörnqvist, M., 2012. *En annan Foucault: Maktens problematik.* Stockholm: Carlsson Bokförlag.

Järvinen, M., 2002. Hjälpens universum – ett maktperspektiv på mötet mellan klient och system. In: A. Meeuwisse and H. Swärd, eds, *Perspektiv på sociala problem.* Stockholm: Natur och Kultur, pp. 253–273.

Justitiedepartementet, 2011. *Förbättrad utsluss från sluten ungdomsvård.*

Kivett, D.D. and Warren, C.A., 2002. Social control in a group home for delinquent boys. *Journal of Contemporary Ethnography*, 31(1), pp. 3–32.

McAlister, S. and Carr, N., 2014. Experiences of Youth Justice: Youth Justice Discourses and Their Multiple Effects. *Youth Justice*, 14(3), pp. 241–254.

McAllister, D., Bottomley, A.K. and Liebling, A., 1992. *From custody to community: Throughcare for young offenders.* Avebury: Aldershot.

Moran, D., 2012a. "Doing time" in carceral space: Timespace and carceral geography. *Geografiska Annaler: Series B, Human Geography*, 94(4), pp. 305–316.

Moran, D., 2012b. Prisoner reintegration and the stigma of prison time inscribed on the body. *Punishment & Society*, 14(5), pp. 564–583.

Moran, D., 2013. Between outside and inside? Prison visiting rooms as liminal carceral spaces. *GeoJournal*, 78(2), pp. 339–351.

Moran, D., 2014. Leaving behind the "total institution"? Teeth, transcarceral spaces and (re)inscription of the formerly incarcerated body. *Gender, Place & Culture*, 21(1), pp. 35–51.

Neumann, C.B., 2011. Imprisoning the soul. In: T. Ugelvik and J. Dullum, eds, *Penal exceptionalism? Nordic prison policy and practice.* London & New York: Routledge, pp. 139–155.

Petersson, F., 2013. *Kontroll av beroende. Substitutionsbehandlingens logik, praktik och semantik.* Malmö: Égalité.

Shammas, V.L., 2014. The pains of freedom: Assessing the ambiguity of Scandinavian penal exceptionalism on Norway's Prison Island. *Punishment & Society*, 16(1), pp. 104–123.

SiS, 2010. *Kartläggning av LSU-utslussning under 2009.*

Ugelvik, T., 2014. *Power and resistance in prison: Doing time, doing freedom.* London: Palgrave Macmillan.

Wästerfors, D., 2009. *Konflikthantering i ungdomsvård ur ett sociologiskt perspektiv.* Stockholm: Statens Institutionsstyrelse.

Werth, R., 2011. I do what I'm told, sort of: Reformed subjects, unruly citizens, and parole. *Theoretical Criminology*, 16(3), pp. 329–346.

Werth, R., 2013. The construction and stewardship of responsible yet precarious subjects: Punitive ideology, rehabilitation, and "tough love" among parole personnel. *Punishment & Society*, 15(3), pp. 219–246.

5 Youth and staff narratives about the time subsequent to youth custody

Petersilia (2001) has noted the importance of implementing re-entry measures and parole activities in order to reduce the high levels of re-offending that characterise inmate populations. It is widely recognised that former inmates have serious problems with unemployment and a lack of education, and also that they have weaker ties to the family and to the social support usually associated with such ties (Petersilia 2001, Seiter and Kadela 2003). These problems are due in part to factors associated with their life situation prior to imprisonment, but also to the effects of the prison sentence itself. Having a prior conviction makes it difficult to get a job, for example (Petersilia 2001), particularly if you are a black male (Pager 2008). Petersilia (2001, see also Seiter and Kadela 2003) also discusses how strategies focused on "getting tough on crime" have intensified these problems by introducing legislation that excludes those with a criminal record from a range of different occupations. Petersilia expresses a particular concern for youths who are sentenced to prison at a young age (and other forms of custodial sanctions may be assumed to produce similar effects). Visher and Travis (2003) argue that in order to understand why certain prison inmates re-offend, while others do not, the entire re-entry process must be examined, i.e. beginning with the conditions prior to the prison sentence, through what happens during the period of imprisonment, what happens directly following release and also what happens in a more long-term integrational perspective. In addition to the significance of treatment factors etc., Visher and Travis note that the maintenance of contacts with family, as well as pro-social contacts more generally, has been found to contribute to a more successful re-entry into society. Schlosser (2015 p. 107) refers to similar ideas in a discussion of cognitive treatment programmes. She argues that it is problematic that the programmes she has studied ignore the contexts in which the inmates are living, and in which they have previously lived, in favour of an emphasis on the choices that are (freely) made by the individual.

A review of evaluations of various measures focused on inmate re-entry found that measures focused on the labour market, drug treatment and education produced positive results in the form of reduced re-offending. The same was the case for measures involving "half-way houses" (Seiter and Kadela 2003), which in the context of the present study may be likened to the pre-release housing alternatives that have been developed by a number of the special approved homes. Travis and Petersilia (2001) also describe the importance of measures in a number of different areas, and research on the life conditions of prison inmates in Sweden shows that these are characterised by resource deficiencies across a range of areas by comparison with the remainder of the population (Nilsson 2002). The same is true of the youths placed in Sweden's special approved homes, and also of those placed in other forms of out-of-home care (Ybrandt and Nordqvist 2015, Vinnerljung and Sallnäs 2008, Shannon 2011).

Research on the youth care system also describes the need for help and support provision subsequent to institutional placements. This is necessary in part in order to sustain change that has occurred during the period of institutionalisation, and in part because these youths are more poorly equipped to succeed in life than young people in general (Andersson Vogel 2012, Andreassen 2003). Research also shows that as a group, youths placed in care subsequently experience problems across a broad range of areas (Vinnerljung and Sallnäs 2008, Andreassen 2003, Andersson Vogel 2012, Shannon 2011). Andersson Vogel (2012) also points to a number of specific problems faced by youths in social care as they make the transition to adult life. For such youths, this transition is both condensed and accelerated. Generally speaking, youths making the transition to adult life often require occasional assistance from their parents, but youths who have been in care often lack access to support of this kind, which makes them more vulnerable. The young people sentenced to youth custody comprise part of this population on the threshold of adulthood; still children when they commit their offences, but often young adults by the time they are released.

This chapter discusses the youths' expectations and hopes regarding the period subsequent to their release from youth custody. It looks at what the youths want and what they say they would need in order to achieve this. This chapter also focuses on the staff's views regarding what could or should be done within the framework of youth custody sentences in order to make a better life possible for the youths subsequent to their release. The chapter also links these discussions to the significance of institutional leave and more open custodial conditions for the youths' lives following their release from youth custody.

The youths' ideas about the period subsequent to release

To desist or not to desist?

All of the youths interviewed were asked about their thoughts on what would happen subsequent to their release and whether or not they would continue to offend. The majority answered that they do not intend to continue offending, or that this was at least their goal or desire. But how should this dominance of answers stating that the youths want to desist from crime be interpreted? Do these answers reflect a client narrative formulated for an interviewer (see Järvinen 2004), or do they reflect what the youths actually want? My own general impression is that the youths' answers reflected what the majority *actually meant* on the occasion of the interview, rather than being something that they only said because it was expected of them.[1] Petersilia (2001, see also Maruna 2001) has also noted that released prison inmates are initially characterised by a strong desire to succeed (in living a better life), and a study of the probation service by Werth (2011) reported that probationers spoke with enthusiasm about "going straight" and changing their lives. Bateman *et al.* (2013 p. 14) also describe convicted youths in England and Wales showing a substantial desire for change in connection with their release, and argue that release may thus be viewed as a "window of opportunity", although these good intentions can rapidly be transformed into disillusion and re-offending if the youths lack the support required to achieve the desired change. On the basis of a narrative interview perspective (Presser 2009, Presser and Sandberg 2015) it can also be added that the narratives, and the decision to present one's current self as a person who desires to desist from crime, are of interest in themselves, irrespective of how they are interpreted, since this type of self-presentation constitutes part of how the youths produce their identities.

Giordano *et al.* (2002) argue that an individual's subjective attitudes are particularly important in the early stages of a transformation process, and it has also been emphasised that the desire to change may be the most important factor in relation to actually achieving change. At the same time, this desire to change should not be viewed as a sufficient condition for ensuring that change will occur (Maruna 2001). There are many other factors that have nothing to do with the individual's own choices that also have an effect on whether or not a person will desist from crime. The greater the level of an individual's involvement in crime, the greater the effects of cumulative disadvantage that the individual will have to deal with, with these effects reducing both the opportunities for change and the chances of experiencing situations that produce the more common types of "turning points", or processes (Carlsson 2014)), such as getting married, finding employment, etc. (Carlsson and Sarnecki 2015, Giordano *et al.* 2002, Laub and Sampson 2009, Maruna 2001).

Desistance from crime may either be viewed as a static event or as a process (Carlsson and Sarnecki 2015, Carlsson 2014, Maruna 2001). It is the latter sense of desistance that I view as the most meaningful perspective for thinking about desistance in the present context, and my point of departure is that the youths' narratives may (or may not) constitute part of an ongoing process of desistance. Whether or not this is the case cannot definitively be determined on the basis of the interviews however, and both the quantitative analysis conducted in the current study (see the next chapter) and earlier follow-ups of youths sentenced to youth custody (Pettersson 2010) rather suggest otherwise, at least viewed on the basis of a static perspective on desistance. Maruna (2001) argues, however, that it can take between seven and ten years from the point at which an individual decides to desist to reach the point at which real change has taken place. Unlike studies focused on individuals who have already (for the most part) moved away from their period of criminal activity, however, the youths included in the current study are instead in the initial phase of what may become a criminal career. In spite of this, however, it is worth repeating that many of the interviewed youths expressed a desire to desist from crime.

There were a few exceptions to the dominant trend of youths wanting to desist from crime. A small number said that they did not know whether they were going to continue offending. Gabriel (youth) put it like this:

> I don't actually know, we'll have to wait and see. */Yes. Okay/* I … buggered if I know. We'll have to see what happens. I hope of course that I won't continue, but…. It might be difficult, it might not happen, so, it … I don't know.

Another of the youths said that he believed things would probably end up being the way they were before, irrespective of what he did himself. The police would keep on monitoring him, and would arrest him irrespective of what he did. That was how things had been, and that was probably the way things would be when he was released too. Another said that it depended on what society had to offer in terms of work and other opportunities. If you don't have (or get) anything else, then you will naturally continue offending. This view is reminiscent of the narratives found in the group of persisters in Maruna's (2001) study. Among other things, these individuals expressed a perception that they were not themselves in control of whether or not they would continue to offend. In the current study, Samir spoke in the following way about his thoughts on the future (at the time of the interview, he had been incarcerated for a long period of time, and he had just been talking about how difficult he was finding this):

SAMIR (youth): Nothing's any fun, like. You don't care what happens any more.

TOVE: What happens?

SAMIR: Er, in the future. Because you think, particularly when you're in youth custody, you're sentenced for a serious crime, you don't see so many opportunities in front of you when you get out.

TOVE: Okay. You don't think it's going to be possible? */No/* Or you don't know what you're going to do, or it's not going to go well?

SAMIR: Difficult to get a flat. Difficult to get a job, because of what you've done, difficult to, or you can['t] get a driver's license until you're 21, 22 or something, I don't know. So you don't see these opportunities, so what do you turn to? Everyone knows what the answer is, crime.

TOVE: Ah, okay.

SAMIR: That's the only way you've got.

TOVE: Is that how it feels?

SAMIR: Yes, that's how it feels for me anyway.

As can be seen, the above interview excerpts do not represent examples of an attitude that views continued offending as a natural or desirable choice. Instead the youths' answers manifest a sense of a lack of alternative opportunities, of not believing that they will end up doing something other than continuing to offend. Although these youths believed, or suspected, that they would continue offending, their narratives nonetheless serve to reinforce the more general picture, that the interviewed youths primarily expressed *not* wanting to continue committing offences. At the same time, the concern that things would not work out this way was shared by a number of the youths who stated more clearly that they did not wish to continue offending following their release from youth custody.

Why do the youths want to desist?

The reasons for the youths wanting to desist from crime vary, and many of them described several different motives. It was not uncommon, however, for the youths (to begin by) not giving any reason at all, other than that they had "made up their minds". At the same time, their reaching this decision was often related to a number of different factors, and when the conversation continued (often in the form of my asking them why they had made this decision), they described clear reasons for having "made up their minds" in this way. They nonetheless often continued to emphasise the importance of having made up their minds, and some of them said that this was actually the only thing that mattered. The youth who perhaps expressed this position most clearly was Ali, who answered in the following way when I asked what might make it possible for him to succeed in staying away from crime:

ALI (youth): It doesn't make any difference.
TOVE: It doesn't make any difference? No.
ALI: To be completely honest, if you want me to be completely honest?
TOVE: Yes, I want you to be completely honest.
ALI: Then it doesn't make any fucking difference.
TOVE: No, okay.
ALI: If I want to commit offences, then I commit offences. It doesn't make any difference *what* you do to me, or *what* you say to me, that's my personal opinion, and I'm 100 per cent certain that everyone else thinks this way too. It doesn't make any difference *where* you're doing time, doesn't make any difference *how* you're treated; if you've made up your mind to commit offences, then you commit offences the whole way; if you've made up your mind not to commit offences, then you don't commit offences. And I actually believe, to be honest, that it's not an illness that can be cured; there's nobody who can talk you out of your ideas, because they're always going to still be there. They might disappear for a week or so, but as soon as you get close to that kind of situation they turn up again. It's like feelings. You can forget your feelings, but as soon as you remember, and someone says something that describes your old feelings, they arise automatically. That's the way it is with all people. So it doesn't matter what you do. How long your sentence is, or where you do your time, it doesn't make any difference.
TOVE: Okay.

ALI: If you choose to keep that idea, the criminal thinking, then you keep it with you for a very long time.

It is not that Ali did not state any reasons for having made up his mind to desist; he in fact described a number of such reasons, among others that offending was not worth it, since for him committing offences produced fear and stress and since he was at risk of being sent to prison in the future if he continued. At the same time, however, he was very clear about saying that the only thing that mattered was making up one's mind. Narratives about the significance of deciding to desist are not uncommon in studies of desistance from crime, substance abuse or other forms of deviant behaviour (Maruna 2001, see also Giordano *et al.* 2002). Bosworth (2007) argues that today's (American) prisons have shifted from an emphasis on treatment and on the staff providing support, to a situation where the inmates are expected to act as rational, free individuals who themselves assume responsibility for their own transformation.[2] Werth (2013) describes similar expectations being placed on inmates by the probation service, as does Hörnqvist (2010) in relation to Swedish prisons and Crewe (2009) in England. Hannah-Moffat (2005) has also discussed these issues. She argues that the correctional focus on the assessment of criminogenic risk and needs as the basis for treatment measures in prisons means that the focus is directed at individual factors and at conceptions of an active offender who makes considered choices about whether to continue or desist from offending. The youths' narratives about making up their own minds constitute part of this discursive context, which is also prevalent in the youth care system. The discourse of the responsible individual is not, of course, limited to the framework of institutional care or the prison system, but is rather one that is also emphasised in society at large (Schlosser 2015 p. 23, Andersson 2004). The youths would no doubt have encountered this attitude prior to their current period of institutionalisation, but it will also have been an integral part of the context and treatment experiences of their youth custody sentences.

It has not been possible on the basis of the youths' journals and files to develop a (sufficiently high-quality and reliable) picture of the extent to which the youths have undergone different types of treatment programme to allow for a quantitative analysis of this factor.[3] At the same time, all of the treatment elements noted in the youths' journals have been coded in the form of a qualitative variable. The coding process focused on including everything that is mentioned that could be interpreted as constituting some form of element of treatment – in some cases, for example, Religious Studies has been included in the information noted in this respect, which may provide a sense of the breadth of the conceptualisation that has been employed. Despite the use of this broad approach, however, there is no mention of any form of treatment measure in 17 per cent of the journals.[4] A review of all of the treatment-related information included in the journals (irrespective of how much treatment the youths have received or how systematic this treatment has been) shows that the measures employed are very much dominated by cognitive treatment programmes.[5] The most commonly employed programmes appear to be Aggression Replacement Training (Goldstein *et al.* 1998) and CBT-focused programmes for criminal behaviour such as "Vägvalet" (Bergström 1997). The use of individual counselling sessions with psychologists also appears to be common (with a CBT focus sometimes being mentioned, while at other times no specific focus is mentioned) and various forms of substance abuse treatment (including both 12-step programmes such as those used by AA and NA and other types of programmes). Thus the treatments that the institutions focus on are clearly dominated by different approaches based on cognitive behavioural science. In addition, virtually all of the institutions employ some form of token economy.

Cognitive behavioural therapy is clearly linked to the perspectives of both individualisation and the criminogenic risk and needs principles discussed above (Andersson 2004). This emphasis on the individual's own choices may in one sense be interpreted as showing that the youths are in this respect manifesting signs of being disciplined subjects, or to borrow Werth's (2011) terminology "reformed subjects", who have internalised the expectations that are placed on them and made them their own (cf. Foucault 1991). Schlosser (2015) has also described a similar tendency towards inmates reflecting cognitive behavioural therapy in their own narratives. At the same time, however, it may be reasonable in our interpretation of what these statements represent to ascribe some significance to a desire on the part of the youths not to want to appear, either to themselves or to me, as passive individuals who lack a will of their own and who are unable to cope without the help of others (with these others in the current instance also being the staff who exercise power over them). Thus the youths' statements that it is they themselves who have made a choice may also be understood as a manifestation of resistance in line with Ugelvik's (2014 p. 239) description, whereby

> [a] person who is positioned as a prisoner may, for example, need to make it clear that the prison does not decide everything, and that the ability to decide things for himself and about his situation has not completely disappeared.

When a youth says that he has made up his mind, or is deciding, to desist from offending, this does not necessarily mean that the youth in question has succeeded, or will succeed, in doing so; this despite the fact that the idea of the responsible and rational individual who chooses desistance would predict the opposite. Unlike Ali, above, who argued that if you make up your mind to desist then nothing else matters, Muhamed (youth), below, describes how he had made up his mind to desist but had not succeeded in doing so for various reasons.

> Then there's this, that I wanted to stop before I got sent down, but I've never been able to. Because everyone, almost everyone, I usually spend time with is a criminal or a drug abuser, so it's quite difficult. But then when you've got away from them, when you're inside, you've got away from them, you've stopped smoking, then it's easier. There's nothing that has

influenced me *here*, the way they've helped me and that kind of thing, I've decided myself. They believe that they're helping me, but I'm only doing it to show that I'm behaving myself. But otherwise I've chosen it myself.

We know from the research that desistance from crime can be difficult when virtually all those one spends time with are offenders, and the significance of the peer group is well established in criminological theory (Sutherland *et al.* 1992, Lilly *et al.* 2014). What is needed, according to Muhamed, is to get away from one's friends and to stop smoking (hash). An institutional placement can produce these outcomes, but according to Muhamed it is not the measures implemented at the institution itself that are important. Another interesting aspect of Muhamed's narrative is the way that he allows the staff to *believe* that they are helping him, since this is a sign of good behaviour (compare the discussions in the previous chapter). This may thus be interpreted as an adaptation strategy in line with Goffman's (1991) discussion of obtaining advantages by showing improvement and compliance, and I would argue it may be interpreted as a manifestation of resistance in the Foucauldian sense (1991, see also Hörnqvist 2012, 2010), in the form of what Goffman (1991) refers to as "working the system".

This idea that what is done at the institution plays no part in either wanting to change or in helping the youths when they have made up their minds to change was a common theme in the youths' narratives about their institutional placements (even though, as will be described a little later, there were exceptions to this). This theme can be seen very clearly in Anders' narrative:

TOVE: So it's not anything here that has got you to stop?

ANDERS (youth): No, no I wouldn't say so. It's like I said to begin with, this is just storage; there's nothing that helps any youth at all. Those who want to keep on offending, they do it despite being in places like this, and those who decide to stop, it's not at all because of this, but because you make the choice yourself.

Talking about the period of institutionalisation as nothing more than storage was, perhaps somewhat surprisingly, not very common in the interviews. Many of the youths did however express a great deal of criticism about the institutions and their work, and their powerful resistance to perceiving themselves as being helped in any way by their institutional placement should also be interpreted as part of this criticism.

Like Ali, who was quoted earlier, several of the youths spoke of continuing to offend as simply not being worth it. It was described as being dangerous, tough, as something that exhausted them, that led them to lose contact with family, friends, partners, etc. They wanted to have a "good life", which was thus viewed as not involving crime. Hampus described this in the following way:

HAMPUS (youth): I'm like … I mean I'm not … I want to get a grip on my life, it, it, er.

TOVE: Yes. What has made you want to do that?

HAMPUS: I've seen most of [what] the criminal world has to offer, and it's not for me. I'm tired of it.

TOVE: Okay. What is it, how, what is it that it has to offer, then, that you've got tired of?

HAMPUS: That it's just miserable, people dying round you and er.... There's no light times, it's just dark the whole time. It's never ... yes (pause). Mm.

That the life of crime can be tough in many ways is something that has previously been described in studies focused on the lack of resources among convicted offenders (Andrews and Bonta 2010, Gendreau *et al.* 1996, Nilsson 2002) and in interviews with former offenders (Carlsson 2014, Maruna 2001). The data from ADAD admission interviews also show that the youths have experienced difficult conditions, and also exposure to crime (see the next chapter). But the youths also spoke of other reasons for wanting to desist. In the following narrative, Patrik describes a number of these:

PATRIK (youth): No, I've made up my mind that I'm going to stop committing offences. I feel that there's no point in it, and I've been doing it for a very long time now, and what have I got out of it? I ... I've got a massive fucking debt at the enforcement agency and I've ... (laughs), and yes, I'm in here. I've been separated from my family for a year. It's not like it's the best thing that's ever happened to me. There's no point in being separated from your family, so for that reason I've been thinking that I'm going to work and I'll get my own flat and start over. That's my plan anyway. Then we'll have to see how it goes. But I'm hoping for the best.

[...]

TOVE: And it's above all that you, that you've been separated from your family and your girlfriend and so on; that's what's made you want to try to do something different? Or is there something else as well that's got you to?

PATRIK: Yes, it's me myself ... I mean ... I myself, I haven't got the energy any more, you have to watch your back, and [name of city] is a dangerous city when it comes to crime. There's a very great deal of crime in [name of city]. And if you're involved in crime and you're in a conflict with someone else or whatever, then you have to watch your back the whole time, and that doesn't feel so good when you're walking with your girlfriend or your family. You don't know; someone jumps out and something happens. So I feel that no, it's crossed the line. It's become too much and now I have a situation where I can give it all up. Just as well.

TOVE: Yes.

PATRIK: And it's better that I do it now. It's like I've said; I'm glad I'm inside now when I'm 17 to 18, rather than it happening when I'm 35 and I've hopefully got two kids and a wife, and yes, having a whole family and how I would have let my kids down. So just for that reason I'm happy that it's happening today, in today's situation.

TOVE: Yes. Is there anything that has happened here at the institution, that has also made you change your mind?

PATRIK: No, I made up my mind before I got here. Before I got here.

Patrik's narrative about the things that led him to decide to desist from crime (a decision that according to his narrative he had already made before arriving at the institution) covers a range of different areas. Patrik, too, mentions that continuing to offend would be too tough and involve too many risks. He also says that it involves risks for his family and not only for himself. The youth custody sentence has itself also meant that he has been separated from his family. And he goes on to say that it would be better to stop now, so that he will not be sent to prison in the future. A future prison sentence would also harm the family that he hopes to have in the future. All of these reasons also turned up in other youths' narratives on why they did not want to continue offending once they had completed their sentences.

The youths described the family and other significant others as being important for their desire to desist in a number of different ways. Casper, for example, described wanting to desist because he wanted to keep his current girlfriend, which he did not believe would be possible if he continued in the same way as before – because who wants to be with someone who hasn't got a job and who is in and out of prison, as Casper put it. Benjamin spoke of future children as a reason for wanting to change his current way of life, saying, "In the future, my little kids coming to visit me in … prison cells … knocking on the window. Fuck no, ugh!" Soltan also spoke of a future with a family and children as a reason for changing his life, but on the basis of a belief that he would have neither a family or children if he continued offending and ended up in prison, and he felt that "almost everyone wants a family and children and to live a good life. I think everyone wants that." In the field of life course research on crime, family formation (primarily in the form of meeting a socially integrated women, since these studies have primarily focused on (heterosexual) men[6]) has been emphasised as an important factor in relation to the shift towards a life without crime (Laub and Sampson 2009, Carlsson 2014, Carlsson and Sarnecki 2015). Among the boys that I interviewed, it is clear that the family is ascribed importance in a number of different ways in relation to the desire to avoid offending in the future, and not only the current, existing family, but also an imagined future family. Leon described the significance of his family and his girlfriend in the following way:

LEON (youth): But then when I came here, my family were there for me more than I thought they would be. And they really showed that … you're like family irrespective of *what* and … that was like what made me want to change. And a lot of it was my … Girlfriend … every time I was on the way down, like … she helped me up. And then maybe, you want to build yourself up for your own sake, [but] above all for the others' sakes. For the ones you love and … yes, that's what it is that means that you maybe develop a powerful desire to change and to get a grip on your life.

TOVE: You get support from others and because it's important to others /*Yes*/ what you do. Mm.

LEON: Because what you do *yourself*, it affects other people too you know. The ones who love you, and the ones you love. And, er … I think it's … important to … I think that everyone can succeed, if only they find like … what's important to *them*.

TOVE: Okay.

LEON: I've never had, if you know what I mean, before I came here, I've never had anyone that I've felt that … I could make someone proud, that if I do this, then my mum is going to be proud of me, if I do that, then my sister is going to be proud of me. I've never felt that. But … since I came here, well … I've thought about it a lot … and when … before, I used to maybe go home to my sister's once or twice week and be there sometimes. Now, like, I talk … to her more or less daily.

[…]

And … I think that … the family is much more important than you think. And they can give you a goal, and a reason, and raise you up and make you the person you want to be.

For Leon, the family has significance in the sense that he does not want to hurt them in the future; what he does matters for those who love him. But the family had also been of significance to his decision as a result of having supported him in a situation when he was in real need of support (cf. Maruna 2001, Schlosser 2015 p. 119). Some of the youths also emphasised the importance of support from the family in relation to whether things would go well for them following their release from youth custody. For Leon, however, it was not only a question of receiving support from his family, but also of wanting to make someone proud, which essentially involved feeling that there was someone who cares about what he does and how things go for him. There were also other youths who said that it was important what their families thought of them, among other things in the sense that they wanted their families to know that they have changed and that they intended to try to desist from crime. These narratives about the family underline the importance of maintaining contacts with the family during the youths' period of institutionalisation, with institutional leave and more open forms of custody playing a role in the youths' being able to maintain these contacts.

Several of the youths mentioned the risk of future imprisonment as a reason for wanting to change. In relation to this, they also said that they had been lucky to be arrested for a serious crime so early in their lives. This was not because they felt that they wanted to be placed in a youth institution, and that this would lead to them being given help, but rather because they would otherwise have ended up (or would come to end up) in prison. Ali spoke of this in the following way.

ALI (youth): No, it was just that I noticed how lucky I'd been because … I got … I committed my offence when I was 17 … […] if I'd been 18 … when I committed my offences, I'd have risked getting six years, from five to six years. So when you're in that situation, you realise how lucky you were.

TOVE: Yes, okay. And then it's not worth it because you'll get long, or a long prison sentence?

ALI: No, but I mean, if I get a long prison sentence, that is to say, even then, while I'm still inside, I'm going to decide that I want to be a career criminal, if you know what I mean. And that's not much fun, you ... you don't want to live your whole life like that.

TOVE: No. Okay. So that if you weren't able to stop offending, and you went to prison, then you think that basically it's all over?

ALI: You could put it like that.

Thus it is both about avoiding prison (which several of the others also spoke about), which means that the youths nonetheless view youth custody as the better option, and also about the fact that sentence length is reduced when a person is under the age of 18. Interestingly, a majority (62 per cent) of those sentenced to youth custody who were interviewed by Palm (2003 p. 50) stated that they would rather have been sentenced to a prison term. This attitude is instead conspicuous by its absence in my own interview material, but I did not ask the youths specifically about this issue. But is this (getting away from friends and being lucky not to have been given a (long) prison sentence) the only way in which the youths mean that their time at the institutions has been of significance to their decision to desist from offending? The answer is no, since there were in fact a number of youths who stated that the institutional placement had itself actually influenced their decision. This was in part due to the contents of their time at the special approved home, in part due to the (enforced) opportunity that it gave them to stop and think about their life situation (cf. Maruna 2001). Following a discussion about how he felt continued offending was no longer worth it, and about how he therefore wanted to desist (although he did not know whether this would be possible), Oscar gave the following description of the significance of ending up in a special approved home for his desistance decision:

TOVE: And is there something here at [name of institution] that has meant that you started feeling this way, or did you feel like this before?

OSCAR (youth): No, I didn't feel like this at all before. Well, I mean, you start to think more when you're inside and obviously you get ideas. Okay, you hear a few things from people [staff], but it's not exactly like "Ping! They said that, yes, it went in." I mean, I thought, "They might, after all, be saying things that it was a good idea to think about." Then you thought about it for a few months, and in the end you think, "Yes, it's actually true; what he's saying is right." But yes, there's not a lot you can do about it.

Oscar's narrative ascribes importance both to the placement itself, which led to him starting to think about things, and also to the content of his stay at the institution, in the form of what the staff had talked to him about. It took a little time, but in the end he digested the staff's "message". The fact that it is not certain that this will help him in the end, that it is unclear whether he will be able to succeed in changing his life, is another question (as can be seen from the final sentence of the above quotation: "But yes, there's not a lot you can do about it"). The desire to change has nonetheless come as a result of having had the time to reflect and having conversations with the staff. It is not clear from the narrative whether these conversations were of a more general character or were part of some form of treatment programme. Some of the youths interviewed by Hermodsson and Hansson (2005) also described having first had a negative attitude towards their placement, but having then been able to see that it had in fact given them something positive. Some of the youths in the current study described their therapy or treatment more clearly in terms of being something important, among other things saying that their placement had given them an opportunity to get help with their problems. Sometimes this meant that they had already wanted to be given help, but some spoke of this desire for help as having arisen during the therapy or the treatment itself. Tore described how he had not previously been given any help, but that the institutional placement had led to him getting the help he wanted:

TORE (youth): And I made that decision quite early, because I wanted to get some treatment, er … because this is the second time I've been arrested, when I came here … and the first time I was sentenced to probation … and I didn't get any help there … and I felt worse (short laugh) which led to me ending up *here* after the second time, and then I felt that I have to take in everything that I can. And I have got help here, which means that I … that's why I really like being here, that I've actually got help for once.

[…]

I don't want, I don't want to do it again because it causes so much harm, so many, even myself. It … it's terrible to see how things have been.

[…]

TOVE: Was it in therapy, then, or was /*No* …/ it something else that led to you …

TORE: No, I felt it already for … I got arrested and put on remand … I like didn't want to experience this anymore. And then they say that I'm going to a special approved home, and I just, like, aha … but when I found out that, when I came *here* then and what happens here, then I felt like, fuck, this is actually really good. Excuse my language.

[…]

It's probably always been there since I got arrested the first time, that I didn't want to be doing this, but when I didn't get any help and then everything just went down and got worse and worse … it just went wrong.

During the same interview, Tore also said that to begin with he had not wanted to participate in therapy at all, but that after a while he had come to regard it as very important, and that he would now in fact prefer to have more therapy than he was being given. A study by Copes (2003) describes youths talking about how, in order to make their time in prison meaningful, they view it as a time for self-improvement. Although the youths in my own study do not describe self-improvement as a means of passing the time and making it meaningful, the interviews do contain descriptions that are reminiscent of this. However, Tore and the other youths who said that they had been helped at their institutions, or by having been placed in an institution, constituted the exception rather than the rule. It was primarily other factors that the youths emphasised as being important – not least simply making up their minds, irrespective of whether or not this is in fact as simple as it sounds. But if a youth has made up his mind, is everything then done and dusted? Is a responsible individual who makes the "right" choice sufficient? Or did the youths identify other factors that were required for them also to be able to achieve what they said they had made up their minds to do, i.e. to not commit offences following their release from youth custody? If the discussion to this point has been focused on what Maruna (2001 p. 24) labels the *why* of desistance, it now shifts to look at what Maruna argues is an even more important issue, i.e. the *how* of desistance.

What is required to stay away from crime?

We know from the literature on recidivism, and from life course studies that have examined what may produce changes that lead towards desistance, that factors such as family formation and getting a job have been ascribed major importance (Laub and Sampson 2009, Skardhamar and Telle 2009, Carlsson 2014). Some studies have questioned how much significance such factors have actually had, however, by asking whether it is having a job that produces the change, for example, or whether some prior change has instead also led to the individual in question getting a job (Skardhamar and Savolainen 2014, see also Giordano *et al.* 2002). In the current study, many of the youths also mentioned factors such as needing to go to school, getting a job and finding somewhere to live as important for them to be able to succeed with their intention to desist from crime. Sometimes all three of these factors were identified as important by the same youths, and research has also shown that measures are required in several different areas in connection with inmate re-entry (Petersilia 2001, Travis and Petersilia 2001, Petersilia 2003, Visher and Travis 2003). The youths sometimes referred to the social services in their narratives about what they needed. Sometimes these references involved the youths describing having received help from the social services, but the references most commonly involved the youths perceiving themselves as being in the hands of a social services office (or a social worker), and not knowing whether this office or individual would either be able to or want to help them (see also Hermodsson and Hansson 2005). Patrik, who had a few months left of his sentence, described his situation in the following way:

PATRIK (youth): It's about, you know, whether they pay, the social services, if they want to go in … just now that I've just turned 18, so I've gone over to being an adult in [name of social services district]. And the adult unit in [name of social services district] is very stingy. They don't want to pay, they don't like … they wait, they want to give money to families instead. They don't put any effort into youths; they don't want to help youths change their lives and I'm scared that they won't want to help me either. But that's something I'll have to wait and see. They were going to have a meeting … is it the fourth today?

TOVE: Er, the fifth.

PATRIK: They had a meeting yesterday, so then they're going to book a meeting here; then they'll come here and so we'll see how it goes.

Thus the social services had held a meeting (without Patrik) about his situation and he was now waiting to hear whether or not they wanted to help him. Patrik also described hoping that he would be able to come to pre-release within two weeks, because he wanted to have time for a short period of pre-release before being discharged. No decision appeared to have been made on this question either, or if it had, he did not himself know what was going to happen. This uncertainty about his situation was something that Patrik shared with several of the youths whom I interviewed. Sometimes, youths who only had a very short period of their sentence left would say that they had no idea what was actually going to happen when they were released. Visher and Travis (2003) have emphasised the importance of post-release preparations for the chances of inmates being reintegrated into the community, and against this background, the narratives of these youths appear to represent a problem in relation to their chances of succeeding subsequent to release. Maruna (2001) noted that one common factor among many of the desisters whom he interviewed was that they perceived themselves as having control over their futures. While it is true that this, for the most part, involved a perceived sense of being in control, it seems likely that the chances of developing such a sense will not be helped by not knowing anything about what is going to happen when one is released. At the same time, however, there were also youths who said that they knew exactly what was going to happen and what they were going to do. Understandably, these youths gave the impression of being less worried about their situation.

While Patrik's view was that the central issue was one of economics, of whether the social services in his local area wanted to devote their limited resources to other areas than young people, the interviews also contained narratives that focused on a perception that the social worker with whom the youths were in contact did not care or did not believe in the youths' desire to change. Kalle was one youth who spoke of this. He was one of the youths who only had a short time left to his release date when I interviewed him.

TOVE: No. Okay, and then you prefer to move somewhere else /*Yes*/ preferably away from [name of county]?

KALLE (youth): Mm.

TOVE: And the social services haven't …

KALLE: No, I mean, I don't know why they, I mean they don't believe me, that's the thing. I mean, I don't think that they believe me. Because I said, "You have to give me a chance, because I don't want to live in [name of county]," ... yes. But I don't want to live there. So they don't believe me. I don't know if they believe me or not. They say ... I'm in for one year and four months and they haven't sorted anything out for me, not a single thing, nothing.

[...]

Yes, we'll have to see what it's like. Otherwise the only thing to do is get a gym pass. Go training. Leisure time, because there's nothing else I want to do. I don't want to meet mates, or get to know new friends; I don't have the energy for anyone any more. I just want to start a new life myself; yes, because I've promised myself that I'm going to stop doing all that. So that ... yes.

Kalle's frustration at not getting any help from the social services was a recurrent theme in our interview and the same frustration could also be seen in the interviews with some of the other youths. The youths interviewed by Hermodsson and Hansson (2005) also sometimes expressed disappointment in relation to the social services, among other things for not listening to them or for not giving them the opportunity to say what they thought. There were also youths in the current study who expressed very clearly that they in no way wanted the social services to be involved in their lives. These statements were sometimes related to the youths saying that up to then the social services had never done anything to help them, and that they had no confidence in them. Staff members also sometimes expressed disappointment over a lack of interest on the part of the social services in relation to the youths sentenced to youth custody. As has been noted above, the research shows that it is reasonable to assume that continued support will be important for many of the youths in the current study (Andersson Vogel 2012). Given the importance that the youths ascribe to feeling that someone genuinely cares about them (see also Hill 2005), it is problematic when these youths perceive the social services to be unwilling to help, or disinterested.

Kalle's narrative also touches upon another common theme that the youths spoke about in connection with our discussions of what they would need in order to be able to stay away from crime subsequent to release. While it was common for the youths to talk about the need of a job or of education, the narrative that was perhaps most common, or at least as common, was the youths saying that they needed to move to somewhere other than where they came from (cf. Maruna 2001). This is a narrative about starting over, without their former (criminal) friends, and about being able to do so in a less risky environment. Some of the youths wanted to move to places with lower crime levels, while others just wanted to move somewhere else, without mentioning the crime level of the new location. It was often the case that they wanted to move from one large city to another, and, in these cases, the crime levels of the two may be assumed to be relatively similar. Thus it was not a question of these youths wanting to get away from a criminal environment in general, but rather of them wanting to move away from the specific environment in which they had been living up to that point. These youths spoke among other things about being worried that it would be difficult to stand their ground in the type of situations that might arise, but also about quite simply having the opportunity to start afresh. However, the youths did not necessarily view the decision to start over somewhere new as an easy one to make; some of them said that doing so could involve a range of consequences. In the following excerpt, Hampus describes his desire to start over somewhere new, and the problems that he feels this might involve.

TOVE: You don't want … to go back to [name of community 1], I understood, but it's not actually because you are *worried?* but it's more because things would go better if you don't move there, is it?

HAMPUS (youth): Yes, I mean, there are too many problems. Because if I go back to [name of community 1], the same problems will be waiting for me there, you know.… Because you don't just live a criminal life like that and then believe that it … I mean that everything will be fine just because you've stopped. It's better to change your environment completely in that case.

TOVE: Yes, okay.

HAMPUS: Then you can give yourself an honest chance.

TOVE: Yes. Okay. So that's the basic idea … mm. Is there anything *more* that you need for this to be successful, other than what we've already talked about?

HAMPUS: Er … I don't know … I, it … I don't know … Friends … friends … help from the social services, financial and housing. Er … I need … I mean I have to … I have to meet people who … who, I mean … you know.… You know I said this to the [name of institution] too; what we're doing *now*, that works *now*. But once I've been *released*, I just, because everyone around me, everyone who cares about me … I mean … when my sentence is *over*, you're not going to be there for me anymore. Because my youth custody sentence has run out. So that's why I want to start, you know; I want to get to know new people in [name of community 2]. That's why it's so important to me, because this is after all a release process. So it's like … yes. I think that's my biggest priority.

TOVE: A new network you could say?

HAMPUS: Yes. Because I don't feel good; I mean you get like this … you know; I'm not even 19 years old yet; I'm 19 in four months, but when you get like this … you feel alone, you know.

TOVE: Mm.

HAMPUS: Mm … because you know, as an 18-year-old and not having any friends left, no one, no one, no one, who you can lean on. No one I can talk to about things, nothing like that; so it's like, I only have my family, so it … I really have to meet new people. Because this works *now*, that I have staff around me. But once I'm released, I'm going to feel so alone in [name of community 2] that I'm going to move back to [name of community 1] and that will result in me re-offending.

Hampus's description illustrates feelings that several of the youths spoke about. They expressed a clear desire and a will to change their lives, but were uncertain about whether they would actually succeed in doing so. Having to, or perceiving oneself as having to, break away from friends in order to be able to avoid re-offending is not a new narrative, but rather one that is quite familiar from previous research. According to Visher and Travis (2003), the development of positive friendships, and also striking up new friendships directly subsequent to release, are central to the successful avoidance of re-offending. Starting over in this way involves major stresses, however, and this was something that clearly worried Hampus. He had also mentioned this to the staff at the institution, and it is here that spending time outside the institution emerges as part of the solution. Hampus described, for example, how he and the staff had discussed him needing to start some form of regular leisure time pursuit in the community to which he planned to move in order to meet new friends there.

As has been noted, the significance of delinquent peers is a widely recognised theme in the field of criminological theory (Sutherland *et al.* 1992, Lilly *et al.* 2014), and several of the youths thought that it was important to stay away from former friends who were involved in offending. In this regard, a small number of the interviewed youths mentioned the significance of electronic tagging as providing a means of being able to stand up to friends when these friends wanted them to participate in things they did not want to do. The youths said that electronic tagging makes it easier to say no, since you could say that the electronic ankle bracelet would start "beeping". Ali described how he felt about the fact that he would be given an electronic ankle bracelet in a short while, saying that it felt "great" that on the one hand he would be free, and on the other hand he would have someone keeping tabs on him. The latter gave him a sense of security in relation to the fact that he wanted to desist from crime but was also worried about whether he would be able to manage this when he had returned to his previous environment. With someone monitoring him via the electronic ankle bracelet during the initial period following his release, he would be able to get used to being in his former environment without committing offences. This line of argument can be compared with Foucault's (1991) discussions of the disciplinary significance of training, and may be regarded as a form of training oneself in not re-offending or getting into problematic situations. In a study focused on substitution treatment for drug abuse, Petersson (2013) showed how the control and rules that those undergoing treatment are subjected to are motivated, sometimes by the inmates but perhaps primarily by staff members, as a form of *support* for introducing some kind of "order" into the lives of clients who are regarded as lacking structure and the capacity to refrain from relapse without this control. In this way, control becomes a form of support similar to Foucault's pastoral power (1982, Järvinen 2002, Petersson 2013), which is also reflected in the youths' narratives on electronic tagging.

Another theme touched on by the youths was the significance of getting a second chance, of being trusted by their environment (and first and foremost the staff). This also involved the staff giving the youths the *opportunity* to show that they could be trusted, and showing the youths that they believed that they wanted to change (or had already changed). In a similar way, Crewe (2011 p. 464, see also Maruna 2001) has described how prison inmates talk about the significance of staff believing in their desire to change. Leon spoke about this at the end of our interview.

TOVE: Then I was also wondering, if there is anything that we haven't talked about, that you would like to, that you think it's important to *bring up* or to say?

LEON (youth): No … I don't know actually … I think rather that, what's important is, you know, that you get a second chance. That you get that before it's too late. That sometimes it can happen that it gets to be too late. And I think that you … not like that you just release the youth, "ah, but now here's your second chance. Now you can go out unmonitored, do what you want." Not like that, but I mean … slowly but surely, but still without too much time passing. That they give you a chance. That you say like that, ah, but … "That's the way it is, you're young, you *deserve* a second chance."… And to take one step at a time … and like … feel your way forwards.

Leon appears to be saying that it is important not to wait too long before giving youths the opportunity to show that they can cope with being outside the institution, but that this should occur in an ordered way, and within the existing frameworks. He later also said that it was important that the staff not only say that they trust the youths, but also *show* that they do so in different ways (by giving the youths various forms of responsibility).[8] It should be noted that none of the youths whom I interviewed advocated simply releasing them just like that; on the contrary, they gave the impression of being well aware that they had been given a sentence that had to be served (this was at least the view they presented themselves as having in their contacts with me). Thus none of them proposed an "open door" policy. In a similar way, Hill (2005) described the youths that she followed and interviewed as in no way advocating an unregulated existence in which they could do whatever they wanted. Instead what they were looking for was comprehensible and reasonable rules that were implemented fairly. In my own study, some of the interviewed youths also described examples of the staff having exhibited exactly the type of trust that they were looking for, among others Leon himself, and these staff members were often described as having a positive effect on the youths' relationships with the staff in general. Benjamin (youth), for example, said that as long as you did what you're supposed to, the staff gave you all the help and support you needed, and he went on to say that

> they open up a load of doors for you; here's a flat for you; behave yourself properly, don't get caught up in crime again and you've got an open future in front of you here; so I mean that's … that's good, you know.

Thus some of the youths felt that they were helped both by their institutional placement and the staff.

Another trust-related theme that some of the youths discussed was the significance of having someone close who trusted and supported them, such as a family member. Tore (youth), for example, said that:

> I need support from my parents. Er … I think, very much. I probably need someone who believes in me.… I believe in myself, but I want somebody else to believe in me … er … and there I think my parents play a very important role … and that … before, I couldn't talk to them at all; now I talk to [my parents], whatever it is.

Tore is one who described having been helped by the staff during his time at the institution, both through the therapy he was participating in and through having developed an improved relationship with his family. Thus in the same way as the family, what it means to the youths and what the youths themselves mean to their families, was described by some youths as a reason for them wanting to *desist* from crime, the family was also described as being an important factor in relation to realising this desire to desist. This thus represents a further argument for the importance of institutional leave as a means of maintaining contacts with significant individuals outside the institution. The importance of maintaining contact with one's family for reduced levels of re-offending has also been confirmed in a Danish study of prison inmates (Monrad Granunböl and Hviid Hornnes 2009, see also Visher and Travis 2003). Studies have also found prison visits to be related to more successful reintegration and lower levels of re-offending (Moran 2013, Visher and Travis 2003). But what did the staff describe as being important, and how would they like the youth custody sanction to work?

Staff views on what would be required for things to go well for the youths

In the staff interviews, I did not pose the concrete question "What is necessary to ensure that the youths do not re-offend?" All of the interviewed staff were, however, asked what they thought an ideal period of youth custody would look like. The staff's answers to this question provide a composite picture of what they feel is needed in order to succeed with their mission, i.e. to ensure that the youths do not re-offend and are given help and support towards a better life than they had prior to their sentences. Sometimes the staff's answers focused on things that they wanted to do better, while at other times they spoke of things that they said were already being done. For the most part, however, their answers revolved around reflections on how the care provided at the special approved homes could be improved.

The staff's answers should be viewed in the context of the fact that the interviews, prior to this particular question being asked (which was most often near the end of the interview), had largely focused on institutional leave. It is, therefore, perhaps not surprising that almost all of the interviewed staff spoke about the degree of custodial openness in their answers to the question on the ideal period of youth custody. Another common theme was that all of those who spoke about this wanted the youths to have increased opportunities to spend time outside the institution, although they did not always have the same ideas about what *type* of custodial openness was needed. This is, of course, very much in line with the findings discussed earlier about the staff viewing time spent outside the institution as being important for a number of different reasons. Many of the staff members also spoke of the pre-release process as being very important, and as something that needed to be extended. The objectives of these pre-release activities should be to give the youths an opportunity to practice being outside the institution and to help them develop the ability to cope with the situations (and the related risk for re-offending) that this entails, as well as building up a context in which they had something to be released into (such as school, a work experience placement or similar).[9] This is also related to the progression through the institutional custody system, that many regard as being necessary, which involves: 1) the secure unit (known as a reception unit); 2) the treatment unit (first locked, and then perhaps open); and 3) the pre-release unit (open). In this connection, some of the staff also said that their institutions currently lacked an open unit that could serve as a transitional form between a locked treatment unit and a pre-release unit. Not all youths were able to cope with being placed on pre-release, which meant that some instead remained on locked units. One reason given for this was that there had been so little demand for open places at the National Board for Institutional Care (and from the social services) that existing open units had sometimes been transformed into locked units. The annual reports published by the special approved homes also show that this has happened on a number of occasions.

A number of the interviewed staff members said that youths were far too often released into uncertainty, and without planning. One of the interview participants spoke of having discussed with colleagues how they should actually begin by planning the end of the sentence. This may be compared with the conclusion drawn by Bateman and colleagues (2013 p. 23, see also Visher and Travis 2003) that "(t)he process of preparing young people for release should commence at the point of entry to the secure estate", which they also identify as one of a number of central tasks for those working with incarcerated youths. One important aspect of the staff's discussions of the problems associated with a period of uncertainty following release from youth custody was that many felt that the social services should assume a greater responsibility for these youths; some went so far as to argue that there should be a legal requirement for the social services to do so. According to staff, the current situation was such that it is quite arbitrary whether this form of joint planning takes place, depending on which municipality the youth comes from, and which social worker is responsible for this issue.[10] This is also reminiscent of the feeling some of the interviewed youths mentioned of being in the hands of a social services system which they sometimes perceived as being unwilling or powerless (particularly at the level of the individual social worker).

Another theme that many of the staff members took up was that they wanted more individually focused treatment measures. This constitutes part of the mission of the National Board of Institutional Care, in that the agency should provide treatment on the basis of the individual's needs. Within the agency's tight organisational framework, characterised by limited staff and financial resources, this is perhaps not being realised to the extent that the staff view as desirable. A number of those interviewed stated that this had constituted even more of a problem in the initial phase of the agency's work with the youth custody sentence, which they in part ascribed to uncertainty and a worry about making errors in relation to the special approved homes' new mandate, which in some ways differed from the existing work of the agency.[11] In relation to this issue, the staff also described the strict specification of the length of youth custody sentences as constituting a problem with regard to the provision of individually focused care and treatment. This would ideally involve activities outside the institution adapted to the needs of the individual youth rather than a focus on a pre-determined time-frame based on the length of the sentence. A more individually focused content also involves the implementation of the youth custody sanction being transferred to "small-scale legal systems" and "parallel judges", as described by Foucault (1991 p. 21). On the basis of the interviews, it would appear that the staff members want to be given this type of a role to a greater extent.

A further theme that recurred frequently during the staff interviews involved a desire to be able to work more with the youths' families and with providing support to their parents. This is something that Visher and Travis (2003) also emphasise as being important in relation to the re-entry of prison inmates. Following their release from youth custody, the majority of the youths return to their parents' home, and according to the staff, it is in the parental home that things eventually need to function well (65 per cent of the youths included in the current study were released to the parental home). The social services were once again mentioned in this context, with some staff members saying that they should adopt a more active approach to providing help and support to the youths' parents. Some staff members also argued that the youths should have a team around them, which should actively work with them outside the institution. By contrast with the interviewed youths, however, it was uncommon for the staff members to say that the youths should move to a new area following their release from youth custody, although this was mentioned.[12] Instead their focus was clearly directed at making things work in the family and in the youths' home communities. Reintegration focused on a return to the youths' former environments has been problematised, however, since for this to work requires that the youths were previously integrated in these environments, which is often not the case (Bateman *et al.* 2013, see also Visher and Travis 2003 regarding the significance of the inmates′ situation prior to a prison sentence).

In the same way as the youths, some staff members also stated that it was important to believe in the youths and that they have to be given a chance. One of the staff members spoke about this issue in the following way, having first discussed the fears associated with allowing youths to spend time on leave outside the institution.

RUNE (staff): But what are we most afraid of? What are we *risking*? Because now, you know, now what we do is reinforce things almost. (pause) We *make things worse*, we reinforce, we make the youths' chances worse if we have the system we have today. We deprive them of the opportunity to ret … to return to society. I mean there was a guy who said this not so long ago, "But you don't get it, I don't know if I can *go on* any more. I don't know if I've got the energy to fight any more now. I mean I haven't done anything other than … I mean I have to get *something* for it." And we talked about it for a while. "But what is it more specifically that you have to *get* for it?" "Ah, but I mean I have to be able to *show* the others." "Who are these others, then, that you have to be able to show?" "But all those who believe that I … I don't know what they believe, they probably think I'm this big gangster or …" And I think it's probably there that I feel a little bit that we maybe, with the vast majority, not all, but I mean that's how it is in all forms of work, no rule without exceptions, but it's there somewhere that I think we end up, that we have to … we *have to* (pause) have to believe in the youths' possibility and desire to, because you know they don't want to be [on the] outside, you know, they want to be [on the] inside.

TOVE: You mean in society now, or do you mean …

RUNE: Yes, I mean society.

This excerpt from the interview with Rune raises the issue of the balance between maintaining security and giving the youths the opportunity, by means of various forms of institutional leave, to prepare for life after their release from youth custody. This is an issue that has also been discussed in studies focused on both prisons (Hörnqvist 2010, Hannah-Moffat 2005, Bosworth 2007) and the probation service (Werth 2013). The chapter now concludes with a discussion of this balance, and of the staff members' attitudes towards it.

(Not) struggling against the wind – on the balance between custodial openness and security

One theme that many of the staff members touched upon in the interviews, and that is closely linked to the youths' opportunities to spend time outside the institutions, relates to the question of a balance between, on the one hand, security issues and, on the other, assessments of what would be best for the youths' treatment or care. This theme did not primarily emerge in discussions relating to what an ideal sentence would look like, but rather in the part of the interview where we discussed what changes the staff members had seen over time in the implementation of youth custody.[13] The discussions within this theme thus related to changes that had occurred in attitudes towards the balance between *security* – keeping the youths incarcerated irrespective of what effects this might produce in order to ensure that they do not abscond – and *openness* – providing opportunities for contact with, or integration into, the community outside the institutions. This issue is also related to Farrington's (1992) critique of the concept of total institutions, in the sense that the concept suggests that these institutions are completely isolated from their surroundings, which thus creates an expectation that the youths (or inmates) will be incarcerated the whole time.

Hörnqvist (2010) discusses productive and repressive interventions in prison (on the basis of the concepts of productive and repressive power) and links the productive concept to the focus on needs found in treatment research, and the repressive concept to the focus on risk and security found in the same body of research. He writes the following in relation to the balancing act which constitutes the focus of this section:

> Productive and repressive interventions in prison have different goals and stand in a tense, if not contradictory relationship to one another. The most common metaphor used in official documents to describe the relationship is that of a balancing act. The National Audit Office speaks about "a balancing act between safe containment and the inmates' motivation to change their attitudes towards crime or substance abuse."
>
> (Hörnqvist 2010 p. 109)

On the basis of the interviews conducted with staff in the current project, it is clear that this balancing act is also an issue in the context of youth custody sentences. On a number of occasions, the staff members spoke of this in terms of a pendulum, which swings between the opposites of, on the one hand, high levels of physical security, and, on the other hand, a focus on treatment. It should also be noted that in the same way as in the above quote from the Audit Office described by Hörnqvist, the staff members who spoke of this issue were also convinced that both elements were necessary, even though they spoke of them in terms of opposites. Thus they needed to balance these two elements against one another. It is also clear from the interviews that the staff members who discussed this question were agreed that there was a very clear swing in the pendulum in 2005, which was linked to a small number of spectacular cases of absconding in the summer of 2005 that received a great deal of media attention. Among other things, these cases led to the majority of institutions with special youth custody places building high fences, and to physical security measures also being expanded in other ways. An internal inquiry was also initiated at the National Board of Institutional Care to examine the security of youth custody institutions.[14] All the directors of the institutions that have special places for youth custody sentences were also summoned to a meeting with the responsible minister, the then Minister of Health and Social Affairs, at which it was made clear that the absconding was viewed very seriously. One of the interviewed staff, Ulla, described the effects of the attention focused on these cases of absconding as being that the institutions were "basically instructed to *lock the doors and don't let them out*".

The Swedish prison system had experienced a similar situation the previous year, beginning in the summer of 2004. In the same way as in the special approved home system, a small number of exceptional prison escapes, which attracted a great deal of media attention, resulted in a great deal of pressure being directed at the responsible politicians and the prison service (Hörnqvist 2010). This led to three prisons with the highest security classification introducing special secure units for inmates deemed to be at "particularly high risk for independent or assisted escape".[15] These events also led to an expansion of security routines (Hörnqvist 2010). A similar process was also witnessed in the UK prison service during the 1990s (Liebling 2008), while Hazel (2008) has noted that media pressure has also led to more positive changes within the field of youth justice.

Another thing that the interviewed staff members who discussed this issue were agreed upon was dissatisfaction with these developments. Some argued that to begin with (during the first years following the introduction of the youth custody sentence), the specified frameworks with regard to institutional leave were rather loose, and perhaps too loose. Others argued that this was a good thing. Irrespective of their attitude on this particular issue, however, all those who discussed the balance between custodial openness and security were agreed that the changes introduced in 2005 were not good. Robin (staff) said that he personally viewed the building of the new fences as a "waste of money" and also said that youths continued to abscond in spite of these. He went on:

> I don't believe in this. I mean you can put people in bunkers and the only thing they're going to focus on, of course, is "how do I get out of here?" (pause) And then it looks fairly grotesque when, I mean, people come from outside, "Wow, there's a five meter fence with barbed wire and stuff."

As can be seen from the above excerpt, Robin felt that the fence produced more powerful feelings in the youths of wanting to get out, simply by further restricting their opportunities to do so. A number of the interview subjects said that the new fences affected the youths, as well as the staff, and that they meant that the youths were perceived and treated as being more dangerous than they actually are. Arvid, for example, said that the fences affected the mentality of both staff and youths since they had made the staff dependent on cameras and physical security measures, instead of on building up a relationship with the youths as a means of getting them to choose not to abscond, as had previously been the case. Similar narratives can be found among the youths followed by Hill (2005), who said that they chose not to abscond because they did not want to disappoint the staff with whom they had developed a relationship. A number of the youths interviewed in the current study also said that when the staff showed that they trusted them, had faith in them and did not simply assume that they would abscond as soon as they got the chance, this resulted in them not wanting to abscond. This does not of course mean that absconding could be completely eradicated by measures focused on relationship building (which would furthermore also require that the staff succeeded in building relationships with the youths, which is not always the case). However, if physical security measures affect the staff in such a way that they devote less time and energy to building relationships, then it has to some extent been counterproductive. Arvid argued that there were benefits associated with the youths knowing that they could "go off" if they chose to. He explained this in the following way:

TOVE: What is beneficial about them knowing that they can go off?

ARVID (staff): They have responsibility themselves. We don't assume their responsibility for staying here, that's a responsibility that they have themselves. I believe that responsibility is not completely unimportant. But *now*, when we go out into the yard, you know, they don't ... even if we're outside, they [the youths] don't have any responsibility, because they *have* to remain here, it is the perimeter around us that takes the responsibility. That's how I look at it. And I thought ... this is not, not an unimportant change.

This view is closely linked to Maruna's discussions about the opportunities available to inmates to take responsibility for their behaviour within the framework of secure institutions. Having noted that it takes more than inmates believing (or repeating phrases about believing) in themselves, Maruna (2001 p. 155) writes that "[e]qually ridiculous is the image of a prison counsellor encouraging inmates to 'take the responsibility for your behaviour' while they are kept in an environment that essentially takes all responsibility and choice away from them". This type of environment instead undermines inmates' opportunities for perceiving themselves as having any personal control. Werth (2011, 2013, see also Bosworth 2007) has also discussed the ambiguity with which released inmates are regarded. They are viewed as being responsible for their own actions, and for improving, while at the same time being seen as potentially dangerous and as lacking the capacity for "improvement". This attitude on the part of probation officers diminishes or completely disregards the challenges that individuals face on release from prison. It also removes any responsibility from the probation officers themselves.

The introduction of the changes (fences and so forth) had thus led to some discontent among at least some of the staff, a discontent that remained more than five years later.[16] Hörnqvist (2012) notes the significance of the organisation for the repressive and productive power that is exercised, and also argues that the staff become representatives of the organisation. The described changes may be understood in these terms, with the staff's personal views about how care and treatment provision should be implemented being assigned a secondary role. According to those interviewed, what was more important was the agency's need to demonstrate efficacy and show that it was dealing with the problem of absconding. As part of the organisation, the staff, irrespective of their own views, simply had to adjust to working in the context of more secure conditions.

The findings of the internal inquiry initiated by the National Board of Institutional Care emphasised that relationship building (so-called dynamic security) was central to the prevention of absconding. The measures proposed by the inquiry nonetheless had a clear focus on physical security measures and risk assessment. Of 17 concrete proposals presented by the inquiry, five may be categorised as physical security measures, five relate to various forms of risk assessment and four focus on the organisation of various routines related to security and risk assessment. Only three of the proposals related to the contents of the care provided at the institutions. These were: 1) to develop the system of custodial progression (from secure to open care provision); 2) that all youths should have a complete programme of activities; and 3) that every youth's treatment plan should be linked to the assessment conducted in relation to the youth in question. It can also be noted that the true nature of proposal number 2 is somewhat ambiguous, since having a complete activity programme is clearly reminiscent of Foucault's (1991) discussion of the way correctional institutions use the micro-management of daily routines in the form of different work tasks as a means of discipline.

Several of those interviewed in the current study mentioned the significance of the media attention for the changes that were introduced (cf. Hörnqvist 2010). Some perceived the National Board of Institutional Care to be a "media sensitive" organisation, and felt that the head office had failed (and also fails in other contexts) to support the institutions in the face of media attention. Instead of defending the care and treatment provided by the institutions, the agency instead decided to quickly introduce various forms of physical security in order to demonstrate efficacy. It is interesting in this context to note that the agency's internal inquiry makes several references to the need to prevent absconding specifically as a result of the risk of attracting media attention, although the stated rationale is that such attention involves a risk that isolated incidents will affect the care provided to all youths admitted to special approved homes. At the same time, this is precisely what the inquiry's proposals led to, and the fact that the inquiry made several references to the media attention directed at incidents of absconding from youth custody as a reason for ensuring that these youths in particular should be prevented from absconding may be viewed as providing confirmation of the "media sensitivity" described by the staff. Another example of this tendency towards sensitivity that was described by one of the interview participants was that the agency was beginning to experience something of a swing in the opposite direction as a result of different forms of criticism that had been directed at the agency by the Ombudsman for Children and the National Board of Health and Welfare (which at the time was responsible for the oversight of special approved homes) (cf. Hazel 2008).[17]

The interviewed staff did not feel that the consequences of the absconding and the subsequent media attention were restricted to the building of the fences and the introduction of other physical security measures. A number also stated that it subsequently also became more difficult to allow the youths to have institutional leave (cf. Hörnqvist 2010). One of the interviewed staff members argued that it created an attitude that the staff should focus on keeping the youths "locked in so that they don't abscond during their sentences", whereas the situation at the time of the interviews had instead moved increasingly towards a focus on ensuring that the youths spent time outside the institution, as a result of new directives relating to the institutions' pre-release activities. A number of the interviewed staff made other similar references to things having once again started moving in the opposite direction, towards a greater focus on the youths' need to spend time outside the institution prior to being released.

A final aspect of the increased physical security that was raised in the interviews was that it has led to open units, along with locked units that had been working with a relatively open approach, being forced to adjust to more secure forms of custody. Tommy, for example, first described that he felt that the agency employed secure forms of custody too often, in part for financial reasons, but also out of a fear that absconding would attract the attention of the media, and then went on to talk about what had happened following the events of 2005. When politicians are put under pressure by the media, they in turn put pressure on the National Board as an agency, and this leads to:

TOMMY (staff): Unfortunately, like what happened for the last time a number of years ago, when they locked everything down, put up fences everywhere, make the youths more dangerous than they actually are, and so on. And put the resources into that. And we all know that if things are going to work out in the future, then they have to be working towards going home, because that's where they're going and they need to be as well prepared as possible in order to be able to (inaudible)

TOVE: Do you see this security, I mean the fence came then, or course, … but do you see this thing with open and secure, that they've also tightened up the unit, from open to secure, is that also a consequence of this? The fences were like so conspicuous …

TOMMY: Definitely. It went out to *everyone* that, number one, absconding cannot be allowed to happen. So the lockable [units] that worked in a fairly open way also had to pull back. The assessment unit that actually had a really open way of working got a fence round it and one [youth] at a time outside [the unit]; it became a completely different way of working for them than they had ever worked with. And then it's … gradually, *now eased* up a bit more, so we're moving, maybe *are* where we were before. But other things are absolutely not like that, I mean, you always have to go with a staff member in the grounds.

TOVE: Before, you went where you were going by yourself?

TOMMY: "Off you go then, you know where you're going"…. So it's about, fear … that's the community protection, so to speak, not being allowed to abscond. And that's probably important, but the question [is] whether it should be number one the whole time; I'm not so sure about that. At the start, yes, that I can agree with…. But it maybe shouldn't follow them the whole way, that it's [the] number one [consideration] the whole time.

Thus the pendulum is swinging back once again, towards a greater focus on the contents of the institutions' activities and on more open custodial forms, but according to Tommy, the changes that were implemented in 2005 are still present in the work of his institution. He identifies the discussions at the agency regarding expanded pre-release activities as one part of this shift back towards more open working methods.

Summary

The majority of the youths expressed a desire to desist from crime following their youth custody sentences. Whether or not they believed they would succeed in this varied, however. At the same time, few of the youths said that the contents of their period of institutionalisation had contributed to their desire to desist. Instead they emphasised their own will, quite simply deciding to stop committing offences, as the most important reason. Behind this expression of desire, and the youths' focus on having made the decision themselves, however, they also described a wide range of reasons for wanting this now, such as consideration for their families, friends and girlfriends, the risk continued offending involved for the possibility of a *future* family, the risk of future imprisonment and the perception that a criminal lifestyle was quite simply too stressful. Thus the essential *willingness* to change (Giordano *et al.* 2002) appears already to be "in place" among the majority of these youths, at least in relation to the way they speak about the time subsequent to their release from youth custody. Like Sandberg (2010), I would argue that speech also generates behaviour, and that for this reason these narratives should not be dismissed as meaningless on the basis of a view that they are merely part of an expected discourse. Although the interviewed youths are not part of the follow-up group, it is nonetheless reasonably safe to assume that many of them will re-offend in spite of their ambition to desist (a large majority of the youths sentenced to youth custody do so, as will be seen in the next chapter). But might this perhaps nonetheless be viewed as the start of a long-term desistance process (Maruna 2001) or is it the case that the youths are still so young that they have not yet started to formulate a narrative of persistence? Irrespective of which interpretation one chooses to focus on, both nonetheless underline the importance of exploiting the desire to change that appears to characterise these youths as a "window of opportunity" (Bateman *et al.* 2013 p. 14).

What then do the youths describe as being important in order to succeed in not continuing to commit offences? For the most part it is a question of having something to do (school or a job) and of having the opportunity to start over in a new environment. For this, support is required from both the institutional staff and the social services, support that according to the youths is not always available, a view that was expressed most clearly in relation to the social services. Having someone who believes, and exhibits trust, in them is also significant. The latter makes the perception of a lack of support from, for example, the social services problematic.

Institutional leave and more open conditions constitute a central tool for being able to provide structured opportunities to have something to do following the youth custody sentence, as well as for the possibility of being able to start over in a new environment (which is likely to require a certain amount of preparation in the new locality). They are also important in order to be able to maintain contact with people who are significant to the youths, in relation to both their desire to desist and their ability to succeed in doing so.

For their part, the staff describe institutional leave and custodial openness as important aspects of their ideal youth custody sentences, and as areas that could be improved. Unlike the youths, the staff were more inclined to focus on how things will work out at home than on making it possible for the youths to start over in a new location, but for things to work well at home also requires institutional leave and that the conclusion of the youth custody sentence be served in more open custodial forms. One issue that was raised by several of the interviewed staff members was the balance between security and openness, and here they described a situation where the focus had shifted over time from the one to the other, and then back again. Even though they said that security, in the form of the prevention of absconding, was necessary, they also argued that too much focus on security can damage the youths' chances of readjustment following their release.

What then does the re-offending of youths released from youth custody look like? And what significance do different forms of custodial openness have for this re-offending? These questions are analysed in the next chapter, which is also the book's final empirical section.

Notes

1 In relation to this particular issue, I also asked the person who transcribed the interviews about her own impressions as to whether these were sincere answers or rather represented what the youths felt they were expected to say. The transcriber's interpretation was that the youths' responses generally reflected sincere answers rather than (only) being based on perceived expectations.

2 At the same time, the prison regulations contain a long list of the rules that the prisoners should follow and of the sanctions associated with deviations from these rules.

3 This has also been noted in previous studies that have made use of information from the journals of youths placed in special approved homes (cf. Shannon 2011).

4 These cases primarily involve youths serving sentences of less than six months duration, but the absence of any treatment information is also found in over 10 per cent of the journals relating to youths with sentences of up to one year. It has not been possible to determine the extent to which this finding is due to an absence of actual treatment measures or to inconsistencies in what is noted in the youths' journals.

5 One factor that should be borne in mind in relation to this apparent dominance, however, is that cognitive treatment programmes are often manual-based and highly structured, which may make references to them more likely to be included in a journal by comparison with more diffuse treatment approaches such as environmental therapy, for example.

6 See Giordano *et al.* (2002), who describe the significance of this factor as being different for women.

7 Referring to a worry (that Hampus thus was not experiencing) that his former friends might somehow dislike his decision to desist, which we had spoken about earlier in the interview.
8 This underlines the importance of the youths also being given unmonitored leave.
9 As I have already mentioned, there were ongoing discussions at the time that I conducted my interviews, which subsequently resulted in new legislation (Justitiedepartementet 2011), on expanded pre-release activities, so this, too, was a topical issue at the time the interviews were conducted. My impression, on the basis of my contacts with individuals who were involved in these discussions at the National Board of Institutional Care, is that the general mood at the Board itself was that the agency wanted to be instructed to expand its pre-release activities.
10 It should be noted that the social services, and their perspective on these questions, are not represented in the study data.
11 Since youth custody involved youths who had been sentenced to a criminal justice sanction rather than youths placed by the social services.
12 It is, of course, possible that the staff would have mentioned this possibility more often if my question had not focused on what an ideal sentence would look like. At the same time, however, the fact that the staff often spoke about the youths needing to be able to cope in their home environment suggests that this is not the case.
13 Many of the interviewed staff members had worked at special approved homes for a substantial proportion of the period since the introduction of the youth custody sentence in 1999, and some had worked there throughout this period.
14 SiS Ref. No. 14-562-05.
15 Available online at: www.kriminalvarden.se/fangelse-frivard-och-hakte/fangelse/sakerhetsklass/ (accessed 3 September, 2015).
16 I myself started to work as research director at the National Board of Institutional Care in the autumn of 2005, at which point this discussion was still ongoing. My own impression at the time was also that there was discontent within the agency about the changes that were introduced.
17 This criticism focused, for example, on the incorrect and/or extensive use of isolation.

Bibliography

Andersson, R., 2004. Behandlingstankens återkomst: Från psykoanalys till kognitiv beteendeterapi. *Nordisk tidsskrift for kriminalvidenskab*, 91(5), pp. 384–403.

Andersson Vogel, M., 2012. *Särskilda ungdomshem och vårdkedjor: Om ungdomar, kön, klass och etnicitet.* Stockholm: Institutionen för socialt arbete-Socialhögskolan, Stockholms Universitet.

Andreassen, T., 2003. *Institutionsbehandling av ungdomar: Vad säger forskningen?* Stockholm: Gothia.

Andrews, D.A. and Bonta, J., 2010. *The psychology of criminal conduct.* Albany: Lexis Nexis/Anderson Pub.

Bateman, T., Hazel, N. and Wright, S., 2013. *Resettlement of young people leaving custody: Lessons from the literature.* London: Beyond Youth Custody.

Bergström, G., 1997. *Kriminalitet som livsstil.* Malmö: Égalité.

Bosworth, M., 2007. Creating the responsible prisoner: Federal admission and orientation packs. *Punishment & Society*, 9(1), pp. 67–85.

Carlsson, C., 2014. *Continuities and changes in criminal careers.* Stockholm: Department of Criminology, Stockholm University.

Carlsson, C. and Sarnecki, J., 2015. *An introduction to life-course criminology.* London: Sage.

Cope, N., 2003. 'It's no time or high time': Young offenders' experiences of time and drug use in prison. *The Howard Journal of Criminal Justice*, 42(2), pp. 158–175.

Crewe, B., 2009. *The prisoner society: Power, adaptation and social life in an English prison.* Oxford: Oxford University Press.

Crewe, B., 2011. Soft power in prison: Implications for staff–prisoner relationships, liberty and legitimacy. *European Journal of Criminology*, 8(6), pp. 455–468.

Farrington, K., 1992. The modern prison as total institution? Public perception versus objective reality. *Crime & Delinquency*, 38(1), pp. 6–26.

Foucault, M., 1982. The subject and power. *Critical Inquiry*, 8(4), pp. 777–795.

Foucault, M., 1991. *Discipline and punish: The birth of the prison.* London: Penguin books.

Gendreau, P., Little, T. and Goggin, C., 1996. A meta-analysis of the predictors of adult offender recidivism: What works! *Criminology*, 34(4), pp. 575–608.

Giordano, P.C., Cernkovich, S.A. and Rudolph, J.L., 2002. Gender, crime, and desistance: Toward a theory of cognitive transformation. *American Journal of Sociology*, 107(4), pp. 990–1064.

Goffman, E., 1991. *Asylums: Essays on the social situation of mental patients and other inmates.* London: Penguin Books.

Goldstein, A.P., Glick, B. and Gibbs, J.C., 2011. *Aggression Replacement Training: A comprehensive intervention for aggressive youth* (rev. 3rd edn). Champain: Research Press.

Hannah-Moffat, K., 2005. Criminogenic needs and the transformative risk subject: Hybridizations of risk/need in penality. *Punishment & Society*, 7(1), pp. 29–51.

Hazel, N., 2008. *Cross-national comparison of youth justice.* London: Youth Justice Board for England and Wales.

Hermodsson, A. and Hansson, C., 2005. *Demokrati i det lilla? Ungdomars delaktighet i sin behandling.* Stockholm: Statens Institutionsstyrelse.

Hill, T., 2005. *Allians under tvång: Behandlingssamarbete mellan elever och personal på särskilda ungdomshem.* Linköping: Institutionen för beteendevetenskap, Linköpings Universitet.

Hörnqvist, M., 2010. *Risk, power and the state: After Foucault.* London: Routledge.

Hörnqvist, M., 2012. *En annan Foucault: Maktens problematik.* Stockholm: Carlsson Bokförlag.

Järvinen, M., 2002. Hjälpens universum – ett maktperspektiv på mötet mellan klient och system. In: A. Meeuwisse and H. Swärd, eds, *Perspektiv på sociala problem.* Stockholm: Natur och Kultur, pp. 253–273.

Järvinen, M., 2004. Life histories and the perspective of the present. *Narrative Inquiry*, 14(1), pp. 45–68.

Justitiedepartementet, 2011. *Förbättrad utsluss från sluten ungdomsvård.*

Laub, J.H. and Sampson, R.J., 2009. *Shared beginnings, divergent lives: Delinquent boys to age 70.* Cambridge, MA: Harvard University Press.

Liebling, A., 2008. Incentives and earned privileges revisited: Fairness, discretion, and the quality of prison life. *Journal of Scandinavian Studies in Criminology and Crime Prevention*, 9(S1), pp. 25–41.

Lilly, J.R., Cullen, F.T. and Ball, R.A., 2014. *Criminological theory: Context and consequences.* 6th edn. Thousand Oaks: Sage Publications.

Maruna, S., 2001. *Making good: How ex-convicts reform and rebuild their lives.* Washington DC: American Psychological Association.

Monrad Granunböl, H. and Hviid Hornnes, J., 2009. *Sociala boder der binder.* Köpenhamns Universitet.

Moran, D., 2013. Between outside and inside? Prison visiting rooms as liminal carceral spaces. *GeoJournal*, 78(2), pp. 339–351.

Nilsson, A., 2002. *Fånge i marginalen. Uppväxtvillkor, levnadsförhållanden och återfall i brott bland fångar.* Stockholm: Kriminologiska Institutionen, Stockholms Universitet.

Pager, D., 2008. *Marked: Race, crime, and finding work in an era of mass incarceration.* Chicago & London: University of Chicago Press.

Palm, J., 2003. *Ungdomarnas upplevelse av sluten ungdomsvård: En jämförelse med LVU-placeringar och fängelse.* Stockholm: Statens Institutionsstyrelse.

Petersilia, J., 2001. Prisoner reentry: Public safety and reintegration challenges. *The Prison Journal*, 81(3), pp. 360–375.

Petersilia, J., 2003. *When prisoners come home: Parole and prisoner reentry.* Oxford: Oxford University Press.

Petersson, F., 2013. *Kontroll av beroende. Substitutionsbehandlingens logik, praktik och semantik.* Malmö: Égalité.

Pettersson, T., 2010. Recidivism among young males sentenced to prison and youth custody. *Journal of Scandinavian Studies in Criminology and Crime Prevention*, 11(2), pp. 151–169.

Presser, L., 2009. The narratives of offenders. *Theoretical Criminology*, 13(2), pp. 177–200.

Presser, L. and Sandberg, S., 2015. *Narrative Criminology: Understanding Stories of Crime.* New York & London: New York University Press.

Sandberg, S., 2010. What can "lies" tell us about life? Notes towards a framework of narrative criminology. *Journal of Criminal Justice Education*, 21(4), pp. 447–465.

Schlosser, A.J., 2015. *Inmates' narrative and discursive discipline in prison. Rewriting personal histories through cognitive-behavioral programs.* Abingdon: Routledge.

Seiter, R.P. and Kadela, K.R., 2003. Prisoner reentry: What works, what does not, and what is promising. *Crime & Delinquency*, 49(3), pp. 360–388.

Shannon, D., 2011. *Follow-up of youths admitted to SiS youth care facilities 1997–2001.* Stockholm: Statens Institutionsstyrelse.

Skardhamar, T. and Savolainen, J., 2014. Changes in criminal offending around the time of job entry: A study of employment and desistance. *Criminology*, 52(2), pp. 263–291.

Skardhamar, T. and Telle, K., 2009. *Life after prison: The relationship between employment and re-incarceration.* 597. Oslo: Statistics Norway, Research Department.

Sutherland, E.H., Cressey, D.R. and Luckenbill, D.F., 1992. *Principles of criminology.* 11th edn. Lanham: Rowman & Littlefield.

Travis, J. and Petersilia, J., 2001. Reentry reconsidered: A new look at an old question. *Crime & Delinquency*, 47(3), pp. 291–313.

Ugelvik, T., 2014. *Power and resistance in prison: Doing time, doing freedom.* London: Palgrave Macmillan.

Vinnerljung, B. and Sallnäs, M., 2008. Into adulthood: A follow-up study of 718 young people who were placed in out-of-home care during their teens. *Child & Family Social Work*, 13(2), pp. 144–155.

Visher, C.A. and Travis, J., 2003. Transitions from prison to community: Understanding individual pathways. *Annual Review of Sociology*, 29, pp. 89–113.

Werth, R., 2011. I do what I'm told, sort of: Reformed subjects, unruly citizens, and parole. *Theoretical Criminology*, 16(3), pp. 329–346.

Werth, R., 2013. The construction and stewardship of responsible yet precarious subjects: Punitive ideology, rehabilitation, and "tough love" among parole personnel. *Punishment & Society*, 15(3), pp. 219–246.

Ybrandt, H. and Nordqvist, S., 2015. *SiS-placerade ungdomars problematik i relation till andra ungdomar.* Stockholm: Statens Institutionsstyrelse.

6 Re-offending and custodial openness

The findings presented in the previous chapters show that opportunities for youths to be given institutional leave or to be moved to more open units play a significant role in everyday life at youth custody institutions. In addition, both staff and the youths themselves described these factors as playing a significant role for the chances of things going well for the youths following the conclusion of their sentences. This does not in itself mean that custodial openness is in fact related to the youths' subsequent re-offending, however. This chapter focuses on this question by examining the youths' registered recidivism following their release from youth custody. The presentation begins, however, by providing a more general description of the young people sentenced to youth custody and their levels of problems in different areas.

Background and prior offending among youths sentenced to youth custody

The study had access to information on both registered offending and social services placements at special approved homes for the period prior to the youths being sentenced to youth custody. In addition, some of the youths have been interviewed about their need for help in various areas using the Adolescent Drug and Alcohol Diagnosis (ADAD) instrument. Table 6.1 presents the youths' registered offending prior to their youth custody sentences.

As can be seen from the table, a large proportion of the youths had been convicted of offences prior to the conviction that resulted in their youth custody sentence. Although the figures are high in general, perhaps the most striking finding is that so many have a prior conviction for violent crime.[1] The proportion with a prior conviction for drug offences may also be regarded as relatively large.[2] It can thus be noted that while 18 per cent of the youths sentenced to youth custody have no prior convictions, the group as a whole is characterised by high levels of prior offending.

Another way of examining the extent of the youths' problems prior to their youth custody sentences is to look at previous institutional placements. As was described in the introductory chapter, the majority of youths admitted to special approved homes are placed there by the social services. These placements may

Table 6.1 Proportions with a prior conviction, prior court conviction, prior conviction for violent offences, theft offences, drug offences and motoring offences. Boys sentenced to youth custody during the period 1999–2006 with a sentence length of between two months and three years. $N=638$

Type of conviction	*Proportion*	*Mean number of offences*
Prior conviction	82	2.3
Prior court conviction	73	1.6
Prior conviction for violent offences	56	0.8
Prior conviction for theft offences	55	1.0
Prior conviction for drug offences	20	0.3
Prior conviction for motoring offences	27	0.5

be due to criminality, substance abuse or other socially destructive behaviour, and placements may be due to two or more of these factors simultaneously. Of the youths sentenced to youth custody, 41 per cent had been placed in a special approved home prior to their youth custody sentence. The youngest was aged 11 at the time of this previous placement. Only 14 per cent of the youths had neither a prior conviction nor a prior special approved home placement.

Fifty-six per cent of the youths sentenced to youth custody underwent an ADAD interview at the beginning of their sentences. Viewed on the basis of all of the variables collected from the convictions register, the youths who were interviewed in this way had lower levels of prior offending, and also re-offended to a lesser extent, than those who were not interviewed using the ADAD instrument, although the differences are not always substantial. Thus the youths who underwent an ADAD interview are characterised by lower levels of offending, and it is therefore reasonable to assume that the problem levels within the group as a whole (including those who were not interviewed) are greater than those described on the basis of the ADAD data.

Table 6.2 presents the help needs (which in turn reflect problems within the different areas) that emerged in the ADAD interviews with the youths sentenced to youth custody, together with the corresponding figures for all youths (boys) admitted to special approved homes and for a comparison group based on a representative population sample of youths (boys) that were collected in the context of another study (Ybrandt and Nordqvist 2015).

As expected, the youths sentenced to youth custody and those placed in special approved homes[3] report significantly higher levels of problems than youths from the reference population. The nature of the problems found among the youths sentenced to youth custody, and among those placed by the social services, is relatively similar, however. Those placed by the social services have somewhat more often been assessed to be in need of help in relation to their families and with drugs, while those sentenced to youth custody are more often assessed to need help in relation to crime, mental health and alcohol problems. None of these relatively minor differences between the groups are unexpected, however, given the reasons for youths being placed in special approved homes.

Table 6.2 Interviewer estimates of youths' needs for help in different areas. Proportions for whom help is regarded as necessary or absolutely necessary. The figures relate only to boys[1]

Problem area	*Youth custody (interviewed 1999–2006)*	*All special approved home youth (interviewed 2010)*	*Reference population (interviewed 2009–2010)*
School	39	42	2
Leisure time and friends	35	31	1
Family	14	24	1
Mental health	31	25	3
Crime	64	47	3
Alcohol	20	13	3
Drugs	31	38	3
$N^2=$	360	432	449

Notes

1 The figures for all special approved home youth and for the reference population (the two columns to the right of the table) have been taken from Ybrandt and Nordqvist (2015).

2 The numbers included for the individual problem areas may deviate from this figure due to internal missing data.

The fact that only 64 per cent of the youths sentenced to youth custody have been assessed to have a substantial or very substantial need for help in relation to crime might perhaps be viewed as somewhat surprising. However, the majority of those not classified as being in need of "necessary" or "absolutely necessary" help lie very close to the threshold for inclusion in the "necessary" category. The fact that the youth custody youths who underwent an ADAD interview have somewhat lower levels of prior criminality than the youth custody group as a whole may also have influenced the results in this particular respect.

It is worth paying particular attention to the fact that almost one-third of the youths sentenced to youth custody who underwent an ADAD interview were assessed to have a substantial or very substantial need for support in the area of mental health. Another relatively serious indicator of mental health problems and depression is having attempted suicide at some point. Eleven per cent both of those sentenced to youth custody and those placed in special approved homes by the social services reported having tried to take their own lives at some point. The corresponding figure in the reference group was 5 per cent.[4]

Thus it may be noted that although the youths sentenced to youth custody have been placed in special approved homes for other reasons than those placed by the social services, they are characterised by similar problems, and the youth custody group is comprised of youths with experience of high levels of problems and adversity even prior to being convicted of a serious offence. What offences, then, were these youths convicted of?

The convictions leading to youth custody

Youth custody sentences should only be imposed for the most serious offences, and a previous study (Pettersson 2010a, Pettersson 2010b) has shown that youth custody sentences are in large part imposed in relation to aggravated violent crime. The principal offences in the convictions for the youths included in the current study are presented in Table 6.3.

As can be seen from the table, the convictions in the current group of youths were also dominated by aggravated violent offences. The most common single offence type was robbery, and a total of 83 per cent of the convictions related to different forms of violent crime. The mean sentence length for the study population was just over nine months. It should be noted, however, that the longest, and the shortest, youth custody sentences imposed during the study period are not included in this figure, and the length of the sentences imposed does not include possible periods of incarceration on remand.

The convictions of only 23 per cent of the youths related to a single offence, with the mean number of offences in the youths' convictions lying at 4.4. At the same time, 13 per cent of the youths were serving more than one youth custody sentence in the course of the same special approved home placement. These youths had thus not had time to complete their first sentences before being given a new youth custody sentence. The most common offences in this latter group of convictions are theft offences and offences against public servants, followed by robbery. These are probably offences that were committed prior to the first youth custody sentence coming into force, but they may also include offences committed after the youths had started serving their first sentence. It is not possible to draw any definitive conclusions on this question on the basis of the data included in the study. It can be noted, however, that the offences that led to the later youth

Table 6.3 Principal offences in the convictions resulting in youth custody sentences of between two months and three years for boys during the period 1999–2006. $N=638$

Offence type	*Per cent*
Murder/manslaughter	1
Attempted murder/manslaughter	4
Aggravated assault (including attempts)	19
Assault	2
Robbery (including attempts)	49
Sexual offences	6
Witness intimidation, perjury, false incrimination	2
Crimes against public servants	2
Property offences	5
Public endangerment offences	2
Drug offences	3
Other	5
Total	100

custody sentences (that were served simultaneously) were less serious than those included in the original youth custody conviction.

The youths sentenced to youth custody were on average aged 17 at the time of both their convictions and their admissions to special approved homes. Some of the youths were sentenced subsequent to their eighteenth birthdays (and there are exceptional cases where the youths have been 19 by the time of their convictions), and a few more had turned 18 by the time they were admitted to a special approved home.

Having presented an initial description of the youths and the offences for which they were sentenced, I now move on to the issue of re-offending and the significance of various forms of custodial openness in relation to this outcome. The presentation begins by looking at re-offending in general, then at the elements of open custody that the youths have experienced during their sentences. It concludes by analysing the significance of these elements with the help of more advanced statistical methods.

Re-offending in general

Before moving on to analyse how institutional leave and spending time on an open unit at the end of one's sentence are related to re-offending, Table 6.4 presents general figures describing the re-offending of the youths sentenced to youth custody.

As can be seen from the table, a large proportion of the youths re-offended within five years of being sentenced to youth custody. Many of them are registered for recidivism in violent crime and drug crime. Given that 56 per cent were subsequently convicted of offences that resulted in a new custodial sentence, as compared with 82 per cent who received a new court conviction, some of these new offences were of a less serious nature. Thus the recidivism rate is high, but this was also to be expected. The recidivism rates described in Table 6.4 may be compared with those among youths given a custodial sentence in England and Wales, where 73 per cent of those under the age of 18 re-offended within a year

Table 6.4 Recidivism in registered crime within five years. Boys sentenced to youth custody for between two months and three years during the period 1999–2006 in per cent. *N*=638

Type of recidivism	*Proportion*	*Mean number of convictions*
New conviction	88	4.3
New court conviction	82	2.6
New custodial sentence	56	1.3
Recidivism in:		
Violent crime	59	1.1
Theft crime	54	1.1
Drug crime	54	1.6
Motoring offences	43	1.3

of their release (Bateman *et al.* 2013 p. 5). The follow-up period in the current study is longer (the shortest follow-up period is two years, the longest almost five years, depending on the length of the sentence) and it is therefore not surprising that a larger proportion of the youths in the current study had re-offended. The fact that almost half of the youths had not committed a new offence that had resulted in a custodial sentences, and thus had not been convicted of a new offence that was as serious as the offence that led to their being sentenced to youth custody, might be interpreted in somewhat different ways. On the one hand, it might be seen as meaning that they have nonetheless been "more successful" following their sentences, not least given the high levels of prior criminality and other problems within this group. On the other hand, it could also be interpreted as a manifestation of regression to the mean (with the youth custody conviction being interpreted as an extreme observation in the context of the youths' offending careers). The finding may also be related to the length of the follow-up period, since some of those who have not been registered for recidivism, or for recidivism into serious crime, within five years, will probably nonetheless be registered for recidivism into offences of this kind at some point in the future. Carlsson and Sarnecki (2015 p. 125) have argued, however, that de-escalation may also be viewed as a form of desistance – or at least as an improvement that may be of interest. Thus they argue that the question of whether or not convicted youths completely desist from crime is not the only question of interest in this context.

Forms of custodial openness

One important element in the idea of a progression through different levels of custodial openness, which has been noted by both the staff (in the interviews) and the National Board of Institutional Care more generally (SiS 2010), and which is also expressed in the instructions to the Board from politicians on the subject of developing the institutions' pre-release activities (Justitiedepartementet 2011), is the goal that the youths' placements should assume more open forms towards the end of their sentences. Table 6.5 presents the types of unit

Table 6.5 Type of unit from which the youths were released, in total and by sentence length. Boys sentenced to youth custody for between two months and three years during the period 1999–2006. *N*=620

	2–6 months	*>6–12 months*	*>12 months*	*Total*
Type of unit:				
Pre-release	2	7	5	4
Open	16	29	30	24
Open and locked places	3	10	10	8
Locked	52	40	41	44
Secure	27	14	14	20
Total	100	100	100	100
N=	238	284	98	620

from which the youths were released at the end of their sentences. Since the extent to which a given youth will have time to experience the ideal progression from secure to open care is in part dependent on how long the youth spends at a special approved home, the presentation is broken down on the basis of the length of the youth custody sentence.

The majority of the youths had been placed in a locked or secure unit prior to release. In some cases, they may have spent time in an open unit prior to this, but have then been transferred back to a locked unit for various reasons. For the most part, however, the youths in the study group have spent their entire sentences in secure forms of custody. One interpretation of this finding would be that the youths have simply not been capable of being placed in more open forms of custody as a result of the demands associated with this form of placement, and that the finding is thus due to the youths' behaviour. There are, however, factors that suggest that this is unlikely to be the only explanation. An internal review conducted by the National Board of Institutional Care (SiS 2010) shows, for example, that it is also due to the availability of open places. The lack of open places was also described in the interviews as one of the reasons why youths remained in more secure custodial forms. A further explanation may be that for those with shorter sentences there is insufficient time to transfer them to an open unit in the course of their sentences, and that it is this factor that the figures reflect. As can be seen from the table, however, this latter explanation can only explain part of the high proportion released from locked or secure units, since even those with long sentences have primarily been released from units of this kind.

One aspect of custodial openness is how often the youths have been given institutional leave over the course of their sentences, and what kinds of institutional leave they have experienced. On average, the group as a whole has been given leave on 18 occasions per 100 days of sentence, i.e. just over once a week. These instances of institutional leave are unevenly distributed among the youths, however, not least depending on the length of their sentences. Those with sentences of up to six months have been given institutional leave an average of 12 times per 100 days of sentence, while the corresponding figure for those with sentences lasting 6–12 months is 20 times per 100 days of sentence, and those with sentences of over 12 months, have been given leave an average of 26 times per 100 days of sentence. The youths' experiences of institutional leave are also unevenly distributed across different phases of the youth custody sentence, with leave occurring more frequently later on in the sentence, which is in line with the rules that regulate institutional leave. Table 6.6 presents the different types of institutional leave that the youths have been given. Since this is also affected by the length of the youths' sentences, the presentation has once again been broken down on the basis of sentence length.

It is common for the youths to have had at least one home visit over the course of their sentences. This is the case for all of the groups, but particularly for those serving longer sentences. It is even more common to have been given leave to participate in what are termed "social activities". These may involve

Table 6.6 Proportion of youths who have experienced different types of institutional leave, by length of sentence. Boys sentenced to youth custody for between two months and three years during the period 1999–2006 in per cent

	2–6 months	*>6–12 months*	*>12 months*	*Total*
Type of leave:				
Home leave	77	95	99	87
Social activities	83	98	99	91
Regular leisure time activity	9	28	58	25
Work/work experience	9	25	51	22
School	7	22	40	18
Other	80	96	100	89
N =	247	291	98	638

more or less anything: going for a coffee, eating at a restaurant, going swimming, visiting a shopping centre or shopping at a newsagent in the vicinity of the institution, or doing other types of errands. It is also common for the youths to have been given leave of kinds that have been coded into the "other" category. These include a wide range of different activities that are, for the most part, things that have to be done rather than activities specifically intended as a form of institutional leave, such as going to the dentist, meeting one's solicitor, appearing in one's own court case, etc. It is less common for the youths to have been to school or work or to have participated in more regular leisure time activities (such as playing football, training at a gym, etc.) outside the institution. It is also in relation to this category that we find somewhat larger differences between those serving sentences of at most six months and those with longer sentences. A little over half of those serving sentences of over 12 months have left their institutions to go to school or work or to participate in regular leisure time activities, as have one-quarter of those serving sentences of 6–12 months. Since so many of the youths, including those serving long sentences, are not transferred to more open forms of custody towards the end of their sentences, this pattern may reflect the staff compensating for this to some extent by also "opening up" locked units towards the end of the youths' sentences. In order to examine this question, Table 6.7 presents institutional leave broken down on the basis of both sentence length and the type of unit from which the youths were released.

Although those released from locked units have also experienced some leave for school, work and regular leisure time activities, it is only in relation to the more common categories of leave (home visits and social activities) that there are no significant differences between those released from open and locked units respectively.[5] Since virtually all youths are given the common forms of leave, it is not surprising that there are no differences in relation to these. There are also differences in the mean number of leave experiences between those released from open and locked units respectively, with those released from open units having had more leave experiences during their sentences. Thus the analysis suggests that there are, in fact, no major compensatory effects whereby those with longer

Table 6.7 Proportion of youths who have experienced different types of institutional leave, by sentence length and whether the youth was released from an open or locked unit. Boys sentenced to youth custody for between two months and three years during the period 1999–2006 in per cent[1]

	2–6 months	*>6–12 months*	*>12 months*
Released from locked unit			
Mean no. of leave occasions/100 days of sentence	11	15	22
Type of leave			
Home leave	74*	92*	98
Social activities	81	97	98
Regular leisure time activity	9	24*	55
Work/work experience	7*	17***	39***
School	5**	8***	30**
Other			
N =	197	182	64
Released from open unit			
Mean no. of leave occasions/100 days of sentence	19	28	34
Type of leave			
Home leave	90*	99*	100
Social activities	90	98	100
Regular leisure time activity	12	37*	65
Work/work experience	20*	40***	74***
School	20**	47***	59**
N =	44	102	34

Notes

* = alpha level of 0.05;

** = alpha level of 0.01;

*** = alpha level of 0.001.

1 While the study represents a census, Chi-2 tests have been conducted in order to show if the differences are significant. These significance tests have been conducted based on comparisons between the youths released from locked and open units respectively, within the different groups based on the length of sentence. Thus those with a sentence of at most six months who were released from an open unit have significantly more often been given home leave (alpha level of 0.05) than those with a sentence of at most six months who were not released from an open unit.

sentences, who are nonetheless released from locked units, are compensated for this by the staff "opening up" the locked units so that they (in relation to leave) produce an experience similar to that which the youths would have had if they had been placed on an open unit. Instead, the analysis shows that those with long sentences who are released from a secure unit have significantly less experience of institutional leave than those with long sentences who are released from an open unit. It is, however, possible that the staff do in fact do this *sometimes* and for *some* youths. Thus we can conclude that, in addition to there being a large number of differences associated with the time spent in secure and more open custodial forms (such as the degree of personal responsibility and the opportunity of experiencing a less institutionalised existence), there are also differences in the level of opportunities for experiencing different forms of institutional leave.

Custodial openness and re-offending

Given that there are differences in the degree of custodial openness, both in terms of the number and type of experiences of institutional leave, and in the type of unit from which the youths are released, are these differences related to differences in re-offending, and if so, in what ways? An analysis of the youths' re-offending based on the type of unit from which they were released (not presented here) shows that the greater the level of security at the unit from which the youth was released (secure, locked, locked and open, open, pre-release), the higher the level of re-offending. In order to produce groups of a reasonable size for the analysis, the different degrees of custodial openness have been combined to produce two categories: "secure units, locked units and units with both open and locked places" and "open and pre-release units". Table 6.8 presents the youths' re-offending on the basis of the types of unit from which they were released, while Table 6.9 presents the relationship between re-offending and the frequency of leave over the course of the youths' sentences.

The proportion who re-offends is clearly higher among those released from a locked unit. Further, these youths also relapse into more serious offences. Just over one-third of those released from an open unit were subsequently convicted of an offence that resulted in a new custodial sentence, as compared with just under two-thirds of those released from a locked unit, and this difference is statistically significant.[6] There are also significant differences in relation to each of the various offence types examined – violent crime, drug offences, motoring offences, theft offences (not presented here). Similar differences (also in relation to different offence types, results not presented here) are found between those with an above average number of leave occasions per 100 days of sentence, and those with fewer than average leave occasions per 100 days of sentence, although the differences between these groups are smaller.[7] The fact that spending time on an open unit at the end of one's sentence appears to be more

Table 6.8 Re-offending within five years (based on the conviction resulting in the most serious sanction) by type of unit from which the youths were released. Boys sentenced to youth custody for between two months and three years during the period 1999–2006 in per cent

	Open unit	*Locked unit*
No re-offending	22	9
Summary sanction order or waiver of prosecution	7	4
New court conviction, non-custodial sentence	31	24
New court conviction, custodial sentence	40	63
Total	100	100
N =	177	443

Table 6.9 Re-offending within five years (based on the conviction resulting in the most serious sanction) by frequency of leave during sentence (per 100 days). Boys sentenced to youth custody for between two months and three years during the period 1999–2006 in per cent.

	>13.5 leave occasions/100 days	*<13.5 leave occasions/100 days*
No re-offending	19	6
Summary sanction order or waiver of prosecution	4	5
New court conviction, non-custodial sentence	28	25
New court conviction, custodial sentence	49	64
Total	100	100
N =	319	317
Mean no. of leave occasions /100 days of sentence	29	7

important than having experienced more leave in relation to one's sentence length would in many ways seem logical on the basis of the interview findings. Both being transferred to and spending time on an open unit quite simply places different demands on the youths, and, in addition to this, leave is generally more frequent for those on open units.

As has been mentioned previously, however, it is reasonable to assume that part of the differences in re-offending are due to factors related to both the possibility of being transferred to an open unit and the risk of recidivism. It may be assumed, for example, that placements in more open custodial forms are dependent on good behaviour (which can be seen from both the internal rules of the National Board of Institutional Care and the interviews with staff and youths), and that this is also related to re-offending subsequent to release. In order to examine this question using more advanced methodological controls, Propensity Score Matching has been employed (see Chapter 3 for a more detailed description), and the results from this analysis are presented below.

Propensity Score Matching

The youths have been matched by means of Propensity Score Matching using the nearest neighbour method and the STATA statistics package with the psmatch2 module. Since being transferred to an open unit appears to be more important than the rate of leave experienced during the youth custody sentence, the analyses have been conducted using release from an open unit as the treatment variable, while the frequency of leave is instead employed as a matching variable. The matching process tested a range of different variable combinations in order to produce the best possible model. This process is described in more detail in Chapter 3. A total of 176 of the 177 youths in the treatment group were matched successfully, and the results of the matching process are presented in Table 6.10.

Table 6.10 Differences between the treatment and non-treatment groups following the matching procedure

Variable		*Treated*	*Control*	*Per cent bias*	*Per cent reduction*	*t-test*	
						T	$p>\|t\|$
Prior convictions	U[1]	1.2147	1.7091	–37.3		–3.97	0.000
	M[2]	1.2159	1.1818	2.3	93.1	0.25	0.799
Prior LVU placement	U	0.31638	0.43864	–25.4		–2.81	0.005
	M	0.31818	0.3125	1.2	95.4	0.11	0.909
Principal offence in youth custody conviction	U	1.8701	1.9727	–14.3		–1.63	0.105
	M	1.8693	1.8864	–2.4	83.4	–0.22	0.824
Leave/100 days of sentence	U	27.286	14.198	87.0		10.53	0.000
	M	26.814	26.052	5.1	94.2	0.43	0.666
No. of days in special approved home	U	286.18	233.97	32.2		3.71	0.000
	M	284.4	288.81	–2.7	91.6	–0.23	0.821
Leave rescinded for bad behaviour	U	0.16949	0.25682	–21.4		–2.33	0.020
	M	0.17045	0.19318	–5.6	74.0	–0.55	0.582
Isolation	U	0.28814	0.25682	–49.6		–5.46	0.000
	M	0.28977	0.26705	4.8	90.4	0.47	0.635
Absconding	U	0.12994	0.43409	–44.4		–4.48	0.000
	M	0.13068	0.11364	2.5	94.4	0.39	0.699
Changed unit because of problems	U	0.12994	0.26591	–34.6		–3.68	0.000
	M	0.13068	0.11932	2.9	91.6	0.32	0.748

Notes
1 Unmatched
2 Matched

Prior to matching, the difference in recidivism resulting a new custodial sentence between those released from an open unit and those released from a locked unit is –0.24 and statistically significant (t=–5.53; p<0.001). After matching, this difference is reduced to –0.14 but remains statistically significant (t=–2.06; p<0.025). If we instead look at the relative risk (which should not be confused with the odds ratio, which is presented in connection with the logistic regression analyses below), and specify a 95 per cent confidence interval around the estimate, the difference in the relative risk is greater than chance for both the unmatched and the matched results. Prior to matching, the excess risk of being given a new custodial sentence for those released from a locked unit by comparison with those released from an open unit is 1.6 (CI: 1.5–1.7). The excess risk following the matching procedure is 1.4 (CI: 1.3–1.4).

If the same analysis (using the matching described above) is instead conducted using any subsequent conviction, rather than recidivism in more serious crime, as the outcome variable, the differences between the groups become smaller. Prior to matching, the difference between those released from open and locked units respectively is –0.14 (t=–4.73; p<0.001) and after matching, the difference is –0.07 (t=–1.47; p<0.100). Thus subsequent to matching, the difference would only be significant given an alpha level of 10 per cent. Since most of the youths are reconvicted, and the differences between the treatment and non-treatment groups are smaller in the context of this analysis, the excess risk are also less marked, 1.2 (CI: 1.2–1.2)[8] prior to matching and 1.1 (CI: 1.1–1.1) subsequent to matching. Both excess risks are statistically significant but they are so small as to be negligible.

Taken together, the findings show that following matching on the basis of a large number of important factors, a treatment effect was identified for being released from an open as against a locked unit, and this effect was greatest in relation to recidivism into serious crime.

Interaction effects

As was noted in Chapter 3, initial analyses indicated the presence of interaction effects, and therefore logistic regressions have also been conducted employing interaction terms. The results of these analyses are presented in Table 6.11. Interaction effects were identified for two background variables: prior court convictions and prior LVU placements.

The odds ratios for the variables that are included in the model as controls (i.e. those not included in the combination variables) should not be interpreted in the same way as in logistic regression models that do not include interaction terms. They are therefore left without further comment. The significance of these variables has also been controlled for in the Propensity Score Matching process, which constitutes the principal analysis. For the sake of clarity, however, two things should be noted. The variables "Leave/100 days of sentence", "Age at admission to special approved home" and "No. of days in special approved homes" are all continuous. This means that the odds ratios for these variables

Table 6.11 Logistic regression analysis of re-offending within five years resulting in a new custodial sentence. Analysis of interaction effects. Boys sentenced to youth custody for between two months and three years during the period 1999–2006. Exp (B)/odds ratio. 95% Confidence Interval. N=620[1]

	Model 1	*CI 95%*	*Model 2*	*CI 95%*
Leave/100 days of sentence	1.0	1.0–1.0	1.0	1.0–1.0
Prior court conviction				
No			1.0	
Yes			2.6	1.7–3.9
Prior LVU placement				
No	1.0			
Yes	2.6	1.8–3.8		
Problems during period at institution				
None	1.0		1.0	
At least one	1.5	1.0–2.3	1.5	1.0–2.2
Age at admission to special approved home	1.1	0.9–1.4	1.2	0.9–1.5
Principal offence				
Violent crime	1.0		1.0	
Robbery incl. attempted	1.0	0.6–1.5	1.0	0.6–1.5
Other, incl. sex offences	0.7	0.5–1.2	0.7	0.4–1.2
No of days in special approved home	1.0	1.0–1.0	1.0	1.0–1.0
Combination variable 1:				
Open unit + no prior court conviction	1.0			
Locked unit + no prior court conviction	2.4	1.1–5.2		
Open unit + prior court conviction	2.9	1.3–6.1		
Locked unit + prior court conviction	6.0	2.8–12.5		
Combination variable 2:				
Open unit + no prior LVU placement			1.0	
Locked unit + no prior LVU placement			1.8	1.1–3.0
Open unit + prior LVU placement			1.9	1.0–3.7
Locked unit + prior LVU placement			5.6	3.2–9.6
Per cent correct predictions null-model	56.5		56.5	
Per cent correct predictions	68.2		68.4	
Hosmer and Lemeshow Test, sign	0.33		0.63	
Nagelkerke R Square	0.21		0.21	

Note

1 Testing for multicollinearity (Field 2013) shows no such problems for the variables included in the models. Note that the values cannot be compared between the models as a result of heterogeneity in unobserved variables (Mood 2010).

presented in Table 6.11 refer to an additional variable: day of leave/day of age/day of sentence served at the special approved home. It is for this reason that the odds ratios for these variables are so small and are non-significant. In this model, however, they function exclusively as control variables, and the analysis is not focused on examining the significance of these particular variables for reoffending. It may also be noted, however, that even when the variables are dichotomised (more/less days of leave than the average), trichotomised (sentence length) or coded into larger categories (age in years), it is only the leave variable that has a significant (independent) effect on the outcome variable (analysis not presented here). Thus having experienced an above average number of leave days per 100 days of sentence has a significant effect on reoffending even when the interaction terms are included in the same model.

Both the interaction between the type of unit and prior court conviction show a similar tendency. As expected, re-offending is lowest among those with no prior court conviction or LVU placement who were released from an open unit. What is interesting, however, is that there are almost no differences between those with a prior conviction or LVU placement who are released from an open unit, and those who lack this background and are released from a locked unit. One possible interpretation of this would be that spending time on an open unit compensates for the higher re-offending risk that is characteristic of youths with a prior court conviction or LVU placement. Further, the excess risks for these two groups, in relation to those with no prior court conviction or LVU placement who are released from an open unit, are statistically significant, but are considerably smaller than for those with a prior court conviction or LVU placement who are released from a locked unit. One interpretation of these findings is thus that it would appear to be particularly important for those with a high risk for re-offending to spend time on an open unit prior to release in order to reduce subsequent recidivism.

Similar interaction effects, in the sense that maintaining contacts with one's family during imprisonment produces the greatest "benefit" for those at high risk of re-offending, have been reported in a Danish study of prison inmates (Monrad Granunböl and Hviid Hornnes 2009). It is difficult to determine how these results might correctly be interpreted, however. They may be due to those at higher risk of re-offending having a greater need to test more open custodial forms and to learn to deal with the responsibility this involves, and also of the possibilities for support related to (re-)integration into the community that are associated with more open forms of custody. The findings might also be interpreted as indicating that there is something that happened with these specific youths during their period of custody, in the form of incidents or processes, which meant that they were able to spend time in more open custodial forms, and which also produced a reduced risk for re-offending. Further, these possible explanations are not mutually exclusive, and they may both be correct. Irrespective of which is correct, or whether both are correct, the findings suggest that staff should endeavour to ensure that youths at higher risk of recidivism are also given the opportunity to move to more open forms of custody during their sentences.

Summary

It is clear from the youths' backgrounds and the other factors for which there is available information, that the youths serving youth custody sentences are drawn from a group characterised by high levels of problems even prior to being sentenced to this form of incarceration. It is also to be expected that a large proportion of these youths will re-offend following the completion of their sentences (both as a result of their high levels of problems, and because this has been shown to be the case in previous studies), and this expectation is confirmed by the results of the current study. For a group of individuals with such high levels of problems, who are at risk of a long period of continued serious criminality, with everything that this involves for themselves, for potential future victims, and in terms of the associated costs to society, any measures that produce reductions in the level of re-offending should be regarded as important, even if their effects are not particularly substantial.

On the basis of the interviews conducted with staff and youths, various forms of custodial openness would appear to have the potential to have an impact on re-offending. This same conclusion can be drawn on the basis of previous research both on youth care provision (Andreassen 2003, Pettersson 2010a, Pettersson 2010b) and on the criminogenic effects of incarceration (Nieuwbeerta *et al.* 2009, Wermink *et al.* 2010, Andersen and Andersen 2012, Andersen 2015, Durlauf and Nagin 2011), and also on the basis of the more theoretical knowledge on total institutions presented in Chapter 2. The analyses of re-offending also show that there appears to be an effect of this kind, primarily in relation to youths having the opportunity to spend time on an open unit, rather than spending the whole of their sentences on secure or locked units. The results also suggest that the opportunity to experience more open forms of custody is of most significance for those youths characterised by a greater risk of re-offending. Further, the most substantial effects were found in relation to recidivism into more serious crime.

This finding can probably be explained by both an (already ongoing) process of change that has made more open forms of custody possible, and by these care forms themselves leading to reduced re-offending. Further, these two processes are likely to be related to one another, which is discussed in more detail, and in relation to the interview data, in the concluding chapter. Before moving on to the concluding discussion, however, it should be noted that the study is subject to a number of limitations, which may be of significance to the findings. The study is not an experiment with youths randomly assigned to spend time in more open forms of custody, and, despite the use of advanced matching techniques, there may be factors that may (at least in part) explain the findings that the models have not taken into account. Further, although the youths have been followed up for five years subsequent to the conviction that led to their youth custody sentence, this observation period is relatively short. Some of the youths who were not registered for new offences within this period will probably re-offend at some point in the future. At the same time, the follow-up period is longer than those employed in many treatment studies, which often employ an observation period of six months subsequent to the conclusion of treatment. Research on recidivism following release from prison has also shown that the majority of those who re-offend do so within a short time of their release (Roxell 2012). In addition, the longer the follow-up period employed, the more difficult it becomes to determine whether it is the relevant treatment measure, or things that happened subsequently, that have produced any observed effects on re-offending. The book's concluding chapter will discuss the results from the interviews and the follow-up on re-offending in relation to one another, and also in relation to theory and previous research.

Notes

1 This proportion may for example be compared with the proportion of violent offences among the total number of convictions for boys (aged 15–17) in 2009, which lay at 17 per cent (statistics from the Swedish National Council for Crime Prevention), and with the finding that the proportion of 15-year-olds suspected of assault in 2005 was 0.8 per cent (Estrada, 2013).

2 Drug offences accounted for 8 per cent of the total number of convictions among boys (aged 15–17) in 2009 (Statistics from the Swedish National Council for Crime Prevention).

3 Some of these youths had also been placed in special approved homes as a result of being sentenced to youth custody. The majority are, however, comprised of youths placed by the social services. Since the periods in which the interviews were conducted do not overlap, however, the youth custody youths who underwent an ADAD interview, and who are included in the current study, are not the *same* youths as those interviewed in Ybrandt and Nordqvist's study.

4 In spite of this, however, only 3 per cent of this group were assessed to be in substantial or very substantial need of help, which might perhaps be interpreted as indicating that, for some of the members of this group, the mental health problems related to earlier rather than current difficulties in this area, since the question related to whether they had *ever* attempted to take their own life.

5 With the exception of leave to participate in regular leisure time activities among those serving sentences of over 12 months.

6 A Chi-square test shows the difference to be significant at $p < 0.001$.

7 A Chi-square test shows the difference to be significant at $p < 0.001$.

8 There is a difference between the lower and the higher CI thresholds, but not after rounding.

Bibliography

Andersen, L.H. and Andersen, S.H., 2012. *Losing the stigma of incarceration: Does serving a sentence with electronic monitoring causally improve post-release labor market outcomes?* Odense: University Press of Southern Denmark.

Andersen, S.H., 2015. Serving time or serving the community? Exploiting a policy reform to assess the causal effects of community service on income, social benefit dependency and recidivism. *Journal of Quantitative Criminology*, 31(4), pp. 537–563.

Andreassen, T., 2003. *Institutionsbehandling av ungdomar: Vad säger forskningen?* Stockholm: Gothia.

Bateman, T., Hazel, N. and Wright, S., 2013. *Resettlement of young people leaving custody: Lessons from the literature*. London: Beyond Youth Custody.

Carlsson, C. and Sarnecki, J., 2015. *An introduction to life-course criminology*. London: Sage.

Durlauf, S.N. and Nagin, D.S., 2011. Imprisonment and crime. *Criminology & Public Policy*, 10(1), pp. 13–54.

Justitiedepartementet, 2011. *Förbättrad utsluss från sluten ungdomsvård.*

Monrad Granunböl, H. and Hviid Hornnes, J., 2009. *Sociala boder der binder*. Köpenhamns Universitet.

Nieuwbeerta, P., Nagin, D.S. and Blokland, A.A., 2009. Assessing the impact of first-time imprisonment on offenders' subsequent criminal career development: A matched samples comparison. *Journal of Quantitative Criminology*, 25(3), pp. 227–257.

Pettersson, T., 2010a. *Återfall i brott bland ungdomar dömda till fängelse respektive sluten ungdomsvård.* Stockholm: Statens Institutionsstyrelse.

Pettersson, T., 2010b. Recidivism among young males sentenced to prison and youth custody. *Journal of Scandinavian Studies in Criminology and Crime Prevention*, 11(2), pp. 151–169.

Roxell, L., 2012. Bättre ut eller snabbare in?: Effekter av ett fängelsestraff. In: Pettersson, L. and Pettersson, T., eds, *Kontrollens variationer*. Lund: Studentlitteratur, pp. 217–238.

SiS, 2010. *Kartläggning av LSU-utslussning under 2009.*

Wermink, H., Blokland, A., Nieuwbeerta, P., Nagin, D. and Tollenaar, N., 2010. Comparing the effects of community service and short-term imprisonment on recidivism: A matched samples approach. *Journal of Experimental Criminology*, 6(3), pp. 325–349.

Ybrandt, H. and Nordqvist, S., 2015. *SiS-placerade ungdomars problematik i relation till andra ungdomar.* Stockholm: Statens Institutionsstyrelse.

7 The significance of custodial openness

Empirical and theoretical insights

As was described in the previous chapter, there were a number of spectacular escapes from Swedish prisons in 2004, which among other things resulted in the construction of a number of high-security units. The above cartoon was drawn at the time by the Swedish artist Magnus Bard. The inmate is peeking out through the tiny hole that remains following the bricking-in process and says "Now I'll be good". The following year, there were a number of cases of absconding among youths sentenced to youth custody, and the same pattern was repeated.

Figure 7.1 Cartoon by Magnus Bard, originally published in *Dagens Nyheter* during 2004.

While no new secure units were built, the majority of the institutions with youth custody places constructed (more) fences and enclosures, with barbed wire, etc. The Bard cartoon has accompanied me over the years for a number of reasons, and it captures very well the central issue examined in the current study. Even though it was drawn as a commentary on a partly different issue – i.e. that of increasing the level of incarceration in order to avoid prison escapes – it also captures the dilemma that exists between "incarceration", in the current context incarcerating children in response to serious offending, and the desire to "make people good", since it is clear that incarceration in many ways functions to produce the opposite effect. It is in relation to this dilemma that attempts to make the total institutions that special approved homes constitute "not-so-total" (Farrington 1992) by means of institutional leave and more open custodial forms should be understood and discussed. In this concluding chapter, I will present a brief discussion of the study's central findings and of the significance for convicted youths of the opportunity to serve their sentences in more open custodial forms.

The significance of custodial openness for the incarcerated boys

As a means of understanding incarceration and the significance that (potential) forms of custodial openness have for the youths' time in special approved homes and for their opportunities subsequent to release, Goffman's detailed analyses of the interactions and relationships in total institutions and Foucault's discussions of discipline both in prison and in society at large have proved to be a fruitful combination. Both perspectives are required in order to understand the ways in which processes and relationships related to incarceration and custodial openness function at the special approved homes, and also how they constitute part of, and contribute to, the continuous process of "making up people" (Hacking 2004) that takes place at these institutions. The experience of the total institution and of incarceration permeates every aspect of these boys' lives (and their bodies) (cf. Goffman 1991), which means that the desire, and the need, for relief from this experience is perceived as absolutely essential. Given the central importance of this desire for relief, the promise of institutional leave and of moving to an open unit becomes an important element in the discipline focused on producing good behaviour in every minute detail of their lives that is built up around them (cf. Goffman 1991, Foucault 1991). But society outside the institution, with its ever increasing demands for responsible individuals who govern themselves into making the right choices, also serves in part to structure the contents of both this discipline and the expectations that the youths are required to meet in order to be given institutional leave (cf. Foucault 1991). Further, institutional leave functions not only as a tool for disciplining the youths but also serves the purpose of monitoring: 1) the situation in the youths' families; 2) how the youths cope with spending time outside the institution and with the situations they are faced with in this context; and 3) how they cope with transferring what they have "learned" during treatment to life outside the institution. Several different forms of control are also woven into the experience of institutional leave, while at the same time leave also contributes to reducing the harms produced by incarceration.

The actions that are produced by the good behaviour requirement for institutional leave in part take the form of participating in programmed activities, and all that this entails, but they also take the form of actions that make the youths compliant during their period of institutionalisation (cf. Hörnqvist 2010). And in this latter respect, I would argue that this primarily involves the production of "docile bodies", i.e. the type of bodies associated with the original version of discipline formulated by Foucault in *Discipline and Punish*. The actions that are produced involve getting up on time, going to bed on time, going to school and staying there throughout the school day, doing the cleaning at the specified time, coming to meals on time and participating in, and being on time for, various required activities (both desired and imposed). This is very much in line with Ugelvik's (2014) arguments that the daily routines of the prison environment are primarily focused on disciplining the body to be in the right place at the right time. But there is also an element of requiring that the youths themselves manifest a desire to change, and thus an obedient body does not constitute a sufficient condition for being granted institutional leave (cf. Crewe 2009 p. 140). Crewe (2009 p. 454) argues, however, that:

> Encouraging prisoners to take "responsibility" for their lives is not intrinsically reactionary. Nor is the belief that prisoners should be challenged in their views of offending. Both carry dangers, however. It is one thing to help someone take control of their life, make informed choices and fulfil their potential, and another thing to remove much of their genuine autonomy, narrow down their options, and force them to conform to a predefined regime.

Thus what is important is not the avoidance of attempts to generate responsibility, reasonable forms of behaviour or the questioning of the youths' offending behaviour. Instead what matters is the way in which such attempts are formulated, and that we are aware of, and avoid, their associated dangers.

The follow-up of re-offending clearly shows that the youths who spend time in more open forms of custody towards the end of their sentences re-offend to a lesser extent than others, particularly in relation to more serious forms of offending. This remains true even following matching on a large number of factors that are of significance, both for re-offending and for the chances of being transferred to more open forms of custody during one's sentence. Spending time in more open forms of custody also appears to be particularly important for youths characterised by a higher risk for re-offending. One conclusion that can be drawn on the basis of the study's quantitative analysis is thus that more open forms of custody are desirable and significant for the re-offending of this group of youths, which is generally characterised by a high level of re-offending. Reducing levels of re-offending is important both for the youths themselves and their future life chances, and also for society at large and potential future crime victims. However, the interviews conducted with youths and staff serve to complicate this picture somewhat.

Custodial openness is desirable and important as a means of reducing the harms produced by incarceration among these young people, and it functions to support them both in choosing not to re-offend and in succeeding in not doing so. At the same time, the study shows that the ability to transfer youths to more open forms of custody may be utilised by staff in counterproductive ways. When the opportunity of experiencing more open forms of custody is made conditional on behavioural criteria that are primarily linked to producing peace and quiet on a given unit, and thus facilitating the staff's position of power and making their work easier, there is a risk that this will produce a range of problems. For one thing, it generates resistance among the youths, which leads to superficial adaptation rather than real change, and it also contributes to less positive relations between youths and staff. Another problem is that it produces a paradoxical situation in which the youths, in order to be transferred to more open forms of custody that will reduce the harm generated by incarceration, must first show that they are able to adapt to the precise conditions that generate this harm. There is thus a requirement that the youths become *institutionalised* (Goffman 1991) in some way in order to be given the opportunity to experience measures that reduce this institutionalisation. All of this means, however, that the potential effects of increasing the degree of custodial openness as a means of reducing re-offending are actually greater than the results of this study show, provided that it is used more wisely and thoughtfully and with less focus on micro-discipline in the form of good behaviour in the unit on which the youth is placed.

It is clear from the interviews that micro-discipline undermines the perception that the staff really care, and instead contributes to producing a more destructive relationship between staff and youths. Ugelvik (2014) argues that in prisons, the exercise of power can be made less painful by treating the inmates kindly. Exercising power in a less painful way would also be of benefit to the relationships between staff and youths, which is something that the youths describe as being important in a number of different ways. The exercise of micro-discipline instead promotes superficial adaptation (Goffman 1991, Petersson 2013, Crewe 2009) and strategies focused on working the system. Bateman *et al.* (2013, p. 18) argue, for example, that:

> [e]ngagement is fundamental to resettlement – a principle that has also been identified as crucial in a youth justice context (Prior and Mason, 2010). Rather than a particular programme, effective resettlement is a dynamic, interactive process, based around high quality relationships between staff and those whom they supervise.

Crewe (2011 pp. 463–464) describes how the shift towards soft power and cognitive treatment programmes changes the staff culture in prisons in a number of ways. While the shift towards self-regulation means that harsh interventions are no longer necessary to maintain order, it also means that active engagement is no longer required from the staff. He also argues that cognitive behavioural programmes are consistent with the explanations of criminal behaviour that dominate among staff, and that this involves (and as I understand him intensifies) a view that crime is a consequence of pure choice. The inmates are viewed as "the architects of their own predicaments" (p. 464). The links to risk reduction in today's prisons also mean that responsibility is left to experts in this area, such as psychologists, which serves to conceal the significance of informal relationships in the process of helping inmates to change their lives. Crewe summarises these trends in the following way:

> If staff fail to engage with prisoners, if they do not get to know their histories, if they doubt that prisoners can change, and if they are obliged to act within highly risk-averse parameters, it is less likely that they can successfully promote desistance.
>
> (2011 p. 464)

It is unfortunate if a positive and important function such as custodial openness instead in part becomes a barrier to these very important relationships.

As can be seen from the interviews, the majority of the youths express a desire to change, a desire that should be made use of. More open custodial forms and the opportunity to maintain contact both with one's family and the community outside the institution are important for the reintegration process that these youths will undergo following their release. This means that it is important that custodial openness is used in a way that does not simultaneously generate resistance and superficial adaptation. Travis and Petersilia (2001) argue that sanctions should be broken down into two parts. The first part has the objective of paying one's debt to society by means of incarceration. The second part, however, should have reintegration into the community as its objective, and here it is not only the convicted offender, but also society and its institutions, that have a responsibility and must participate. Travis and Petersilia advocate that central institutions such as the healthcare sector, employment support (the employment agency), the childcare system (the social services), should become more involved, not only while the offender is in prison but also subsequent to the completion of the sentence. To borrow Farrington's (1992) terminology, one could say that Travis and Petersilia are proposing that prisons should be "not-so-total" in order to facilitate the integration of inmates into the community. The results of the current study confirm the need to work towards making Sweden's special approved homes "not-so-total".

Another question raised by the interviews with the youths is that of whether resettlement during the period following release should perhaps be more focused on giving the youths the chance to start over somewhere new, since many of them want this and believe that this is what they need. In the current system, the youths for the most part return to their families and their former neighbourhoods following their release, an environment that they may well not have been integrated in prior to their sentences (Bateman *et al.* 2013). The staff also describe one of the central tasks of institutional care as being that of ensuring that the youths are able to function in their home environments subsequent to release, and that this is very difficult. By contrast with the youths, however, the staff focus less on alternative solutions. It might perhaps be wise to instead provide them with support to build a new life. Their peers are starting this process, building a life outside the parental home, whereas for the youths serving youth custody sentences, this process is put on hold, and they thus fall behind in this respect during their period of incarceration (cf. Andersson Vogel 2012).

Foucault (Foucault 1991) argues that prisons primarily produce criminals and criminality. Recent studies of the criminogenic effects of prisons may be said to provide support for this view (Durlauf and Nagin 2011, Nieuwbeerta *et al.* 2009, Andersen and Andersen 2012, Bales and Piquero 2012). The current study has not examined the possible criminogenic effects of the special approved homes and the youth custody sanction. Instead, the focus has been directed at the issue of whether a potential effect of this kind may be reduced through the use of more open custodial forms over the course of the sentence. The study provides substantial support for the view that custodial openness is important both for making the life of incarcerated children more humane, and for the chances of things going better for them following their release. The power that the youths' desire to move into more open forms of custody gives the staff, however, needs to be dealt with in a constructive manner, and must not be used for short-term strategies intended to produce a calm environment on a given unit.

Bibliography

Andersen, L.H. and Andersen, S.H., 2012. *Losing the stigma of incarceration: Does serving a sentence with electronic monitoring causally improve post-release labor market outcomes?* Odense: University Press of Southern Denmark.

Andersson Vogel, M., 2012. *Särskilda ungdomshem och vårdkedjor: Om ungdomar, kön, klass och etnicitet.* Stockholm: Institutionen för socialt arbete-Socialhögskolan, Stockholms Universitet.

Bales, W.D. and Piquero, A.R., 2012. Assessing the impact of imprisonment on recidivism. *Journal of Experimental Criminology*, 8(1), pp. 71–101.

Bateman, T., Hazel, N. and Wright, S., 2013. *Resettlement of young people leaving custody: Lessons from the literature.* London: Beyond Youth Custody.

Crewe, B., 2011. Soft power in prison: Implications for staff–prisoner relationships, liberty and legitimacy. *European Journal of Criminology*, 8(6), pp. 455–468.

Crewe, B., 2009. *The prisoner society: Power, adaptation and social life in an English prison.* Oxford: Oxford University Press.

Durlauf, S.N. and Nagin, D.S., 2011. Imprisonment and crime. *Criminology & Public Policy*, 10(1), pp. 13–54.

Farrington, K., 1992. The modern prison as total institution? Public perception versus objective reality. *Crime & Delinquency*, 38(1), pp. 6–26.

Foucault, M., 1991. *Discipline and punish: The birth of the prison.* London: Penguin Books.

Goffman, E., 1991. *Asylums: Essays on the social situation of mental patients and other inmates.* London: Penguin Books.

Hacking, I., 2004. Between Michel Foucault and Erving Goffman: Between Discourse in the Abstract and Face-to-Face Interaction. *Economy and Society*, 33(3), pp. 277–302.

Hörnqvist, M., 2010. *Risk, power and the state: After Foucault.* London: Routledge.

Nieuwbeerta, P., Nagin, D.S. and Blokland, A.A., 2009. Assessing the impact of first-time imprisonment on offenders' subsequent criminal career development: A matched samples comparison. *Journal of Quantitative Criminology*, 25(3), pp. 227–257.

Petersson, F., 2013. *Kontroll av beroende. Substitutionsbehandlingens logik, praktik och semantik.* Malmö: Égalité.

Travis, J. and Petersilia, J., 2001. Reentry reconsidered: A new look at an old question. *Crime & Delinquency*, 47(3), pp. 291–313.

Ugelvik, T., 2014. *Power and resistance in prison: Doing time, doing freedom.* London: Palgrave Macmillan.

Index

Page numbers in *italics* denote tables, those in **bold** denote figures.

For Product Safety Concerns and Information please contact our EU representative GPSR@taylorandfrancis.com
Taylor & Francis Verlag GmbH, Kaufingerstraße 24, 80331 München, Germany

www.ingramcontent.com/pod-product-compliance
Ingram Content Group UK Ltd.
Pitfield, Milton Keynes, MK11 3LW, UK
UKHW011017180926
475701UK00004B/799